CRITICAL INSIGHTS

American Road
Literature

CRITICAL INSIGHTS

American Road
Literature

Editor
Ronald Primeau
Central Michigan University

SALEM PRESS
A Division of EBSCO Publishing
Ipswich, Massachusetts

GREY HOUSE PUBLISHING

Cover Photo: Radius Images

Editor's text © 2013 by Ronald Primeau

Copyright © 2013, by Salem Press, A Division of EBSCO Publishing, Inc.

Critical Insights: American Road Literature, 2013, published by Grey House Publishing, Inc., Amenia, NY, under exclusive license from EBSCO Publishing, Inc.

∞ The paper used in these volumes conforms to the American National Standard for Permanence of Paper for Printed Library Materials, Z39.48-1992 (R1997).

Library of Congress Cataloging-in-Publication Data

Library of Congress Cataloging-in-Publication Data
American road literature / editor, Ronald Primeau, Central Michigan University.
    pages cm. -- (Critical insights)
  Includes bibliographical references and index.
  ISBN 978-1-4298-3819-1 (hardcover)
  1. Travel in literature. 2. American literature--History and criticism. 3. Travelers' writings, American--History and criticism. I. Primeau, Ronald, editor of compilation.
  PS169.T74A54 2013
  810.9'355--dc23

2012049038

ebook ISBN: 978-1-4298-3835-1

PRINTED IN THE UNITED STATES OF AMERICA

Contents _____

Critical Contexts

Critical Readings

Resources

About This Volume

Ronald Primeau

This volume of original essays is the largest and most diverse collection to date on American road literature. Eighteen contributions were commissioned to provide a comprehensive overview of the genre's historical development, its main forms of expression, and the wide range of values discovered, created, and shared in journeys along highways through America's heartland. Represented here is commentary on Native American travel legends, the Underground Railroad, and traditional writers in the American canon such as Mark Twain, Theodore Dreiser, Sinclair Lewis, and Jack Kerouac, alongside emerging and more recent figures and the usually overlooked accounts of early women writers. Poets such as Theodore Roethke and Robert Fanning, blues songs, and travel guides all contribute to the amazing range of the literature of quest, discovery, and settlement that continues to define us as a diverse people on the move.

The first four essays survey major critical approaches applied to the enjoyment and interpretation of the genre. They also apply critical and cultural theory to some of the earliest road stories and to French philosopher Jean Baudrillard's views of how the heartland functions in the symbol-making processes of our lives. A comparison of two works by Mark Twain suggests further ways in which we can read and contextualize these books.

The Critical Readings section presents fourteen discussions of significant road books, beginning with the paradoxes of gender in the novel that has been considered the bible of American road literature: *On the Road* (1957) by Jack Kerouac. The three essays that follow address some lesser-known works and important themes taken on by Sinclair Lewis, Wright Morris, and Cormac McCarthy. Deborah Paes de Barros reviews the almost-buried history of women's early travel narratives and assesses their modifications of road-genre conventions more recently. The next three selections turn to topics often missed along the highway, first with David Bain surveying the road's ventures into dark fantasy and horror fiction. Christian Knoeller next considers how Michigan's Pulitzer Prize–winning poet Theodore Roethke's meditations on nature and mystical yearning inform his masterful use of journey tropes in *The Far Field* (1964). In a companion piece, Caroline Maun shows us Robert Fanning's creation of a counterpoint dysphoria in *American Prophet* (2009) that comes up against road-literature conventions that have lost their appeal and power. Fanning's prophet sets out with predictable optimism, comes up empty, and tries to warn his listeners about what Braun calls the extremes and the excesses he experiences. Unable to communicate the warnings he tries repeatedly to convey, his prophetic voice becomes parodic, underscoring both the failure and the personal cost of the collapse of what had for so long been reliably heroic and healing.

The final grouping of essays illustrates the cultural diversity of the genre and returns to the rich values and insights that have been discovered and nurtured along the highways through the heartland. Maureen Eke explores the long tradition of Underground Railroad literature in the clandestine and arduous work of moving toward freedom and the achievement of civil rights. Matthew Low provides similar insights on the particular patterns of movement in M. Scott Momaday's reworkings of Kiowa Tsoai legends. Phil Patton listens closely to the lyrics of blues songs and the cultural geography they map onto the highways through the heartland—like the freedom road and road of escape Highway 61, a home in motion to Bessie Smith, Magic Slim, Bob Dylan, Robert Johnson, Ike Turner, and so many others.

Finally, these selections share examples of the ever-evolving genre in action, as Mary Beth Pringle underscores images of home and travel in Mary Morris's nonfiction and Arvid Sponberg composes a hybrid genre rolling across roads that limn Lakes Michigan, Huron, and Superior in a creative-nonfiction exploration of teaching, writing, politics, marriage, parenthood, and religion, combined with commentaries on heartland writers Bonnie Jo Campbell, Chad Harbach, and Bruce Norris. Steven

K. Bailey scrutinizes a form of road literature often read but seldom analyzed: travel guidebooks and road atlases. In these most practical household packagings of discourse, he identifies genre conventions and finds camouflaged ideologies and lines of power often so subtle as to be nearly subliminal in their rhetorical and political agendas. Bailey argues persuasively that readers need to first recognize and then challenge the naturalized ideologies in order to open up space for counternarratives with more nuanced insights about places, people, and cultures.

Equipped with guidebooks they may adhere to or resist, today's drivers and readers along the highways through the heartland occupy the same physical and mythical space traveled by Native Americans, slaves escaping on the freedom trails, pioneer women combining settlement and quest motifs, beat poets and other countercultural heroes, blues singers and poets chronicling the untold stories of everyday people, and even visiting French philosophers, joining the worries of John Steinbeck and his French poodle, Charley, that we are trading genuine experience for homogenization and simulations of the concocted and the unreal.

In many new and diverse ways, the contributors in this volume examine the rich history of literary road travel and show how the genre has moved in directions that open up spaces for new quest journeys, identities, and places in hybrid literary forms. Each essay in the volume traces how every new road trip unsettles and undermines our assumptions about race, class, and sexual identity. Being in motion invites new ways to look at the realities and values we have been taught. From the buoyant leaps into the unknown to the darkest dystopias of splatter-horror fiction, the journeys through America's heartland reinforce even as they subvert and parody the pilgrimage tradition. The journey truly does become more important that the destination as the road itself becomes home, rather than merely the place one sets off on to get somewhere else.

Along rivers and railroad tracks, dirt roads, blue highways, and interstates, on foot and on two, four, or more wheels, walkers, bicyclists, motorcyclists, truck drivers, and dreamers in souped-up sedans have encountered the excitement of new beginnings, the horrors of the road's darkest sides, and, for some, the collapse of a genre that can perhaps expect too much. In prose, poetry, and song, on film, canvas, and computer screens, the literature of the American highway remains resilient, innovative, and experimental—limited only by the new travelers and readers it beckons. The essays in this volume point the way for adventurers who start the engine, find meaning in the writing of their stories, and turn pages to create worlds waiting to be found or created.

On American Road Literature _____

Ronald Primeau

Travel narratives are found in the earliest American literature across regions, in many genres, using several modes of transport. From pioneer diaries to science fiction, movement has been a central subject and theme of a national literature of exploration and self-discovery. The journey has been central to the mythic dimensions of the quest motif as well as an energizing force of literature of social protest. In this recurring fascination with pilgrimage, picaresque exploration, and the quest romance, the midwestern heartland has been crucial as both a central location and a defining state of mind. While most literary road trips move through several geographical regions, often portraying a cross-country trek, the highways through the heartland are in many books either the major setting of the story or the significant space through which travelers must pass on their way toward their destination.

Along the literary highways winding or zooming through the midwestern heartland, three major groupings have emerged. First, there are books by notable midwestern authors in which most or all of the experiences on the road occur in that region. Because the region is small compared to the wide expanse that beckons for the long trek, and because departures, arrivals, and reentries generally take place elsewhere, books set entirely in the heartland are rare. Second is a grouping of many more books in which the region is a prominent, though nowhere near dominant, setting. More important than mere location, these road narratives emphasize crucial midwestern subjects, themes, or views as major influences on the genre on the whole. Examples include Jack Kerouac's fascination with cornfields, Chicago blues, and the Iowa Pooh Bear in *On the Road* (1957) and Robert M. Pirsig's suggestion that midwestern "nowhereness" is a central ingredient in the American experience of Zen peacefulness (*Zen and the Art of Motorcycle Maintenance*, 1974). Finally, a third grouping of books might be thought of as those in which the travelers are just "passing through"—where the landscapes, people, and values of the heartland are important as a place and a literary theme, but the emphasis in the books overall is elsewhere.

In all three types of midwestern road narratives, the region stands for a place of wholesomeness, friendliness, and paradoxically meditative motion. It is often a place to slow down, to capture lost values and ways of life, and to regroup, recharge, and sort out the complexities of the quest. The Midwest is the literal and figurative place of intersection that recalls Walt Whitman's "Song of the Open Road":

> I inhale great draughts of space,
> The east and west are mine, and the north and south are mine.
> I am larger, better than I thought,
> I did not know I held so much goodness. (5.6–9)

Midwestern authors created literary road quests long before the invention of the automobile. Mark Twain relates what he calls "several years of variegated vagabondizing" in a famous stagecoach journey from Missouri to Nevada (*Roughing It*, 1872). He also created some of the most unforgettable river journeys of all time in *The Adventures of Huckleberry Finn* (1865) and *Life on the Mississippi* (1883). (English author Jonathan Raban retraced Twain's journeys down the Mississippi in *Old Glory: An American Voyage*, 1981). Other early road trips by Midwestern authors include Margaret Van Horn Dwight's *A Journey to Ohio in 1810* (1912), L. Frank Baum's famous *The Wonderful Wizard of Oz* (1900), and Theodore Dreiser's *A Hoosier Holiday* (1916), the first midwestern automobile road narrative.

More recently, several well-known road narratives by midwestern authors have emphasized the importance of place and celebrated the culture and values of the region. In *Blue Highways* (1982), William Least Heat-Moon begins his circular trip on the back roads of the country in Missouri. Though he circles the country following the coming of spring, Least Heat-Moon's journey is ultimately inward. The road is therapy, travel becomes a metaphor for an inner quest, and the highway is sacred space where true inquiry is at last possible. From Black Elk he learns the power of the circle, and from the Hopi evolution through four worlds he learns that "a human being's grandest task is to keep from breaking with things outside himself" (Least Heat-Moon 186). What began as a quest for order becomes in *Blue Highways* something akin to Whitman's lesson of reception. The culmination of his quest takes place in New Harmony, Indiana, where the Rappites' labyrinth teaches him "the Harmonist concepts of the devious and the difficult approach to the state of true harmony" (411).

While the westward journey of *Zen and the Art of Motorcycle Maintenance* begins in Minnesota and its midwestern setting is short-lived, the Zen-like meditation along the way is anchored in the acceptance of boredom and monotony that brings peace in the endless grass of the prairies. Pirsig's quest is not only a travel narrative but a compendium of the history of Western philosophy. In his acceptance of "stuckness" (284) and embracing of a "preintellectual awareness" (272) that allows one to experience Quality, Pirsig's midwestern values take him very far east: "The Buddha, the Godhead, resides quite as comfortably in the circuits of a digital computer or the gears of a cycle transmission as he does at the top of a mountain or in the petals of a flower. To think otherwise is to demean the Buddha—which is to demean oneself" (17). Several midwestern authors bring this same message to a range of audiences, as in the young-adult book *Grandpa and Frank* (1976), where Janet Majerus recounts the story of twelve-year-old Sarah, who engineers a plot to save her grandfather from the conspiracy planned by her Uncle Frank. Set on the roads from central Illinois to Chicago, Sarah's escape includes her "borrowing" a pickup truck on a pilgrimage of love in this leapfrog-generation rescue.

Midwestern authors also create gentle parodies or ironic underminings of the quest itself. Charles Dickinson (*The Widows' Adventures*, 1989) combines the highway quest with a bittersweet commentary on aging in America. Two sisters travel from Chicago to California to visit relatives. Helene is blind and drives the car with the assistance of her sister, Ira, who cannot drive at all. They travel only between midnight and 4:00 a.m. at low speeds and on back roads. On this trip featuring "you and me bickering across America" (Dickinson 150), they bring 120 cans of beer and $12,000 in twenty-dollar bills. The book also spends a good deal of time at the widows' home in Chicago, where Dickinson critiques our culture's willingness to take advantage of the elderly who try to continue living on their own.

"I come from Des Moines. Somebody had to" (3), quips Bill Bryson in the opening of *The Lost Continent: Travels in Small-Town America* (1989). As soon as he was old enough, Bryson moved to England so he could "*be* somewhere" (7; ital. in orig.). Years later, he returned to America's Midwest—first to retrace his boyhood vacations, then in search of American popular-culture myths, and finally on a quest for the perfect small town. Subsequently, this transplanted midwesterner has written well over a dozen books, but in the end the Iowan finds staying away harder than he thought. "I could live here," he concludes, and "for the first time in a long time," he feels "serene" (299).

The most overly parodic road narrative by a midwestern author, Jim Harrison's *A Good Day to Die* (1973), follows a group of disinherited antiheroes on their sacred cross-country quest to blow up a dam and save the Grand Canyon from destruction. Following the breakup of his marriage, the narrator travels with a Vietnam veteran named Tim and Tim's girlfriend, Sylvia, on a wearying and unproductive pilgrimage. It does not matter that their quest fails; their tenacity becomes heroic existentialist angst that follows the conventions of the road quest while parodying them. The bittersweet resolve of Chief Joseph's words "Take courage, this is a good day to die" (Harrison 139) advances the genre's hopeful escapism to a new kind of optimism.

The nation's heartland is also important as both mythology and an actual place, as well as a set of values and beliefs, in many significant road narratives by authors from outside the region. Midwestern prairies, plains, and small towns are prominent in the settings of many novels. Creative nonfiction authors also spend considerable time traveling through and discussing the region. Many road quests feature cross-country treks in which the Midwest serves as a place for taking stock along a flat landscape that frees the mind for meditation. Often road protagonists enter the region the way pilgrims move into sacred space. For Kerouac in *On the Road*, the area is wild and lyrical; Pirsig recognizes a Zen contentment with "hereness and nowness" (5); Sissy Hankshaw in Tom Robbins's *Even Cowgirls Get the Blues* (1976) finds in the midwestern prairies the ultimate feminine embodiment of the life force. Common to such accounts is the recognition of a magical expansiveness and a unifying power in the landscape's simplicity. In *Travels with Charley* (1962), John Steinbeck finds distinctive regional qualities he thought had vanished. Midwestern people are more open and outgoing than people elsewhere, he finds, as they exhibit an electrifying flow of energy. The people are generous and take their cues from a rich and beautiful countryside. He worries that speech rhythms and accents as well as distinctive regional values will become homogenized; against this dystopic vision, Steinbeck finds the Midwest a welcome corrective.

In *Roads* (2000), Larry McMurtry sets out on a nomadic exploration of movement on what he calls "the great roads, the interstates" (12), which have as their predecessors the network of rivers that long formed our nation's arteries. "What I want to do," he explains, "is treat the great roads as rivers, floating down this one, struggling up that one, writing about these river-roads as I find them, and now and then, perhaps, venturing a comment about the land beside the road" (19–20). McMurtry devotes one chapter and one winter month to a journey from Duluth, Minnesota, to Oklahoma City, and along that stretch, he philosophizes at length about the culture and values of the Midwest. McMurtry's openness on things midwestern is varied and provocative. While he bemoans the erosion of family farms—"recent generations of midwestern farmers have to cope not only with the slow failure of their farms but with a sense that they have failed their ancestors as well" (37) —he acknowledges that "the midwest symbolized by amber waves of grain and large solid families has rarely been the midwest I've found" (38). He concludes that midwesterners lead dull lives enlivened by shopping trips and that they are "compromisers" (40) who learn to be resigned to ordinariness and a less-than-exciting life. McMurtry says that in the Midwest, it is difficult to find much of the glamour that has become "part of the American promise" (39) and "longing for prettier things" (40) can even lead to murder. He cites a large number of midwesterners who "go postal," or "blow one's stack and murder as many people as possible." This, he feels, is born of the frustration and repression found in a region that has become "the home, or at least the venting ground, for quite a few of our natural-born killers" (39).

Emphasized often in the midwestern leg of the road pilgrimage is the way seemingly infinite space is defined and punctuated by road-side sculpture, a phenomenon that Karal Ann Marling in *The Colossus of Roads* (1984) compares to the way the pilgrim's shrine became "a stopping place in time, where the everyday rules of reality are sus-pended and idyllic dream commences" (101). In this grand scale and sweeping scope, the iconography of the colossus represents the fron-tier myth and the American dream. Because the East is too small for Paul Bunyan, the midwestern expanse becomes the ground on which to work out what Marling calls the American riddle of "how the finite individual can find his bearings in the infinite immensity of space" (6).

More than in any other road narrative, Jack Kerouac's *On the Road* expresses adulation for the sprawling landscape and heroic values found on the midwestern plains and prairies. Sitting in a gloomy hotel on the plains, narrator Sal Paradise finds that he is "halfway across America, at the dividing line between the East of my youth and the West of my future" (15). Alternately expansive and confining, life is slower and the roads faster, capturing what Ann Charters calls "the rhythm of the midwest" (82). Sal celebrates funky Chicago, the open-ness and expanse of Iowa and Nebraska, and, in Detroit once again, a convergence of the "strange Gray Myth of the West and the weird dark Myth of the East" (Kerouac 245). In Omaha, Sal celebrates the residual values of the Western frontier, reenergized by "the wild, lyrical, drizzling air of Nebraska" (22). *On the Road* became a benchmark for the evolution of the American road narrative, and over the next half century, many road authors would pause a while in the heartland to take stock and reassess the direction of their quest.

Many road narratives intersect the midwestern landscape and culture only briefly, affirming nonetheless the significance of the region as a place and a network of symbols. In Mona Simpson's *Anywhere but Here* (1987), Ann August and her mother, Adele, set out from Bay City, Wisconsin, to seek adventure and a better life in Hollywood. Adele wants to escape the suffocation of small-town life; she compulsively runs away from the fear that her daughter will become "a poor nothing girl in a factory town in the midwest" (350). In *This Is My Country, Too* (1965), an African American recasting of road conventions in the direction of the freedom quests found in the spirituals, slave narratives, and poetry of the black oral tradition, John A. Williams first drives in New England and then flies to Detroit, where he purchases a car for the trip south. William Saroyan starts out in London, Ontario, and travels to South Dakota in *Short Drive, Sweet Chariot* (1966), spending considerable time in the Midwest in this book about freedom and the psychological healing that is released in car talk and what he calls "the built-in listener" (42) in us all that brings us closer to "the healing of God" (43) while on the road. In *The Air-Conditioned Nightmare* (1945), Henry Miller passes through a Midwest that epitomizes America's monotonous fabric of life on his way to the Southwest, where "the secret of the American continent" is contained and "everything is hypnagogic, chthonian and super-celestial" (239). Finally, Dayton Duncan sets out from St. Louis in his retracing of the journeys of Lewis and Clark (*Out West*, 1987.) Duncan moves through the edges of the Midwest on a pilgrimage to stir up our settled past for reinterpretation and a regenerative act of healing. For Duncan, the lessons learned are a corrective history lesson on the facts of our past and the mythologies we substitute for the realities we want to escape.

In addition to works by midwestern authors and adventures set in the Midwest, a considerable body of the literature of the American highway passes through the region in an almost tangential way. Charles Kuralt featured many Midwestern people and locales in his books and videos. Richard Reeves discusses the cementing over of the Saginaw Valley in Michigan in his *American Journey* (1982), a revisiting of Alexis de Tocqueville and Gustave de Beaumont. Douglas Brinkley and his students include Springfield, Illinois, and Lawrence, Kansas, among the midwestern stops in *The Majic Bus* (1994). Duncan's retracing of Lewis and Clark begins in Saint Louis. Henry Miller touches down briefly in his rental car. Peter and Barbara Jenkins meander through the region in *Walk across America* (1979). Even L. Frank Baum gives Dorothy and Toto a famous chat about Kansas. From Whitman's "Song of the Open Road" to Twain's *Roughing It* (1872) and Lesley Hazleton's *Driving to Detroit* (1998), the Midwest achieves a modest and often indirect but significant place in the overall road-quest pattern. Even tangentially, the Midwest is a literal and symbolic place of great value in the lure of the open road.

Two midwestern authors epitomize the region's central place in the evolution of the American road narrative. In *Zen and the Art of Motorcycle Maintenance*, Pirsig equates the most admirable elements of "stuckness" and "Quality" with a midwestern peacefulness often found only in Buddhism. In *Blue Highways*, Least Heat-Moon circles around and through the region in an inner quest for harmony. Less peaceful quests, as in Harrison's *A Good Day to Die*, Bryson's *The Lost Continent*, and Dickinson's *The Widows' Adventures*, emphasize the midwestern landscape and values as pivotal in longer and more expressive journeys.

Among works by non-midwestern writers, Kerouac's *On the Road*, Steinbeck's *Travels with Charley*, and Saroyan's *Short Drive, Sweet Chariot* devote considerable time and emphasis to the region. This emphasis is found in historical predecessors as well, from Whitman's "Song of the Open Road" to Twain's *Roughing It* and *Life on the Mississippi* and Dreiser's *A Hoosier Holiday*.

Most notable among books that pass through the region in meaningful ways are Williams's *This Is My Country, Too*, Douglas Brinkley's *The Majic Bus*, Hilma Wolitzer's *Hearts* (1980), Miller's *The Air-Conditioned Nightmare*, Mary Morris's *Nothing to Declare* (1988), Reeves's *American Journey*, Bill Moyers's *Listening to America* (1971), Anne Roiphe's *Long Division* (1972), and Charles Kuralt's *My Life on the Road* (1990).

Today, road stories traveling through the American heartland are more popular and significant than ever. Major book stores feature large displays of "travel narratives" located near but distinct from travel guides, maps, and road atlases. Most journeys are still undertaken not in groups but as a solitary escape from routine, an effort to clear one's head, or a quest for meaning in one's life. We find still many adventure tales reflecting the residual values of the frontier and the wanderlust that endures long after there appear to be clearly demarked places to go. Pilgrimages are still prominent; we go in search of personal identity, to seek or clarify a sense of national purpose, or to protest establishment values. The heroic quest now invites more diversity than ever as women and people of diverse ethnicities make their own space in what used to be the privileged terrain primarily of white males. Road literature is also expressed in as many media as ever, with poetry, road songs, film, the visual arts, the blues, and other forms of the oral tradition joining traditional nonfiction prose, road novels, electronic books, and hypertexts as the genre adapts to new readers and travelers. Through it all—in actual vehicles, mythologies, and states of mind—drivers and readers crisscross the nation as the American heartland holds anchor as a departure point, a rite of passage, and a residual mythology of values tied to the land.

The American road narrative is, most of all, absorbing storytelling about exploration and self-discovery. In the quest myth and the hero journey, we see played out our long-standing negotiation between imperialism and exceptionalism. The former recalls a forced occupation of another's land and homes, a rejection of the robber barons old and new, countercultural protest against McCarthyism, jingoism, and the flight to the suburbs that began in the Eisenhower years—speaking out all the while against the dominant culture's efforts to normalize or naturalize itself to the disparagement of the Other. At the same time, many road quests look to validate manifest destiny, the theory of the elect and the exceptionalist privileging of a nation perceived to have been chosen as a model for how the rest of the world should live. Such paradoxical themes in the genre mirror the complexity of the American heartland, where conservative and activist values have flourished alongside each other and where the restless return seeking renewal, validation, and ongoing exploration.

Further Reading

Robert R. Hubach's *Early Midwestern Travel Narratives* (1961) is an indispensable record of diaries, journals, and other accounts of the frontier and early settlement periods in the Old Northwest Territory. Hubach's bibliographies, summaries, and interpretations are most helpful. My own work *Romance of the Road: The Literature of the American Highway* (1996) includes discussions of midwestern writers of road narratives in several categories: journeys of self-discovery, the search for a national or regional identity, and works of social protest. Cynthia Dettelbach's *In the Driver's Seat: The Auto in American Literature and Popular Culture* (1976) and Patrick Holland and Graham Huggan's *Tourists and Typewriters: Critical Reflections on Contemporary Travel Writing* (1998) extend the genre to include not only traditional narrative forms but also virtual places, hypertexts, the hyperreal, and ectopias. Phil Patton's *The Open Road* (1986) also places the genre in a historical framework that includes the emergence of a variety of popular-culture formats.

More recent critical commentary has shown how women have re-shaped the American road narrative in crucial ways. In *Through the Window, Out the Door: Women's Narratives of Departure from Austin and Cather to Tyler, Morrison, and Didion* (1998), Janis P. Stout traces "women's appropriation of the traditionally masculine mode of travel writing and narrative tropes of journey" (xii). Other informative scholarly studies include *The Land before Her: Fantasy and the Experience of the American Frontiers, 1630–1860* (1984) by Annette Kolodny, *Felicitous Space: The Imaginative Structures of Edith Wharton and Willa Cather* (1986) by Judith Fryer, *The Home Plot: Women, Writers, and Domestic Ritual* (1992) by Ann Romines, and *The Feminization of Quest Romance: Radical Departures* (1992) by Dana A. Heller.

Many related studies, though not discussing directly the road-narrative genre itself, contribute significantly to an understanding of the quester in motion. Marling's *Colossus of Roads* looks at roadside sculpture as important stopping places on the American pilgrimage. In *Driving Passion: The Psychology of the Car* (1987), Peter Marsch and Peter Collett examine the role of the automobile as jewelry, clothes, weapon, and badge of identity. John A. Jakle's work *The Tourist: Travel in Twentieth-Century America* (1985) provides an important historical perspective on the development of tourism and considerable insight on the structural components of the journey and its evolving literary documents.

Works Cited

Bryson, Bill. *The Lost Continent: Travels in Small-Town America*. New York: Harper, 2001. Print.

Charters, Ann. *Kerouac: A Biography*. New York: St. Martin's, 1994. Print.

Dickinson, Charles. *The Widows' Adventures*. New York: Morrow, 1989. Print.

Harrison, Jim. *A Good Day to Die*. New York: Delta, 1981. Print.

Kerouac, Jack. *On the Road*. New York: Penguin, 1976. Print.

Least Heat-Moon, William. *Blue Highways: A Journey into America*. Boston: Back Bay, 1999. Print.

Marling, Karal Ann. *The Colossus of Roads: Myth and Symbol along the American Highway*. 2nd ed. Minneapolis: U of Minnesota P, 2000. Print.

McMurtry, Larry. *Roads: Driving America's Great Highways*. New York: Simon, 2001. Print.

Miller, Henry. *The Air-Conditioned Nightmare*. New York: New Directions, 1970. Print.

Pirsig, Robert M. *Zen and the Art of Motorcycle Maintenance: An Inquiry into Values*. New York: Harper, 2005. Print.

Saroyan, William. *Short Drive, Sweet Chariot*. New York: Phaedra, 1966. Print.

Simpson, Mona. *Anywhere but Here*. New York: Random, 1992. Print.

Stout, Janis P. *Through the Window, out the Door: Women's Narratives of Departure, from Austin and Cather to Tyler, Morrison, and Didion*. Tuscaloosa: U of Alabama P, 1998. Print.

Whitman, Walt. *Leaves of Grass*. Ed. Sculley Bradley and Harold W. Blodgett. New York: Norton, 1973. Print.

CRITICAL CONTEXTS

Critical Meeting Places: Major Approaches to the American Road Narrative Genre_____

Ann Brigham

The road may be long and well traveled, but scholarly analysis of the road narrative is a newer and much less populated landscape. Even though road narratives date back to the early twentieth century (and even further, as some writers in this volume argue), the first book-length study to define the genre did not appear until 1996. This is somewhat surprising, especially when considering the road trip's status as an iconic American experience. The lack of abundant scholarship is certainly not due to the unpopularity of the road trip or road texts; in fact, perhaps popularity has something to do with the scarcity of scholarly books. Could analysis of this cultural form really constitute a serious academic pursuit? Do road narratives develop meaningful observations about social experiences, identities, or ideas? Is there complexity in plots about rebellious romps or aimless wanderings? Thankfully, many scholars think the answer to these questions is a resounding yes.

This essay focuses on the work of several of those scholars; in particular, it discusses seven scholarly monographs that demonstrate how the road narrative offers important insights into the workings of society and that highlight the unique significance of this genre. Some examine the genre's definitive forms and figures, especially as they resonate with audiences. Some analyze the genre's intrinsic Americanness; others argue that the texts present prevalent cultural myths and social relations that demand analysis.

Overarching Themes

For writers, directors, protagonists, scholars, and audiences, the road endures as a realm of possibility and promise. This association begins with its spatial character. As a space and a symbol, the road represents expansiveness and open-endedness. It may lead out of somewhere specific, but it could go anywhere. In the vast United States, and in our vaster imaginations, the road twists and turns, offering new directions, exciting detours, unprecedented access, and a beckoning horizon. Think, for instance, about its difference from another prevalent space, the street. Streets are readily and carefully mapped, and they are anchored by buildings and addresses and situated by businesses and residences. They are often bound by a grid system, and some may even be gated. In short, even when they are the bustling streets of urban centers, streets signify settlement. In opposition to a spatial pathway that represents the known, the road holds out the promise and possibility of the unknown—or unrealized. On the road, nothing seems settled. As scholar Katie Mills writes, people "expect something better down the road" (34).

This expectation stems from the sense that the road is in opposition to, or outside of, the social and spatial territory mapped by the street. The road promises escape, freedom, and discovery, three themes repeatedly explored in critical analyses. Viewing the road as distinctly different from the space of home, scholars emphasize how it offers an "escape from routine" (Lackey 130), a mode of getting away from constraints—whether those be family, the familiar, society, or one's self. In addition to releasing protagonists from tangible annoyances such as "schedules, commitments, memberships, and credentials" (Primeau 69), the road offers a more philosophical or profound change of scene. In Ronald Primeau's words, the road trip "suspends for a while definition according to one's origins, profession, and geography" (69). In women's road narratives, argues Deborah Paes de Barros, the road functions specifically as "an outside space" that escapes and subverts patriarchy (188). In these and other cases, then, the road releases travelers from the forces that have shaped them.

Once released, travelers find that the road promises a transformative change in orientation. Kris Lackey suggests that road protagonists set themselves "outside the mainstream for the purpose of reflection upon self and society" (111). In this way, the road functions as a mode of expansiveness, whereby protagonists—and, perhaps by extension, audiences—learn new ways to understand themselves, others, and their country. The road trip's change in orientation may also symbolize an explicit form of countercultural protest, an idea that, according to many literary critics and fans, defines (among other texts) Jack Kerouac's now-legendary 1957 novel *On the Road*. David Laderman argues that the physical space of the road is what enables critique because it "celebrates subversion as a literal venturing outside of society" (2). Some scholars investigate the ways this particular vantage point "outside the mainstream" is occupied by a range of already socially "marginal" figures: the picaro, the rebel, and the nomad, as well as larger groups such as women, people of color, and LGBTQ communities. Such analyses argue that the meaning of the road-story genre takes shape through an understanding of the importance of *who* takes to the road.

This focus on outsiders suggests that the escape offered by the road may be particularly appealing to those who already hold tenuous positions in relation to social structures. But, as evidenced by the large number of road narratives that feature white men, the road also appeals to those who are secure in their home lives and social situations. In other words, the road story tracks the movements of dominant social groups as much as it concerns outsiders. Some scholars embrace this tendency as evidence that road stories represent values that unite people and "affirm the value of everyday people and celebrate the ordinary" (Primeau 12). In short, they emphasize sameness rather than differences; people yearn to escape and seek something better, and the road represents both this universal desire and the mode for pursuing it. Others question what might be called the politics of the road, examining how the road story, with its overwhelmingly white, male protagonists, exemplifies the experiences of those with specific social privileges. Many critics analyze this privilege or examine what happens when the protagonist of the road story challenges the conventional profile. In relation to issues of who travels, scholars' inquiries address two fundamental questions: Is the road story expansive and open, bringing into focus a wide range of personas and viewpoints, especially those that challenge the status quo? Or do narratives ultimately reveal and reiterate cultural mythologies and social power?

Although critics' individual answers to these questions are varied and complex, collectively they document the persistence of a widespread cultural impulse or proclivity. The road narrative seems to represent a form that is characteristically, perhaps uniquely, American in the way that it explicitly links the road with a larger national ideal of freedom. As Rowland A. Sherrill points out, there is an American tendency to locate individual freedom "in the more or less unfettered capacity for personal mobility, afforded by, indeed beckoned by, the expansive 'space' of the continent" (212). "In road stories," according to Katie Mills, "the concept of liberty is most consistently defined as freedom of movement" (26).

Several scholars focus on this theme of a liberating spatial movement, often suggesting how it points to the persistent "restlessness of American culture" (Primeau 18). Americans, it seems, are hardwired to move. And, as Primeau points out, it is "the power of movement itself," rather than reaching a specific goal, that promises to "bring happiness, success, and fulfillment" (18). Some writers—including Laderman, Mills, Primeau, and Paes de Barros—discuss restlessness as a countercultural gesture of protest aimed at a rigid or unchanging social order, sometimes arguing that it appears as its own space of non-belonging. Sherrill argues that it signals the American readiness for change. But its appearance has also prompted less celebratory assessments. It has been deemed a sign of male privilege as well as a transcendentalist-inspired "pursuit of an ideal self" (Lackey 130), which reveals the underbelly of American freedom in its expression of a personal manifest destiny by white male travelers (125).

Crucial to this American idea of freedom as movement, and central to many scholarly arguments, is the sense or pursuit of an unanchored self who refuses "a fixed place" (Ganser 309) in relation to identity or location. Several critics interpret the mobility of the road as producing more "fluid, permeable, and transient conceptions" (309) of identity, space, and social relations, and their work explores crucial questions about the cultural work of the genre: To what degree does such fluidity destabilize social categories and hierarchies, perhaps offering new configurations of identity or social relations? Alternatively, how might this mobile, unanchored self depend upon the fixity—that is, the immobility—of others, thus continuing the legacy of manifest destiny, for instance?

Before global positioning systems and satellite-based navigation, one of the common occurrences, if not appeals, of road travel was getting lost. In thematic terms, the road story emphasizes the road as a method of discovery, the route to finding oneself. Scholars suggest that this process of discovery is twofold, often emerging as a "search for personal *and* national identity" (Primeau 19; emphasis added). Leaving home to discover their country, protagonists discover something transformative about themselves. Or a personal journey unearths enduring American values that unite the vast nation. The desire to discover is often prompted by a profound dissatisfaction with the way things are. Primeau links the national search to road authors' sense that "their country's history is short by world standards," and so they look to discover what is unique about America, a search that often turns to a nostalgic study of regional attitudes and values (15). Mills links the personal search to the larger national ideal of independence, maintaining that since World War II, road stories have offered "a vision of how we might break free of unwanted loyalties and obligations to create new identities for ourselves" (223). For Sherrill, the road traveler demonstrates ways to navigate the complex and alien landscape of contemporary America. Lackey analyzes how the search for a transcendent experience and self (135) that is free from social constraints ignores important realities of industrialization and racial history, ultimately fostering an illusory pastoral ideal (64).

Even though the number of scholarly studies is still relatively small, there exists an exciting range of ways to analyze and contextualize the road story. The following sections discuss how sets of scholars develop the ideas presented above. As these arguments show, the road genre, a distinct and diverse American cultural form, consistently focuses on avenues of identity (trans)formation. Its appeal, in Primeau's words, extends beyond the realm of literary setting to "a mode of expression in which a culture explores and defines itself" (4).

A Common Core: Defining the Genre's Shared Features and Values

Offering wide-ranging surveys, both Ronald Primeau's *Romance of the Road: The Literature of the American Highway* (1996) and Rowland A. Sherrill's *Road-Book America: Contemporary Culture and the New Picaresque* (2000) focus on identifying the genre's shared characteristics and "cultural norms" (Primeau 16) across a diverse range of road stories. Although focused exclusively on road films, David Laderman's *Driving Visions: Exploring the Road Movie* (2002) also offers important insights about the fundamental features of the genre.

Fittingly, as the first major study of the road story, *Romance of the Road* aims to describe and justify the makings of a genre. That aim is realized, in part, through the classification of repeated "formulaic patterns" (Primeau 15) that have evolved around four subgenres. Three of these were introduced above: social and political protest, the search for a national identity, and self-discovery; in the fourth, "experimentation or parody," authors recombine genre conventions to reflect changing tastes (15). In his discussions of the road genre's questioning of the status quo, creation and celebration of an American identity (67), and search for self-knowledge and rebirth (133), Primeau is less interested in "text-centered interpretation of an individual work" (16) than in the ways this genre creates a dialogue among writers and readers about identity and social values. That is, he stresses the communal nature of the form and explains why this genre is particularly suited to this characterization: "As narrators converse with the people they meet, as well as others along for the ride, readers are drawn into participation in the questioning and reshaping of values and attitudes," resulting in a "dialogical road of self-searching" (88). Ultimately, "the genre's transforming power is . . . its ability to get us talking together" (15). It does this through its use of conventional and recognizable formulas that give "authors and readers a base on which to build" (14). Once this common core is established, the genre evolves through readers' and authors' ongoing ability to draw from a known set of stories in order to produce new creations or understandings.

For instance, Primeau identifies Kerouac's *On the Road* as establishing a long tradition of approaching the road as a place for those who were "beat down" to question social order, voice "what went wrong with the American dream" (36), and regroup to "restore a lost harmony" (38). The effect—and the importance—is that the road story draws readers "into dialogue with authors, texts, and critics as cultural beliefs and values are reaffirmed, redefined, or otherwise renegotiated" (106). His foundational study suggests a distinctive relationship between form and content. That is, the road genre's elastic, dynamic form matches, and even enacts, its thematic focus on movement.

Published four years after *Romance of the Road*, Sherrill's *Road-Book America* also concerns itself with the relationship created between genre and audience. But whereas Primeau emphasizes an interactive dialogue, Sherrill views the genre as an instructive one. He identifies a "new American picaresque" that presents a "road curriculum" (270) for navigating the disorienting changes taking place in the second half of the twentieth century.

As his terminology suggests, Sherrill defines the genre not as a collection of its own specific conventions, like Primeau, but as the revival of a previous literary genre. Tracing the history of the genre, he argues that the picaresque emphasizes the "theme of motion," appearing during times of "social and cultural upheaval" (32). The task of the new picaresque is to discover coherence and connection as a way to belong in a newly diverse and tumultuous America (42).

The theme of motion is embodied in the picaro (or picara), a figure who inhabits the margins of society and wanders from place to place. As "strangers in exile" (Sherrill 260) with no fixed social or spatial location, picaros are uniquely suited to gain access to an "enormous range" of places and people that are usually outside of the reader's purview (177). Picaros become "narrative agents" for readers, enabling audiences to vicariously cover the vastness of the country and its inhabitants (177). Furthermore, because they interact with new surroundings in a democratic and nonjudgmental way, the picaro offers instruction to the reader in how to empathize with "others" that the reader might have heretofore seen as "unapproachably alien" (171).

As his picaro takes stock of America, so Sherrill surveys a vast catalog of texts, defining the road story more loosely than Primeau, including titles like E. L. Doctorow's *Billy Bathgate* (1989), S. E. Hinton's *The Outsiders* (1967), and Cormac McCarthy's *All the Pretty Horses* (1992)—anything with a road in part of the text. A wanderer himself, he moves through lists of examples that expose readers to "countless items in the cultural inventory": the Texan and Mexican borderlands, a Creek Nation bingo hall, Armistice Day ceremonies in Oklahoma, a Jack Daniel's distillery, and the Castro in San Francisco (Sherrill 183–4).

Collectively, the protagonists of these texts represent and disclose some of the "maladies of contemporary American life" (Sherrill 264): marginalization, alienation, homesickness (269). But their episodic interactions function as a mode of discovery that teaches how, in trying times, to "cope with exile," to "start over," to see things anew, to be resilient, and to cross social boundaries (262). Ultimately, the cultural work of the picaresque is to revive contemporary America by recalling the long-standing American "habits" of "movement and change," firsthand experience, improvisation, and hopefulness (220).

Though focused exclusively on road movies, David Laderman's *Driving Visions* introduces ideas about the road genre that have relevance for studying other road texts. He argues that the genre's "core impulse" is the "rebellion against conservative social norms" (1). Understanding the road journey "as a means of cultural critique," Laderman argues that because the road is a physical route "outside of society" (1–2), it offers a unique vantage point for critique. That is, it brings into view the very borders of American society—the limits and "status quo conventions" one must adhere to in order to belong (2). The road movie's "deliberate rebellious impulse" (20) focuses on escape from such conventions, and Laderman complicates the idea of escape by enumerating two distinctive forms that it takes. First, the quest road movie emphasizes "a movement *toward* something (life's meaning, the true America, Mexico, etc.)," while the outlaw road movie presents "a more desperate, fugitive flight *from* the scene of a crime or the pursuit of the law." Identifying the genre as one of countercultural subversion, Laderman maintains that "*both* types link transgression and liberation with mobility" (20; ital. in orig.).

Mobility and Cultural Mythologies

Both Primeau and Sherrill discuss the road story as a genre of repeated patterns and shared norms that highlight commonality. The next two studies, Kris Lackey's *RoadFrames: The American Highway Narrative* (1997) and Katie Mills's *The Road Story and the Rebel: Moving through Film, Fiction, and Television* (2006), foreground change over continuity. Both writers contend that the mythologies central to road stories—in their respective studies, transcendence and rebellion—must be critiqued and historicized. While the first two scholars largely focus on the identification and affirmation of defining characteristics, these two ask questions of the narrative features and patterns they find.

Lackey's inquiry develops around the philosophy of self and other that the project of discovering America expresses. Understanding road narratives largely in relation to the literary tradition of transcendentalism, he argues that the road is viewed as a space of freedom where travelers shed the unnecessary constraints of a narrow society in pursuit of an essential self and experience (Lackey 135). Escaping from home, travelers finds release in a "western pastoral space, where it is possible, imaginatively, to recover both the virgin land of preindustrial America and the experience of having the land all to yourself, of projectively mastering it" (68).

Rather than create an encyclopedic catalog of dozens of texts, Lackey concentrates on close readings of a small set of road stories in order to show their internal complexities and contradictions. Specifically, his analysis discerns "shadow texts," the unacknowledged "ignored or repressed antithetical messages that lie beneath the authors' assertions" (ix). In the neo-transcendentalist project outlined above, the landscape and its inhabitants become raw material for the traveler, to the point that the journey ultimately becomes a mode of "enlarging and dramatizing the perceiving self" (31–32). The shadow text is that the "myth of conquest is reborn" and the expansiveness of self is "underwritten by the privilege of race" (118).

In charting this thematic territory, Lackey focuses on the diverse racialized experiences of male travelers. For whites, the road produces the transcendental subject—the "illusion of an expansive, omnipotent self" (125). By contrast, African American writers from the 1950s forward challenge this neo-transcendentalism by showing there is no getting outside of, or beyond, the social and historical. Lackey argues that "unlike the boss or family or routine the white traveler abandons to discover America or himself, the black traveler cannot shed his blackness" on the road (119). There is no release or escape. Instead, African American road stories challenge the American ideal of spatial movement as a form of freedom.

Especially in road narratives by white men, "labor and class, racial conquest and exploitation are expunged from the map or relegated to the distant past" (Lackey 48)—leaving a romance for the individual imagination. In his own search to uncover the meaning and shadow texts of highway literature, Lackey debunks the mythology of the road as a sacred space of freedom and transcendence. In order for the road to be that, he argues, the traveler must engage in a kind of historical forgetting.

Katie Mills is also concerned with historical forgetting, but in a different way. Focusing on road stories across media, she insists that we must historicize road narratives and our readings of them. While Primeau and Sherrill consider issues of audience consumption, Mills turns our attention to the production of road narratives, arguing that when and how texts are produced make a difference in what they mean. Historical contextualization, she argues, allows us to understand how road stories reflect larger sociohistorical issues.

In discussions of literature, film, television, and even the internet and video games, Mills examines one of the most common ways the theme of escape is represented, defining the post–World War II road story as a "genre of rebellion" (2). Like Sherrill, she analyzes the genre in relationship to who travels. Both locate an outsider at the center of the genre. However, Mills counters Sherrill's largely ahistorical account of the picaro with an analysis of the rebel that specifies the figure's meaning and effect in relationship to its historical moment and technological production.

Although Mills argues that the road genre becomes an explicitly countercultural one in postwar America, she also maintains that the idea of rebellion is never static. She identifies an ongoing remapping of the genre, tracking a repeated cycle of innovation and commodification (189) that oscillates between creations for "people in the margins of society" to create a sense of autonomy and mobility and highly commercial productions that "capitalize on the profitability of the rebel image" (84). She argues, for instance, that the mainstream hot rod and biker films of the 1960s capitalized on the success of the beat road story but "popularized a backlash against the very 'mysteries'" the beats advocated: "homosexuality, racial difference, and an intermixture of literary and visual qualities in the avant-garde" (120).

Performing and advocating critical media literacy, Mills argues that scholarly analyses must not only identify the genre's structuring themes, like rebellion, but also evaluate whether particular stories serve a conservative or progressive function (120). In her discussion of the appearance of female characters in road films from the 1970s, for instance, Mills contends that the road genre, unlike other postwar film genres, accepted "the destruction of traditional gender roles," portraying "the awkward search for new roles between the sexes" (148). However, she finds that the "increasing presence of women" (158) ultimately reflects the male-dominated Hollywood film industry, as road films convey a conservative politics that "champion[s] the sexual revolution, not women's liberation per se" (148).

Mills argues that remapping of the rebel story does not focus on the perspective of the lone, individual traveler but instead represents the viewpoint of subcultures—beats, hippies, women, African Americans, gays and lesbians, for example. Like Primeau, she understands the form as an interactive, evolving genre, specifically documenting "the ways in which emerging minority storytellers twist old stories to challenge formal conventions that have excluded them" (Mills 28) and to assert their autonomy. In the 1990s, for example, minority filmmakers construct a rebel position by using the road story to "raise political consciousness" and rebel against "unvoiced expectations about gender, sexuality, or race" left unquestioned in previous texts—or culture—while giving voice to the "collective longing for transformation of a minority community" (196–97).

Women's Road Narratives

Mills's work, and Lackey's to some extent, represents a critical tendency that becomes much more developed in the next two studies: the discussion of themes in relation to issues of identity. This tendency may be influenced by the development of identity politics, a form of political activity emerging from "the women's movement, the civil rights movement, gay rights struggles, and the New Left in the 1960s" that emphasizes "the importance of recognizing—and valuing—previously denigrated or devalued identities" (Kaplan 125). Focused on the concerns of those who identify with a particular a social group, rather than a specific political party or ideology, identity politics expands the fight for economic and legal rights to include the challenging of demeaning characterizations through "representation, voice, and self-determination" (125). Deborah Paes de Barros' *Fast Cars and Bad Girls: Nomadic Subjects and Women's Road Stories* (2004) and Alexandra Ganser's *Roads of Her Own: Gendered Space and Mobility in American Women's Road Narratives, 1970–2000* (2009) both focus on bringing attention to the cultural representations of women as a social group. But why did two studies on women's road narratives emerge in such a short period of time? In addition to challenging the road's association with masculinity, these writers suggest that the road may have particular appeal for a group that is overwhelmingly defined by domesticity. That is, for women, the road offers a mode for exposing and escaping the social and spatial configurations that restrict them.

Framing her study with Rosi Braidotti's feminist, postmodern theory of the nomad, Paes de Barros examines a female "nomadic consciousness" (18) exemplified by writers and characters who resist fixed territories (7) that are both spatial and social. These "bad" girls of road stories "ignore the regulating effect of masculinity" (8) by freeing themselves from an imposed domesticity and escaping to the road as a space outside of "cultural definitions" (10).

For these women, the road can provide a "temporary adventure" and respite from patriarchy or a "solace for the marginalized and unhappy woman" (186). At its most subversive, the road marks a space of exaltation and power (186). Paes de Barros's main point is that, in all cases, women's movements outside of social order are subversive.

As outsiders in society, women move to exist outside of patriarchal spaces, relationships, and definitions, rejecting "all universal rules and categories" (Paes de Barros 17). In the "outside space" (188) of the road, their subversion takes place, in part, as the transformation of identities and purposes defined by patriarchal culture. In road novels by Dorothy Allison, Barbara Kingsolver, and Mona Simpson, for instance, the female nomad does not express "rugged individualism" (96), nor does she seek to domesticate new terrain (18), two tendencies of men's road stories. Instead, she uses the road "as a path toward fulfillment, community and attachment between mothers and daughters" (96). This relationship presents an alternative to patriarchal heterosexuality, reclaims the maternal, and forges elastic connections between women. While the masculine tradition of the road emphasizes destinations and possession of space, Paes de Barros argues that the female nomad seeks a dynamic space of community and self-expression, reveling in a resistant and ongoing movement.

Paes de Barros's nomadic women seem not unlike Sherrill's picaros; both represent perpetually transient figures, "invisible outsiders" (Paes de Barros 11) who resist cultural limits with movements that, in turn, express fluid identities that challenge rigid classification. Although this can seem confusing, especially because the writers are very free ranging in their definitions of road texts and concepts, these overlapping arguments exemplify a critical tendency (also represented by Laderman) to view the road as an unequivocally subversive space outside of or oppositional to the status quo—however that is defined.

Alexandra Ganser, like Paes de Barros, challenges the perception of road literature as "masculine territory" (307), and she shares an interest in how women's narratives participate in the myth of the open road. However, she is also interested in their rejection of the myth. Rather than view women's road narratives as a "homogeneous group" (50) with a "unified narrative" (305), she categorizes them in relation to three paradigms of mobility: quest narratives, paranomadism, and the picaresque. As women's road stories question, subvert, and appropriate these paradigms, they envision not one but many roads (311).

Taking up issues of genre definition and identity politics discussed by other scholars, Ganser also draws from recent work by cultural geographers in order to highlight the ways women's texts challenge dominant "spatial formations" (14). Scholars have not discussed home much at all, except to argue that the road traveler's "quest for freedom" represents a "flight from domesticity" (14). Ganser complicates this dichotomy, first by showing how different forms of mobility construct different relationships to home: the quest seeks "the ideal home," the nomad "dismantles the duality of home and away, private and public," and the picara disdains "the necessity of home altogether" (35). Second, she argues that women may take to the road to escape confining domesticity, but they also find spatial limitations on the road (18–19). In short, roads are not always a space of liberation.

This second point is developed through Ganser's approach to identity. Rather than argue that the road, or any space, is structured according to a single category of identity, such as gender, she attends to the "multiplicity of differences"—race, class, age, sexuality—that shape women's mobility or immobility (306). For instance, quest narratives search for a place that "represents the idea of a better, more meaningful, more liberated life" (33). However, they also suggest how this very search must come to terms with "the colonial and gendered legacy of the journey West and the concept of the frontier" (308).

Ganser's category of paranomadism offers an important critique of the "somewhat romanticized" theories of "nomadic mobility" (34) by stressing that paranomads' paths are "chosen under pressure more than out of pleasure" (180). Rather than "wanderlust and adventurousness," their ongoing journeys are "motivated by economic or political necessity" (34) and reveal the multiple differences that produce different kinds of mobility. Cynthia Kadohata's novel *The Floating World* (1989), for instance, explores the "conflicting mobilities" (Ganser 218) of three generations of a Japanese American family: immigration, relocation and internment, and a subsequent diasporic migrancy. Theirs is a transgressive way of life, but it is not romanticized (181).

Where Now?

Each of these writers has mapped out important territories, so to speak, that also suggest possible directions for future scholarship. Ganser proposes, for instance, that critics question the "liberatory theorization of travel" (16). This task can be undertaken, first, by devoting additional critical attention to particular texts that offer this critique (like African American narratives), and second, by complicating the understanding of the road story as, by definition, a form of liberation or subversion.

In particular, as scholars, we need to consider more deeply the ways that road narratives offer complex understandings of transgression. Many critics understand transgression—the violation of cultural, moral, and legal codes or limits—to be an inherently positive and liberating form of subversion. But, as we might learn from those figures whose road travels include the possibility of personal danger, those who are deemed too mobile are viewed as problematically transgressive. Such analyses can lead to a greater understanding of the ways that mobility, as a spatial and ideological practice, works for some and against others and is always a cultural, rather than merely physical, enterprise.

By extension, future scholarship should continue to focus on "the spatiality of society" (Mitchell 3) in order to interrogate the term, and terms, of the road. Because the road is a geographical construct, the insights of geographers seem particularly important to help literary critics develop an approach to it that goes beyond viewing it as a metaphorical and physical space outside of social reality and structures. Indeed, like "real" roads, literary and filmic representations of the road are a part and production of society. Even if a text does construct the road as completely outside of and immune to society, how can we analyze that representation as a cultural construction that tells something about how we divide up our social world or about power relations? Finally, as this question suggests, and as reviewer Neil Campbell has called for, future road scholarship can further convey the genre's importance by determining the ways in which road narratives "reveal explicit social and cultural issues" (Campbell 285). In particular, we can continue to discern the road genre's significance as an American cultural form by analyzing its engagement with, and elucidation of, historically specific questions and concerns. Such a focus will make a valuable contribution to scholarly efforts to understand how the road's meaning and significance, as well as its role as a social construct and mode of knowing, emerge and change across texts and over time.

Works Cited

Campbell, Neil. "Road Narratives and Western Identity." *Western American Literature* 36.3 (2001): 279–90. Print.

Ganser, Alexandra. *Roads of Her Own: Gendered Space and Mobility in American Women's Road Narratives, 1970–2000*. Amsterdam: Rodopi, 2009. Print.

Kaplan, Carla. "Identity." *Keywords for American Cultural Studies*. Ed. Bruce Burgett and Glenn Hendler. New York: New York UP, 2007. 123–27. Print.

Lackey, Kris. *RoadFrames: The American Highway Narrative*. Lincoln: U of Nebraska P, 1997. Print.

Laderman, David. *Driving Visions: Exploring the Road Movie*. Austin: U of Texas P, 2002. Print.

Mills, Katie. *The Road Story and the Rebel: Moving through Film, Fiction, and Television*. Carbondale: Southern Illinois UP, 2006. Print.

Mitchell, Don. *The Lie of the Land: Migrant Workers and the California Landscape*. Minneapolis: U of Minnesota P, 1996. Print.

Paes de Barros, Deborah. *Fast Cars and Bad Girls: Nomadic Subjects and Women's Road Stories*. New York: Lang, 2004. Print.

Primeau, Ronald. *Romance of the Road: The Literature of the American Highway*. Bowling Green: Bowling Green State U Popular P, 1996. Print.

Sherrill, Rowland A. *Road-Book America: Contemporary Culture and the New Picaresque*. Urbana: U of Illinois P, 2000. Print.

Real, Romantic, Modern, and Natural: Midwestern Hybridity and the Frank Booth Illustrations in Theodore Dreiser's *A Hoosier Holiday*

Marilyn Judith Atlas

A Hoosier Holiday (1916) documents an August 1915 journey by automobile from New York to Terre Haute, Indiana, where Theodore Dreiser (1871–1945) was born. It demonstrates that the memory of emotion increases the likelihood that a "language-based narrative" memory will stick from childhood, as well as that "body" memory, somatic memory, exists without a semantic or narrative component. Dreiser shares the emotions as well as the traumas of his childhood, rethinking both his present life and his childhood using all of the tools in his artist's box: dialect and dialogue, humor and philosophy, images and narrative. This five-hundred-page memoir is worth considering because through it, a major writer explores his controversial ideas and perspective, reviewing a radical life both thought and felt, both traumatic and privileged. Like essayist Ralph Waldo Emerson, Dreiser refuses easy labels, preferring ambivalence and hybridity to orthodoxy. Although he can be self-consciously sentimental and nostalgic, as scholar Carolyn Heilbrun points out in her introduction to *Writing a Woman's Life* (1988), "nostalgia, particularly for childhood, is likely to be a mask for unrecognized anger" (15). Dreiser had much to be angry about: he despised his oppressive Catholic education and the repression of normal sexual urges that his Midwest upbringing demanded. He also thought his father difficult and the size of his family ridiculous given the family's economic difficulties: "As I have said, there were ten [children] all told—a restless, determined, halfeducated [sic] family who, had each been properly trained according to his or her capacities, I have always thought might have made a considerable stir in the world" (*Hoosier* 15).

But that anger in no way undoes the fact that his travel memoir is dedicated to his mother and that it begins with a stunningly beautiful chapter, "The Rose Window," in which Dreiser refuses to forget how he dreamed as a boy: "In the eaves of our cottage were bluebirds and wrens, and to our trumpet vines and purple clematis came wondrous humming birds to poise and glitter, tropic their radiance" (*Hoosier* 17). Dreiser creates a palimpsest in which layer is added to layer and the world in which he travels is allowed its many moods and tastes and shades of light. Dreiser made the trip at the suggestion of illustrator Franklin Booth (1874–1948), another Indiana native, who proposed it when they saw each other at a New York party celebrating the publication of midwestern poet Edgar Lee Masters's *Spoon River Anthology* (1915). Booth wanted Dreiser to accompany him to Indiana in order to visit the scenes of Dreiser's childhood years: Terre Haute, Sullivan, Evansville, and Warsaw. They made a deal: Dreiser would document the trip, and Booth would illustrate it. Dreiser, nearly forty-four years old at the time, had left Indiana at sixteen. Here was his chance to revisit and reinterpret the spaces that had molded him.

Indiana had proved disheartening for Dreiser as a permanent home, but as the trip frequently demonstrated to him, it was "pleasing enough as a spectacle or the temporary scene of a vacation" (*Newspaper* 459). The two-thousand-mile road trip was to be taken in Booth's automobile, an Indiana-made Pathfinder, and was to be chauffeured by two young men, first Speed and then Bert. Miss H——, one of Booth's models, also accompanied them for a short part of their journey west (39). But it was Booth who most interested Dreiser. Early in *A Hoosier Holiday*, he describes Booth and their relationship:

I first met Franklin ten years before, when he was fresh from Indiana and working on the Sunday supplement of a now defunct New York paper. I was doing the same. I was drawn to him then because he had such an air of unsophisticated and genial simplicity while looking so much the artist. I liked his long strong aquiline nose, and his hair of a fine black and silver, though he was then only twenty-seven or eight. It is now white—a soft, artistic shock of it, glistening white. Franklin is a Christian Scientist, or dreamy metaphysician. (13)

Franklin sketched and Dreiser wrote. Both men were famous by the time the trip was taken, neither defined himself as a traditional Christian, and both hungered to recapture their lost Midwest—to taste the past and experience the present. They were drawn to new, modern ideas, and also to beauty. Sexually insecure, they were caught in a patriarchy that both benefited and restricted them (361). It was a remarkable trip, and it resulted in a remarkable road-trip book.

By 1915, Booth was successful enough to have a studio in Carmel, Indiana, where his parents lived, as well as one in New York, and Dreiser, who had published many novels, was recognized as a serious modern writer. *Sister Carrie* (1900) had been his biggest success, but other books in various genres followed. Dreiser published a book of short stories, *Old Rogaum and His Theresa* (1901), and a series of novels—*Jennie Gerhardt* (1911), *The Financier* (1912), *The Titan* (1914), and *The "Genius"* (1915)—in short succession. In between, he wrote and published a memoir of his European tour, *A Traveler at Forty* (1913), and collected and published some plays in the same year that *A Hoosier Holiday* appeared in print.

Written more than forty years before Jack Kerouac's groundbreaking road narrative *On the Road* (1957), *A Hoosier Holiday* is one of the first road-trip books. It demonstrates Dreiser's ability to straddle several worlds, write creative nonfiction effectively, and examine with fresh eyes and midwestern modernity the world that molded his personality and art. From his days as a literary journalist in the 1890s and the early twentieth century, Dreiser had learned to observe and record facts; as a turn-of-the-century novelist, he had demonstrated his ability to create and develop memorable midwestern characters and spaces. Recording his trip home to Indiana gave him an opportunity to write something else truly innovative. He was helping to create the American road book—a still-unclassified genre.

Val Holley, author of the essay "H. L. Mencken and the Indiana Genii," has examined iconoclast journalist Mencken's many connections to Indiana. As Dreiser's confidant and correspondent, Mencken worked to promote Dreiser's novels as well as his travel memoirs. As a newspaperman, he valued "reminiscences" as primary documents and Dreiser's as helping to push the world of literature back into relevance. Mencken saw Dreiser's memoir as valuable to understanding the reality and foibles of the Midwest. This was an Indiana cultural product, one of which the forward-thinking Mencken approved. He wanted a new vision of the Midwest and, through writers such as Dreiser, was bringing this vision into print. As coeditor of the magazines *Smart Set* and *American Mercury*, Mencken fought against the northern branch of the Ku Klux Klan, which was located in Indiana. He needed a writer such as Dreiser to help him further his modernist political and aesthetic agenda. Although the two men did not always agree and over the years had an increasingly volatile relationship, as Robert Elias documents in *Theodore Dreiser: Apostle of Nature* (1969), for a time Mencken helped promote Dreiser's writings. In October 1917, Mencken wrote in the *Smart Set* that *A Hoosier Holiday* marked a "high tide" of Dreiser's writing—praise that helped to sell this road book.

Dreiser valued realism. While *A Hoosier Holiday* is sprinkled with sentiment and mysticism, it never stops being a realistic text in which Dreiser shares what he saw and remembered. As a young writer, he had admired Midwest humorist and realist George Ade, perhaps a bit too indiscriminately. In *Two Dreisers* (1969), Ellen Moers notes that Dreiser reused a small section of Ade's *Fables in Slang* (1899) in the first chapter of *Sister Carrie*. Moers argues that in that first important novel, Dreiser was attempting to create a realistic portrayal of character Charles Drouet as not only a "drummer," or traveling salesman, but also a "masher," a man who tries to seduce women, and suggests that Dreiser must have felt that Ade drew his "masher" particularly well. When Dreiser was questioned about "borrowing" this passage, Ade came to his rescue, generously dismissing accusations of plagiarism and explaining that he was quite willing to allow Dreiser the privilege of a small cut-and-paste theft. By 1900, Ade saw himself as a minor player and Dreiser as a global one, and he was therefore willing to protect Dreiser's career from this type of stain (Moers 113).

Booth was an illustrator for such popular magazine as *McClure's*, *Cosmopolitan*, *Scribner's*, *Harper's*, the *Saturday Evening Post*, *Good Housekeeping*, *Ladies' Home Journal*, and *Collier's*. Between 1910 and 1930, his work was widely recognizable, his signature almost unnecessary. He was famous not for realism or "immorality"—unlike Dreiser, who was known for creating characters who behave badly but go unpunished by the author, such as *Sister Carrie*'s Carrie Meeber—but for his poetic sense of space. He was admired by later artist Norman Rockwell, who in turn became famous for his idealization of American life. Booth was known as a master of the pen and brush, a mostly self-taught artist who used techniques modeled after wood engraving. He became known for his methodology because it allowed more freedom than either steel or wood engraving allowed. In his biography of Booth, Howard C. Caldwell explains, "Booth used almost every kind of line in almost every possible combination and with these lines of different strength and different spacing, he produced hitherto unsuspected tone values in black and white" (11). His pen looked like paint, his black lines like colors, and so he was able to capture, beauty, mood, and thought—imaginative qualities that, combined with his craft, made his work complex and popular. Although Booth was capable of meticulousness, Dreiser preferred that his work in *A Hoosier Holiday* be "rough," stressing realism and impressionism rather than romance. Somehow, presenting the Midwest finely did not suit Dreiser's memory of the midwestern places of his youth or the way he wished to depict the trip in words.

In his introduction to the 1997 Indiana University Press reissue of *A Hoosier Holiday*, historian Douglas Brinkley notes that Booth was also the respected illustrator of the radical magazine *The Masses*. So it was the radical Booth who illustrated for the radical Dreiser, whose early influences included Herbert Spencer, the social scientist and political theorist who coined the phrase "survival of the fittest," and the French novelist Honoré de Balzac, one of the founders of realism (Dreiser, *Newspaper* x). Naturalism, realism, and romance were reflected in both men's philosophies and art, and in *A Hoosier Holiday*, they would meet in the form of illustrations and language.

In *Sister Carrie*, set in the 1880s and 1890s, Carrie Meeber and George Hurstwood travel by train, but in 1915, Dreiser and Booth made their pilgrimage via modern automobile. Dreiser was self-consciously aware that what he was doing was technically modern: "We clambered up the bank on the farther side, the car making great noise. In this sweet twilight with fireflies and spirals of gnats and 'pinchin' bugs . . . we tore the remainder of the distance, the eyes of the car glowing like great flames" (*Hoosier* 39). This passage, with its motion and emotion, narrative, personification, and embodiment, is typical of *A Hoosier Holiday*. Here Dreiser feels and thinks, and Booth's illustrations complement the experience of traveling from the East to home in the Midwest, where both Lew Wallace's Christian novel *Ben-Hur* (1880) and the first automobile were created: a mythic and technologically savvy space.

Brinkley reminds his readers that the Western tradition of travel writing is an old one and can be traced back to Norwegian and Icelandic epic narratives. During the mid-nineteenth century, with the emergence of the American Renaissance, writers traveling and writing their stories in various genres was much in vogue. Emerson, Walt Whitman, Henry David Thoreau, and Margaret Fuller each wrote about his or her travels. Thoreau famously proclaimed, in an article published posthumously in the *Atlantic Monthly* in 1862, that walking is a spiritual and metaphorical activity: "Every walk is a sort of crusade preached by some Peter the Hermit in us, to go forth and reconquer this Holy land from the Hands of the Infidels" (qtd. in Brinkley 4). Thoreau's infidels may have been, as Brinkley says, "the industrialists who preached the gospel of unfettered commerce" (4), but not so for Dreiser. Dreiser's holy land was Indiana, and the infidels were the demons of his child-hood—his stern father, his Catholic upbringing, and the poverty that flavored too much of his youth and caused him to move from home to home and city to city. Dreiser needed to face his own Midwest mythologies, disappointment, and anger. His fight was to be part of the middle class, to respect his place in the world. His youth had been none too easy, and it required a second look from him.

Ironically, the industrialism and commerce that Thoreau opposed made this modern genre of highway literature possible. Dreiser appreciated the automobile; as Brinkley observes, "the owner of a car could go whenever and wherever he pleased" (6). For Dreiser, the automobile was a liberator. Almost four decades earlier, he had left Indiana, dreaming first of being a big-city reporter and then of being a novelist. Now he was helping to invent a new genre: road literature.

So in 1915, Dreiser traveled west by automobile as a social realist taking the pulse of a nation as well as his own pulse. By turns he was an adventurer, a philosopher of democracy, and a man revisiting the place of his birth and youth. This was his travel to the "interior," his "heart of darkness" and of light, his journey down variously paved Midwest roads. He was not author Joseph Conrad, nor narrator Charles Marlow, nor antihero Mistah Kurtz, but all three. When he visited each small town's major hotel, he was the youthful, impoverished Dreiser looking in, the appreciative Dreiser in the lobby, and later the ambivalent Dreiser viewing small-town realities from the perspective of a successful writer who had sat in Paris's cafes, visited its art museums, and written to tell the world about it several years earlier in *A Traveler at Forty*.

Dreiser, Booth, and Speed were making history, writing and illustrating a road book. Their Pathfinder was powerful, letting them choose to take less traveled, more scenic routes. It was also musical. Dreiser explains, "It was a smooth-running machine which, at its best (or worst), gave vent to a tr-r-r-r-r-r-r-r-r which became after a while somewhat like a croon" (*Hoosier* 26), and he repeats the sound at several junctures in the text to entertain the reader.

This automobile trip inspired Melvillean metaphysical questioning. At the end of chapter 3, "Across the Meadows to the Passaic," Dreiser waxes eloquent, giving the reader some combination of *Moby-Dick*'s (1851) Ishmael and Pip:

> What if it *is* all a mad, aimless farce, my masters? Shan't we clown it all together and make the best of it?
> Ha ha! Ho ho! We are all crazy and He is crazy! Ha ha! Ho ho!
> Or do I hear someone crying? (*Hoosier* 28; ital. in orig.)

He begins chapter 15, "A Ride by Night," as if he were Ishmael experiencing the unctuousness of the try-pots for the first time or watching schools of whales, mothers and infants together in the great Pacific, before even one harpoon is thrust: "It was a glorious night—quite wonderful. There are certain summer evenings when nature produces a poetic, emotionalizing mood. Life seems to talk to you in soft whispers of wonderful things it is doing. . . . All nature improvises a harmony—a splendid harmony—one of her rarest symphonies indeed" (116).

Dreiser borrows without apology, playfully documenting his road trip through oceans of American and world literature and history. He begins another chapter in a manner reminiscent of colonial-era teacher Sarah Kemble Knight's travel journal, written while she was traveling from Boston to New York: "Next morning I was aroused at dawn, it seemed to me, by a pounding on a nearby door. 'Get up, you drunken hound!' called a voice which was unmistakably that of the young man who had rented us the room" (*Hoosier* 123). Dreiser tries out many personas throughout the memoir, and he peppers his narrative with literary references. Hamlin Garland's 1891 collection *Main-Travelled Roads* is mentioned (134), as is Homer's *Iliad* (153). French writer and Nobel Prize winner Anatole France makes an appearance (154), and Dreiser uses a poem by Euripides to explain his belief that the world was never just (196). While he toys with entropy, he does not remain depressed. His life force is too strong.

But the memoir is filled not only with roads but also, interestingly for a road book, with trains. Wherever the Pathfinder goes, it meets trolleys and railroads: "I looked up a cliff side—very high up—and saw a railroad station labeled Manunka-Chunk" (*Hoosier* 38). Dreiser later writes, "Below us, under a cliff, ran a railroad, its freight and passenger trains seeming to thunder ominously near" (40). Dreiser is always noting the sound of trains, their tracks, the world left behind making itself known. He revels in and notes the quality of the road taken, "the eyes of the car glowing like great flames," and the speed and the beauty he passes and touches (39). Nowhere in the memoir does he stop being amazed at what nature is or what humans have made; he notes the errors and he notes the wonders. Dreiser thinks about and feels the architecture and the flora, the water and the sky, the storms and the poverty, the wealth, the pretension, and the possibilities. Like Saul Bellow's Henderson the Rain King, he "wants" as he moves self-consciously through time and space.

Dreiser and Booth's chauffeur, Speed, is described as "a blond, lithe, gangling youth with an eerie farmer-like look" (*Hoosier* 22). Speed was a mechanic who could fix a flat, a boy-man from the Midwest. Their trip was to be a modern-day Midwest adventure. Booth, who had brought his charcoal to sketch the countryside, assured Dreiser that Speed had been "one of the chauffeurs who led the procession of cars from New York over the Alleghenies and Rockies to the coast, laying out the Lincoln Highway" (22). He was a symbol of modernity, from his name to his role. Speed would lead the way on this modern-day epic journey of discovery.

In this memoir, Dreiser enjoys visiting the grand hotel found in every small town, and these visits fill him with a collage of conflicting emotions. A young and poor Dreiser, yearning and ambitious, is only one of the many Dreisers the reader meets on this road trip. He rants against the brutality of capitalism and the silliness of some midwesterners who do not seem to understand or remember that money cannot buy "certain delicacies of perception" (*Hoosier* 46).

Dreiser shares with the reader the geographical, idyllic, and architectural details of the midwestern scene, examining tinsel and ordinariness, pretension and cuisine. He loves the regional dialect and makes sure his readers share his pleasure. There are stories to be told in the automobile: "'That's a very fine darg ye have.' 'Yes, stranger; he's the finest dog in the county'" (*Hoosier* 89). The words remind the reader that the Midwest has its own culture and texture. Coal pits, sidewalks, beaches, Lake Erie, farms—here in *A Hoosier Holiday* is Dreiser's chant of middle America.

As soon as he leaves New York, Dreiser feels he is in the extended Midwest: "I was out of New York and back home, as it were—even here at the Delaware River—so near does the west come to the east" (*Hoosier* 48). Dreiser means this to be a study of his Midwest, a rural Midwest that begins in New Jersey and Pennsylvania, where the people are more intelligent and free in their souls than the Europeans he visited just a few years earlier and wrote about in *A Traveler at Forty*. In sum, Dreiser explores provincialism and rethinks democracy. Examining machinery, production, and midwestern heroes such as Abraham Lincoln and William Jennings Bryan, trying to separate the Midwest of his youth from the Midwest of 1915, Dreiser creates a palimpsest of dullness and passion, backward and progressive thinking.

This sentimental and realistic text was written while Dreiser's eyes should perhaps have been focused on the Great War in Europe. He does mention the war briefly, speculating that perhaps the Germans, being stronger, will win and hoping that the United States will stay out of the fray (*Hoosier* 180), and he cannot fully erase its presence from the book. In chapter 39, his host accounts for his inability to keep an organized inn by explaining that he is depressed and traumatized by the loss of first his wife and then his son: "I've just suffered a great blow in the death of my oldest boy over at the Dardanelles. When he left the navy he went into the Australian Army, and they made him a captain and then when this war broke out his company was sent to the Dardanelles and he went along and has just been killed over there"

(311). The United States had not yet entered the war officially, but midwesterners nevertheless were dying because of it.

Dreiser falls in love with country life. He is sick of the city; he fumes about the industrial cities "intent on building cheap skyscrapers at the expense of architectural integrity." He laments the "misguided downtowns," imitations, and copies of "great whales" (Brinkley 9). But the tone of this road book fluctuates; it is sometimes a picaresque frolic and at other times a painful exploration of nostalgia and the buried emotions of an exhausted boy. In Terre Haute, Dreiser has the wrong address for his birthplace, so he cannot find his first home. He turns forty-four in Bloomington, his old college town, and again expresses ambivalence about who he has been, who he is, and where he is heading. Throughout the narrative, Dreiser moves in and out of time, in and out of place. His memoir sounds notes of both pleasure and despair.

While many later road books are better known, *A Hoosier Holiday* nevertheless deserves to be remembered and read. Here the ideal and the real meet, and Dreiser's sexualized, sometimes feminist but more often sexist worldview helps establish the culture of the United States in 1915. The author's confusion and ambivalence and the illustrator's talent, textures, and choices of where to place his gaze combine to make this a memoir worth reading and seeing.

In *A Hoosier Holiday*, Dreiser crosses the line many times between nostalgia and cynicism, just as Booth's illustrations move from architecture to nature, from narrative to still point. The drawings used in the memoir were begun on the road, but Booth intended to develop them using ink. Dreiser, however, was so charmed by the "rougher" versions that he asked Booth to leave them be, a request Booth honored. Perhaps that lack of polish was meant to reinforce Dreiser's "rough" vision of Indiana: a home where the Ku Klux Klan was gaining power; a home where his past desires for privilege, such as being a guest at the grand hotels, collided with his knowledge that Gilded Age values had helped to kill his beloved characters, such as *Sister Carrie*'s Hurstwood, who failed to remain economically viable in "robber baron" America.

Dreiser and Booth complemented one another. Both had troubled youths. Booth's father withheld approval from his artistic son, while Dreiser's might have preferred a religious, conservative, less sexual child. Like Dreiser, whose brother was the musician Paul Dresser, Booth had creative siblings; also like Dreiser, he was inspired by architecture and space. Neither man was formally well educated; Dreiser was a committed reader and largely self-taught, and Booth had studied briefly at the Chicago Art Institute and the Art Student's League and had gained some technical knowledge from art correspondence classes. Both had traveled to Europe. Caldwell, in his introduction to *Franklin Booth: American Illustrator* (2006), quotes Booth's humorous response regarding the ultimate value of his European trip: "While I did not come back any better artist than I was before I left, my three months in Europe gave me a wonderful talking point." When he returned, he was better able to sell his illustrations to magazines such as *Scribner's* (17). So when Booth and Dreiser made their trip to Carmel, Indiana, a studio Booth had built in 1912 was waiting for him. His parents, who had retired, lived in the town, and Booth's studio was at the back of their property. He preferred to work in Carmel rather than in New York (19). The thirty-two full-page illustrations for Dreiser's *Hoosier Holiday* were completed in Booth's Carmel studio.

This travel book's form and content explore Dreiser's and Booth's ambivalent responses to the Midwest: the Midwest they had left, the Midwest they were visiting, and the Midwest of their fantasies. They worked together well; they cared for one another. In chapter 27, "A Summer Storm and Some Comments on the Picture Postcard," Dreiser explains that since Booth wanted to sketch and neither had an umbrella, Dreiser laid his mackintosh on Booth's head "like an awning" (*Hoosier* 215). As Booth sketches a bridge, Dreiser half-jokingly considers their joint legacy: "It may be written that 'In A.D. 1915, Theodore Dreiser, accompanied by one Franklin Booth, an artist, visited the site of this bridge, which was then in perfect condition, and made a sketch of it, preserved now in that famous volume entitled "A Hoosier Holiday," by

Theodore Dreiser.'" Booth reprimands Dreiser for omitting his name from the book's title page, and Dreiser gives him full credit and suggests that Booth will proofread the text, thereby ensuring that Booth will get his due and that his name will also be preserved for posterity (216). This is the case in the University of Indiana Press's republication of the memoir and illustrations, which includes Dreiser's name as well as Booth's on the title page.

This is a travel book worth knowing. From Dreiser's commentary on Whitman to his perspective on the Midwest's melting-pot fiasco—he recounts an encounter with a clearly Japanese American woman who insists on erasing her Japanese heritage—to his discussion of the lynching of Jewish factory supervisor Leo Frank, the book expresses Dreiser's Midwest. Even Anatole France gets a cynical line at the beginning of chapter 31—"robbery is to be condoned [sic]; the result of robbery respected" (qtd. in *Hoosier* 244)—as Dreiser experiences the downside of the region.

Together, Dreiser and Booth—a world-class author and a world-class illustrator from the "golden age of American illustration"—took this trip and immortalized the Midwest in prose and illustration. They represent what Moers astutely recognizes as the contradiction inherent not only in Dreiser's art (and Booth's as well) but also in the American cultural experience. Neither Dreiser nor Booth can be placed neatly in any one period or tradition; both bridge the worlds of science and art, naturalism, realism, and romance.

A Hoosier Holiday is steeped in midwestern contradictions. As Dreiser writes in his attempt to convey his sadness and ambivalence about being in Indiana, "a dead world like this is such a compound—a stained glass window at its best; a bone yard at its worst" (*Hoosier* 284). In Warsaw, Dreiser attempts to gain some usable perspective, to study the idea of "memory" (290). He is trying to figure out the universal by studying the specific, and he is experiencing modernity, ambivalence, and in-betweenness. Appropriately, he offers his readers an abrupt and awkward but poetic ending: "Of dreams and the memory of them is life compounded" (513). Dreiser leaves the reader with a sentence fragment and much to consider about the road-book genre and about the Midwest—its racism, classism, sexism—firmly reminding the reader in a prescient way that emotions are not a luxury but an essential part of rational thinking and that people are all works in progress who cannot do better than look and listen and think and feel as best they can.

Neither Dreiser nor Booth apologizes. They were democrats and artists working together. Descartes might have believed "I think, therefore I am," but Dreiser and Booth both knew better. For them, the heart was as essential as the head; the past and present went hand in hand.

Works Cited

Bellow, Saul. *Henderson the Rain King*. New York: Viking, 1959. Print.
Brinkley, Douglas. "Introduction: Theodore Dreiser and the Birth of the Road Book." *A Hoosier Holiday*. By Theodore Dreiser. Bloomington: Indiana UP, 1997. 3–11. Print.
Bryson, Bill. *The Lost Continent: Travels in Small-Town America*. New York: Harper, 1990. Print.
Caldwell, Howard C. "Franklin Booth Biography." *Franklin Booth: American Illustrator*. Ed. Manuel Auad. San Francisco: Auad, 2006. 11–22. Print.
Damásio, António. *Descartes' Error: Emotion, Reason, and the Human Brain*. New York: Putnam, 1994. Print.
Dreiser, Theodore. *Best Short Stories*. Ed. Howard Fast. Chicago: Dee, 1989. Print.
___. *A Hoosier Holiday*. New York: Lane, 1916. Print.
___. *Newspaper Days*. Ed. Thomas P. Riggio and Lee Ann Draud. Philadelphia: U of Pennsylvania P, 1991. Print.
___. *Sister Carrie*. New York: Doubleday, 1900. Print.
___. *A Traveler at Forty*. New York: Century, 1913. Print.
Dreiser, Theodore, and H. L. Mencken. *Dreiser-Mencken Letters*. Ed. Thomas P. Riggio. 2 vols. Philadelphia: U of Pennsylvania P, 1986. Print.
Elias, Robert H. *Theodore Dreiser: Apostle of Nature*. Ithaca: Cornell UP, 1969. Print.
Fitzpatrick, Vincent. *H. L. Mencken*. New York: Continuum, 1989. Print.
Garland, Hamlin. *Main-Travelled Roads*. Lincoln: U of Nebraska P, 1995. Print.
Heilbrun, Carolyn. Introduction. *Writing a Woman's Life*. New York: Norton, 1988. 11–31. Print.
Holley, Val. "H. L. Mencken and the Indiana Genii." *Traces of Indiana and Midwestern History* 3.1 (1991): 14–18. Print.
James, Henry. *The American Scene*. Bloomington: Indiana UP, 1986. Print.

Kerouac, Jack. *On the Road*. New York: Viking, 1957. Print.

Lackey, Kris. *Road Frames: The American Highway Narrative*. Lincoln: U of Nebraska P, 1997. Print.

Lingeman, Richard. *Theodore Dreiser*. 2 vols. New York: Putnam, 1986–90. Print.

Manchester, William. *Disturber of the Peace: The Life of H. L. Mencken*. New York: Harper, 1950. Print.

Marx, Leo. *The Machine in the Garden: Technology and the Pastoral Ideal in America*. New York: Oxford UP, l964. Print.

Moers, Ellen. *Two Dreisers*: *The Man and the Novelist As Revealed in His Two Most Important Works,* Sister Carrie *and* An American Tragedy. New York: Viking, 1969. Print.

Primeau, Ronald. *Romance of the Road: The Literature of the American Highway*. Bowling Green: Bowling Green State U Popular P, 1996. Print.

Wade, Wyn Craig. "Ain't God Good to Indiana?" *The Fiery Cross: The Ku Klux Klan in America*. New York: Simon, l988. 215–47. Print.

West, James L. W. "Theodore Dreiser." *Sixteen Modern American Authors: Volume 2; A Survey of Research and Criticism since 1972*. Ed. Jackson R. Bryer. Durham: Duke UP, 1989. 120–53. Print.

Ziff, Larzer. *Return Passages: Great American Travel Writing, 1780–1910*. New Haven: Yale UP, 2000. Print.

Baudrillard in the Heartland: The Construction of the Midwest in American Road Literature _____

Barry Alford

> Where is the sea, that once solved the whole loneliness
> Of the Midwest?

James Arlington Wright

The Midwest has been carved up so often it is hard to see it as coherent. Wagons, trains, and highways have bisected it in pursuit of something other than itself, rendering it indistinguishable on its own terms. The road narratives of the post–World War II era—a subgenre often referred to simply as road literature, coming as it did at the dawn of a bicoastal America knit together by the shining networks of new highways and fast cars—reduce the Midwest to what the French cultural theorist Jean Baudrillard has called a simulacrum, a copy without an original (1). The heartland in these constructs is available only through excavation and archeology, and then only as an image emptied of content and meaning. The construction of the Midwest in road literature is never about reclaiming the region as part of the cartography that opens America to the hipster nomads moving in space and time in opposition to emerging conformity and consumer capitalism. Instead, road narratives use the simulacrum of the Midwest to buffer the eruptions of discontent and provide comforting alternatives to the nightmare of the road.

This treatment of the Midwest is unique to this type of road literature. Previous treatments of regional identity were much more specific, much more interested in what made each part of the country different from any other part of the country. But in this subgenre of American road literature, there are very few distinguishing characteristics that are part of the narrative. It is almost as if the territory of the heartland has to remain unmarked and unmapped for the narrative to proceed. There is little here to suggest a nod toward traditional wisdom or homespun tales of initiation or insight. These travelers are not at home in the Midwest, and they are not coming home to the Midwest. The country they traverse is more symbolic than actual. There may be the odd piece of memorable pie served in William Least Heat-Moon's *Blue Highways* (1982), but the absence of detail marks a shift in the way literature imagines and portrays America.

Road literature is about the reconstruction of America. It is a reconstruction situated at a particular time in the nation's history, in a particular cultural struggle for authenticity and alternative identities. Every construction of America contains a construction of the Midwest. Introducing Baudrillard is a way of reminding ourselves that the construction is purposeful, a literary illusion. There is, of course, a Midwest of specific and historical dimensions, but road literature is not about that construction. There are vital and interesting narratives that have their roots in the heartland—the Underground Railroad, for example, and much of the history of the progressive labor movement—but road novels empty out the particulars of this region, leaving behind something essentially American but devoid of distinguishing characteristics. The Midwest was once a frontier itself, but it was eclipsed because it lacked an ocean to prevent its obsolescence. The construction of the heartland, the simulacrum, is interesting for what is left out as much as or more than for what it contains. Much like the constructions of "whiteness" and "maleness" that operate as default settings in much road literature, the Midwest is interesting precisely because of what is not said.

One of the things that make American road literature unique is the ability to translate space into time and speed, to transform movement into meditation. The journey in a road novel is only superficially a physical journey. The deeper journey is always one of self-discovery. In *On the Road* (1957), Jack Kerouac's "holy road" (124) of cars and highways becomes a place to reflect and dream, and that requires space. Rolling a Cadillac through Kansas at one hundred miles per hour, on roads "straight as an arrow" (252), frees the mind and elevates the spirit, but it requires an emptiness, a monotony of landscape and lifestyle that makes the eventual arrival in the mythic West a revival that goes deeper than geography. The journey transforms the traveler. The Midwest is the space of liminality, as Ronald Primeau puts it (6), that lifts the traveler/hero out of the now and into a suspension that has marked travel and pilgrimage for as long as stories have been told. The Midwest becomes that space of road that lies between the old consciousness of the East and the emerging consciousness of the West. In doing so, it relinquishes its own identity. It is emptied of its particular and specific qualities and made to stand for something else.

Of course, this view of the Midwest is not entirely new to road narratives. As James Arlington Wright's poem "As I Step over a Puddle at the End of Winter, I Think of an Ancient Chinese Governor" suggests, the Midwest is often seen as something to be escaped, a loneliness to be solved. In his essay about science-fiction writers, "Rockets Rise on the Wabash," Henry Golemba goes so far as to suggest that the reason that so many mainstream practitioners of that genre come from the Midwest is that the emptiness of the region promotes extreme imagination. These writers escape this "inferior culture" (4) but hold on to the sense of place, of timelessness and solidarity, that comes from growing up in the heartland. Golemba captures the contradiction that the Midwest generates for travelers in road literature. The heartland operates as a placeholder in the ongoing narrative for the possibility of a new identity and a new cultural landscape, but it does so as a memory, not a reality. Sal can think of himself as being a "patriarch" in Iowa in *On the Road* (161), but the real Kerouac could not survive more than a couple of months in Grosse Point. The slowness of the heartland is alluring as an antidote to the speed it takes to escape it. Golemba's construction of the Midwest matches the way road literature constructs it: alternately solid and empty, necessary and unremarkable.

The specific emptiness of road narratives, however, differs in a significant way from Golemba's construction. Golemba sees the Midwest as boring but substantial, too specific and mundane to fire the imagination of authors engaged in the emerging genre of science fiction. In contrast, in road novels, the heartland exerts no gravity at all. The heroes of road novels are not languishing in the fields or working away in the mills. They are exercising a new kind of freedom, one that isolates the storyteller from the emotional space. Unlike science fiction, road novels do not take the time to make the heartland "strange" or alien. They do not follow the plot of an Alfred Hitchcock movie, with hypocrisy or evil lurking behind every picket fence. Instead, they erase the heartland from the narrative, leaving only the hint that they have passed through.

Baudrillard, in the opening of *Simulacra and Simulation* (1994; *Simulacres et Simulation*, 1981), quotes Ecclesiastes: "The simulacrum is never what hides the truth—it is truth that hides the fact that there is none. The simulacrum is true" (1). So it is with the constructions of the Midwest that populate road literature: they do not hide the truth; they are the truth. Whether it is Dean and Sal rocketing through the Midwest in someone else's Cadillac in *On the Road* or George Gastin highballing a rig high on speed through the heartland in Jim Dodge's *Not Fade Away* (1987), what they pass becomes insignificant compared to the act of passing through. The real—or, in Baudrillard's terms, the hyperreal—becomes what we expect the Midwest to be, what we need the heartland to stand for, and not what it actually is. Even in more benign constructions, the heartland is little more than prelude. Robert Pirsig warms up to narrative in the Great Plains, and William Least Heat-Moon circles through the Midwest, but both of them find their vision in high country. Road literature creates a heartland to fit its needs and, in the process, leaves a trace of what road narratives since World War II take for granted.

The reason the Midwest is so important to contextualizing and understanding road literature is that it makes it possible to see what this literature assumes as its core principles. That is, because the heartland is an illusion, it can help us better see what the genre is really about.

The real question is why the Midwest has to be constructed this way. What is it that these quest narratives are after that makes it so important not to get stuck, to be able to maintain speed and liminality? The road, especially in its early forms, offers an escape from the decay of the postwar culture. It was obvious that the culture was undergoing a significant change; the question was how that change would be constructed and who would be included. The lore of the beat generation, the rejection of the increasing materialism of American culture, the beginning of a youthful counterculture—these are well documented. In the PBS documentary *The Source* (1999), the beats are credited with starting almost all of the countercultural formation of the 1960s. Although that is no doubt true in part, it is worth looking at what is not said about the novels that follow *On the Road* in a quest for a new America. Primeau calls his 1996 book *Romance of the Road*, and it is worth unpacking just what kind of romance this is.

The "romance" of the postwar traveler has a different texture to it than previous versions of the road. Although the beats often cite Walt Whitman as foundational to their work, their novels lack the joy or rootedness in America that Whitman celebrated. Beat travelers are always already trapped by the contingencies of their everyday existence. Recently divorced, fighting mental illness, going home to die, they take to the road not to sing of the common man but to lose their identity in the new invisibility of the highway. The heartland holds no interest for them because in the heartland, people know who you are. There is none of the anonymity that allows these questers to look for something not yet imagined and not available to everyone.

The first observation, one confirmed by Primeau's expansive cataloging of road literature, is that road literature is essentially a white, male privilege. There are exceptions, of course, but not that many, and the major works in the genre are male dominated. It is important in recovering the historical context of these works to recognize this sense of privilege. The story of the beat writers in almost every critical analysis greatly underestimates and marginalizes the role that the "beat chicks" played in both bringing the gaggle of students and hangers-on at Columbia after the war into contact with each other and nurturing the movement into existence. The role that Kerouac's first wife, Frankie Edith Parker, played in the movement and in Kerouac's life and fiction should stand as a primary example. The birth of the road novel is contiguous with the postwar suppression of women in American society. The blue-collar working women of the war effort, romanticized as Rosie the Riveter, were being forced out of jobs and coaxed back into domesticity by everything from consumer capitalism to propagandizing sitcoms just as men were heading out on the highway to find "it." The open road and the visions of individual freedom are, for the most part, gender specific. It would not be out of bounds to simply say they are misogynistic. The point is not that this focus makes road literature "bad" but that it marks a cultural definition of what male privilege looks like in action.

The same thing can be said for the role whiteness plays in road narratives. The era of the 1960s is the setting of the greatest number of road novels, but only one of these was written by an African American. In 1965, John A. Williams, a travel writer for *Holiday* magazine, published *This Is My Country Too*, a chronicle of his travels in search of America. It is not surprising that Williams's observations, often written from the relative security of a Howard Johnson, do not match the idyllic, Whitmanesque freedom that white authors discover. In an even more audacious example of white privilege, the country that road narratives traverse, and that these travelers claim as their own, no longer shows any signs of the Native American cultures that were forced from the land. Road literature "explores" and appropriates a landscape that does not have to bear witness to the struggle, exploitation, and genocide that allow the authors to claim any sense of ownership to their experience. Kerouac makes a nod in that direction in Mexico—and, to be fair, Kerouac can at least claim Native American ancestry—but his observations, as always, end up being about his inability to connect and sustain, rather than the larger cultural issue. Even when Least

Heat-Moon offers his vision of the hoop dance in *Blue Highways*, the vision is presented not as culturally specific, as grounded in a sacred understanding of place and time, but as a boutique insight equally available to all. This America was not cleared or struggled over. It was not ever a home or an ancestral space. It was always already empty, always already devoid of meaning or identity. So much of American literature is about what has made the country unique and valuable. This is literature about the lack of those qualities, the inability to spark some sense of the true and beautiful in the whole vast expanse of the continent. These storytellers have not just lost track with the people who preceded them, they have lost track of themselves.

One of the mysteries of road literature is that the characters in flight should feel secure and privileged. They are not fleeing a diaspora or struggling to have a chance in life. Dean has his own checkered past, with his missing father and reform-school background, but why would Sal, and the countless others who take up his trek, flee to the road to find "it"? The lack of diversity in the structure of the road novel offers both a glimpse into their promise and a cautionary tale. It is part of American exceptionalism to believe there is still more there—more to discover, even when the ocean argues otherwise. There is a sense of entitlement, a privileged feeling that this form of existence is too small, too confining, for someone so special. This is already the first sense that the glitz that America started to embrace in the media and advertising age following World War II was a hollow vision. The speed of the road is an attempt to break through to something real, to burn away the illusions of the emergent commercialization, but because the goal was never any more real than the image the characters try to escape, the quest must fail.

Primeau talks about the problem of reentry (127) that to some extent is part of any quest or initiation rite of passage. What is unique to these road novels is the context of the quest. At precisely the moment that America becomes transcendent, it vanishes into its own mythology. These storytellers leave because their own stories have no real meaning, but they discover that nothing else does either. So much of what we have become and failed to become in the period since World War II is captured in these novels. They make it clear, as no other form of fiction is quite able to accomplish, that the specter of the simulacrum is already invasive in American culture. If these privileged souls cannot find an anchor point to their lives and cannot push through the illusion far enough to bring back, as Whitman tried to do, a vision that was expansive and positive, the only conclusion is that the culture has lost the ability to fashion that narrative.

Road narratives have to be contextualized and held accountable for the things that are occluded in the telling. They should also be challenged on their most widely granted cultural capital: their resistance to the rampant consumer capitalism of postwar American culture. It is true that road narratives offer an alternative cultural experience, but it may not be accurate to say they avoid consumerism. To be sure, no one hits the road with a new refrigerator in tow, but these narrators are engaged in a different kind of cultural consumption: the devouring of the exotic. For almost all of them, it is the West that beckons. For Sal, the new and raw atmosphere of Denver seems like the perfect cure for the stale streets of Lowell and the haunted piers of New Jersey. When that disappoints, there is always San Francisco as a last stand in America, before Mexico City offers the last chance for salvation and redemption. Road narratives cultivate an appetite for new scenery that in the bicoastal frenzy of postwar America almost always translates as the West. As Jim Morrison and the Doors once sang, "The West is best, get here and we'll do the rest." Road narratives follow the migratory patterns of the culture itself. The cultural formation that Theodore Roszak eventually labels a "counterculture" is driven by lifestyle alternatives and destinations that often can be condensed to "California." But the consumerism that the beats fled follows their new cultural artifacts. At the end of *Desolation Angels* (1965), a broken and bitter Kerouac confronts the counterfeit versions of beatness that his writing spawned. The urban legend of *On the Road* being kept behind the bookstore counter because kids still steal it remains. The road may be an attempt to resist, but it, too, translates into commercialism.

The trick of liminality in road literature is that none of this should be remembered, that the old America or the real America should be replaced by an America that is not played out or restricted. The coming decades of industrial monotony that make one hotel chain or fast-food restaurant the same as the next, obliterate regional distinctions in favor of faux-universal accents, and sell surfer shirts to kids in Nebraska are part of the same formation. By the 1950s, Daniel Boorstin was already alarmed by the process of replacing the real with the staged. In the early 1960s, when John Steinbeck took to the road in his camper to see if the America he used to know was still there, he decided it was not. Even the search for the "five-calendar restaurant" (Least Heat-Moon 26) in *Blue Highways* is juxtaposed with the commercialization of the freeway. Road novels are predicated on the notion that the trip is still there to make, still there to be transformed into an original quest. The question is whether or not it is still possible. Some commentators have observed that the "road" is closed, that the end of innocence—of hitchhiking and back roads less traveled—has come. Perhaps what is "lost" is best understood as the inevitable saturation and decline of an America that no longer sells, that has been reduced to clichés.

The danger of road literature is that it forces a reading of the cultural landscape that lacks the specificity to be sustainable. The Midwest is made vulnerable in these narratives because its only value is as empty space. Gone are the lived practices and histories that made the land and its people significant, if only to themselves. In this way, the heartland is treated in the same way that Raymond Williams, in *The Country and the City* (1973), observes the country being framed and reframed in its relationship to the city. Williams warns that this endless contrast and comparison, which in this case creates a nostalgia for the country to counter the modernism of the city, leaves both localities poorer for the comparison.

For what is at issue, in all these case, is a growth and alteration of consciousness: a history repeated in many lives and many places which is fundamentally an alteration of perception and relationship. What was once close, absorbing, accepted, familiar, internally experienced becomes separate, distinguishable, critical, changing, externally observed. (297)

The only way to make the Midwest matter in road literature is to read it into the narrative, to reconstruct an alternative narrative of the struggles and lived histories of the region and of the people who have lived in the spaces reduced to highways through the night. Williams shows that territory, like the Midwest, is always contested, always a mix of alternative narratives that make some realities accessible while obscuring others.

The best way to understand road literature is to read back into it the complexities of the regions and times that have produced it. This sub-genre of American literature is interesting because it was produced in an era that is critical to American art and consciousness but is not that well understood or critiqued. The beats were part of the first generation of American artists, along with abstract expressionist painters and postwar jazz musicians, to have the world as their stage. They occupied an American moment of cultural dominance brought about by the war and the confluence of energies, such as jazz and modern poetry, that made this period critical to the new formation of culture and the role that race and gender would eventually play in it. Road novels are situated in an America constructed out of a past that never existed, and they project a future that never arrived. In a formal sense, they are not that interesting. As Primeau points out, they tend to follow a fairly predictable set of principles. But the cultural space they occupy is another matter.

Road literature inhabits the same moment as the invention of "cool" and the leveling of high and low culture and art based on a rejection of the high art of modernism. Cool has an avant-garde phase, but the gatekeepers are not credentialed in the same way. Being able to listen to Miles Davis or John Coltrane or to read the mad rantings of Allen Ginsberg's *Howl* (1956) or the jazz prose of *On the Road* is not grounded in the same kind of cultural elitism. It is just as antibourgeois as high modernism, but it is also anti-intellectual. Cool requires a romantic authenticity that is immediate, not the dispassionate gaze of the modern. Every road quester seeks a "real" experience to replace a stale vision of the future exemplified in movies like *The Man in the Gray Flannel Suit* (1956). Every road novel is predicated on the belief that this time the trip will reveal the real America, that this time the wound can be healed. But the trip is always already confined to the personal; it is undertaken by a shaman, intent on a personal vision, an individual glimpse behind the veil. In the cultural and artistic landscape of the cool, there really is no authority to sort or stratify creative experience. The critic is rejected in favor of personal experience and taste. Sal does not end up the only narrator of the road, just the first in the long line of individuals that fail in the end. The idea promoted here is that we are on our own, with no relevant past to account for and no way to connect to a future that recognizes or honors the visions from the road.

Understanding road literature requires the kind of genealogy suggested here. It is not enough to see this subgenre as broadly American or in the tradition of quest literature; these generalities are less interesting than the particular historical and artistic contexts that both created and sustained it. It holds the place it does with generations of readers because it still feeds the myth of individual discovery and resistance. Road novels emerged at exactly the point in our cultural evolution when radical individualism and alternative identities became possible. The first people to exercise those options in prose form were educated white males searching for something beyond the postwar consumer blitz. Their novels carve out a space that both articulates and obscures the options available, leading to an individual awareness of the limitations of the quest. Sal ends up back home with his aunt, or married in the original scroll version, and Kerouac's character is in even worse shape in *Desolation Angels*, drunk on the bus home to his mother's place to die. What is passed up is an alternative history, an alternative postwar experience that does not succumb to the romantic quest of the alienated individual. Even Sal sees the possibility at several points in *On the Road* to settle, to love and work his way to salvation, but he never has the courage to choose that option. Neither does America. Road novels help us see what we chose: decades of chasing something that we can never bring back off the mountain and share with anyone else. The idea that the quest belongs to the individual, that it does not have to be infused with sacrifice for the whole, drives the literature and the era toward an American identity that is both confused and isolated from its communal roots.

Reconstructing the Midwest in these literary works is critical to making the choices of the genre and the period manifest. Because it is left out, the heartland is never really co-opted in the project that reduces identity to extreme individualism. The road through the Midwest is a road waiting for its own, alternative narrative of community and identity. The promise of the West did not save America. The mirage of California in today's emerging era of communal sustainability looks very different than it did after the war, in the blitzkrieg of suburban sprawl and shopping malls for everyone. An alternative narrative of national identity and purpose will require a new horizon and a new sensibility. As readers and as a culture, we have been on the road for more than fifty years now. It is time to come home, to the heartland, to tell a new story.

Works Cited

Baudrillard, Jean. *Simulacra and Simulation*. Trans. Sheila Faria Glaser. Ann Arbor: U of Michigan P, 1994. Print.

Boorstin, Daniel J. *The Image: A Guide to Pseudo-Events in America*. New York: Harper, 1961. Print.

Dodge, Jim. *Not Fade Away*. New York: Atlantic Monthly, 1987. Print.

Doors, The. "The End." *The Doors*. Elektra Records, 1967. LP.

Ginsburg, Allen. *Howl, and Other Poems*. San Francisco: City Lights, 1956. Print. Pocket Poets 4.

Golemba, Henry. "Rockets Rise on the Wabash." *Great Lakes Review* 5.1 (1979): 1–6. *Texas A & M U Science Fiction and Fantasy Collection*. Web. 5 Oct. 2012.

Kerouac, Jack. *Desolation Angels*. New York: Coward, 1960. Print.

___. *On the Road. Jack Kerouac: Road Novels, 1957–1960*. Ed. Douglas Brinkley. New York: Lib. of Amer., 2007. 1–278. Print.

Least Heat-Moon, William. *Blue Highways: A Journey into America*. Boston: Little, 1982. Print.

The Man in the Gray Flannel Suit. Dir. Nunnally Johnson. Twentieth Century Fox, 1956. Film.

Pirsig, Robert M. *Zen and the Art of Motorcycle Maintenance*. New York: Bantam, 1975. Print.

Primeau, Ronald. *Romance of the Road: Literature of the American Highway*. Bowling Green: Bowling Green State U Popular P, 1996. Print.

Roszak, Theodore. *The Making of a Counter Culture: Reflections on the Technocratic Society and Its Youthful Opposition*. Garden City: Doubleday, 1969.

Steinbeck, John. *Travels with Charley*. New York: Viking, 1962. Print.

Williams, John A. *This Is My Country Too*. New York: New Amer. Lib., 1965. Print.

Williams, Raymond. *The Country and the City*. New York: Oxford UP, 1973. Print.

Wright, James Arlington. "As I Step over a Puddle at the End of Winter, I Think of an Ancient Chinese Governor." *Above the River: The Complete Poems*. New York: Farrar, 1992. 119. Print.

American Odysseus: Mark Twain, Travel, and the Journey Home_____

John Rohrkemper

The nineteenth-century United States saw few travelers as restless as Mark Twain. By the time he was thirty, he had been a riverboat pilot working up and down the Mississippi, had lived and worked in the great eastern cities of Philadelphia and New York, and had roamed the silver fields of Nevada, the played-out gold fields of California, and the lush paradise of the Sandwich Islands (now Hawaii). When the opportunity came to convince a newspaper to pay his way to Europe and the Middle East, he leapt at it, and when all was done, he had established himself as a travel writer. He wrote five travel books and many travel essays, and his fiction is suffused with travel. As he neared sixty, he embarked on a yearlong round-the-world reading tour that took him from the United States to such locales as Canada, Fiji, Australia, India, and England, an extended performance that could be seen as a prototype of a modern rock band's world tour.

Twain's first book was a collection of sketches that he would have preferred to have left unclaimed, though it did contain "The Celebrated Jumping Frog of Calaveras County," the 1865 story that had first brought him fame. The book that he thought of as his first true book was *The Innocents Abroad* (1869), the rambunctious account of his journey to Europe and the Middle East with a shipload of affluent Americans. On a bitterly cold Sunday in February 1867, Twain took sanctuary in the Plymouth Church in Brooklyn, New York. He was there not only to escape the cold but also to hear a sermon by Henry Ward Beecher, a preacher who had become a star by virtue of his erudite and witty sermons and his brilliant presentations of them. Twain, who had already begun what was to be a resoundingly successful career as a lecturer, probably saw some of himself, or what he aspired to be, in Beecher the performer. He was impressed. He also was intrigued by a prospectus he found at the church advertising a journey to Europe, the Mediterranean, and the Middle East, on which travelers would be accompanied by Beecher, the Civil War hero William Tecumseh Sherman, and other luminaries—the United States' first celebrity cruise. Twain arranged for a newspaper, the *Alta California*, to underwrite the cost of the trip and pay him a salary in exchange for a series of "letters" chronicling the six-month sojourn.

Beecher, Sherman, and the other star attractions all withdrew from the trip before setting sail, but when the *Quaker City*, a recently decommissioned Civil War navy vessel, embarked in June, Twain had plenty of material for his letters in the several dozen wealthy Americans who were his cruise mates. Scholar Bruce Michelson vividly describes the tour:

> The first invasion of the old world by the American "guided tour" was so unprecedented an act that the steamship and its passengers were objects of wonder—and suspicion. [At one port, authorities] detained the ship in the harbor for several days, never having seen the like and fearing some dark ulterior purpose. They were right to be uneasy. The *Quaker City* contained the vanguard of the largest and richest invasion of wandering pleasure-seekers in history. The Americans were coming to turn Europe into one vast amusement park, to transform every gallery, palace, cathedral, and house of state into a hometown sideshow, to gape at the "foreigners" and have themselves a good time. (391–92)

Coming just two years after the end of the Civil War, the tour of the *Quaker City* heralded a new postwar era, one marked by the rise of a new, moneyed leisure class and the desire of members of that class to make the continental tour. This trend was to be most fully explored by Twain's contemporary Henry James, who examined this international theme in works such as *The American* (1877) and *Daisy Miller* (1878), among others, but Twain may well have been the first to examine the theme in literature.

In the letters that Twain sent to the *Alta* over the next six months and the manuscript that would become *The Innocents Abroad*, he had a twofold purpose: to poke fun at what writer H. L. Mencken would later call the American "booboisie"—the uncultured American—and, in the end, to make the Old World, the sacred shrine to which the *Quaker City* pilgrims had journeyed, seem a little less awe inspiring to his American readers. The Old World and its inhabitants as depicted in his work are as varied, quirky, and even comical as the New World and the Americans he chronicled. Twain clearly delights in exaggerating the tics and idiosyncrasies of his fellow travelers, even inventing colorful characters and incidents to serve his purpose, but he also suggests that the institutions and inhabitants of the Old World should inspire no special reverence in and hold no particular sway over any American. In his 1953 essay "Mark Twain as Critic in *The Innocents Abroad*," scholar John C. McCloskey offers a corrective to a tendency to see the book as a rant of American chauvinism, an onslaught of Jacksonian criticism of a moldy and decadent Europe. McCloskey points out that Twain is nearly as likely to be lavishly complimentary as he is to be harshly critical of the Old World he experiences on the tour. Indeed, Twain praises some aspects of Europe and the Middle East and criticizes others, just as he is charmed by some of his fellow pilgrims and amusedly mortified by the behavior and attitudes of others. The narrative stance of *The Innocents Abroad* is comic, asserting that all people—European, North African, Middle Eastern, and American alike—are strange and curious creatures, always some degrees smaller than they think they are. But it is important for Twain, and presumably for his American readers, to keep in mind that their foibles are no more egregious than anyone else's. In a sense, then, *The Innocents Abroad* is a cultural declaration of independence: America need no longer pay obsequious service to its presumed betters.

Upon its publication in 1869, the book became an instant and rousing best seller. It made Twain the premier travel writer in the United States, cemented his reputation as a humorous writer, and established him as one of our most important writers of any genre. The book was also an invaluable stylistic laboratory for Twain. In "The Celebrated Jumping Frog of Calaveras County," he had established a distinctive, wry narrative voice that appealed to readers. But *The Innocents Abroad* presented a new challenge: maintaining a compelling narrative voice across a book-length narration. In a sense, Twain appears to have solved the problem by ignoring it, for the book is a kaleidoscope of various narrative voices. Michelson argues that *The Innocents Abroad* is more than the account of a pleasure tour by rich Americans; it is also

> a pleasure tour through modes of narration. It ranges through sentimentality and parody, patriotism and anti-Americanism, whimsy and plodding factuality; the persistent, overriding assertion of the prose being that "I Mark Twain am out to have myself a good time." And we are meant to enjoy his narrator's pleasure trip, his tour through the world of literary voices, just as we enjoy his tour of foreign lands.

Michelson concludes, "*The Innocents Abroad* is a stylistic experiment with the principle of improvisatory play. And it works" (395–96). Twain was a great improviser; it was perhaps his greatest gift as a writer. Never a methodical intellectual, the spottily educated Twain might have said that his true university was the novels, stories, and sketches that he wrote. In his finest work, Twain was open to learning from himself, from what he was learning through the act of writing. His finest characters—Tom Sawyer, Hank Morgan, Pudd'nhead Wilson, the slave Roxy, and particularly Huck Finn—are also great improvisers, living their lives from moment to moment and by the seat of their pants. In writing *The Innocents Abroad*, Twain learned to master the improvisational narrative voice that would serve him so well throughout his career, particularly in *The Adventures of Huckleberry Finn* (1884).

The Innocents Abroad was a phenomenal success from its first appearance, so it is no surprise that Twain, like his readers, began to think of himself as a travel writer as well as a humorist. But what to write next? He thought of setting off on and chronicling another journey, but instead he hit upon the idea of mining his own past experiences, ones that antedated his trip to the Old World. The result was his 1872 book *Roughing It*. If *The Innocents Abroad* suggests that Americans should hold no particular reverence for all things Old World, by extension it implies that all things American could be fit subjects for a writer's—and reader's—attention. In *Roughing It*, Twain took the chance that his own experiences could capture and hold the attention of his readers.

Twain had created himself as a character in his first travel work, but that character principally observed and commented rather than acting. *Roughing It*, on the other hand, is as much memoir as travel narrative. The book begins with a lengthy account of an eventful, often arduous, and always humorous stagecoach ride from St. Joseph, Missouri, to Carson City, the provincial capital of the Nevada Territory, in 1861. Twain's brother Orion had won a patronage job for his support of Lincoln and the Republican Party in the 1860 election. Orion was to be the secretary of the Nevada Territory and invited his younger brother to be secretary to the secretary. But Twain, always restless, was not content to spend his time buried in governmental paperwork in sleepy Carson City. He was first lured to the nearby boomtown of Virginia City, site of the recently discovered Comstock silver lode. The town had everything: overnight millionaires, saloons, prostitutes, and characters of every description. But soon the lure of the road led him farther afield. Twain describes his restlessness as inchoate wanderlust, an itchiness to get back on the road that has since been echoed repeatedly in the literature of the American road:

> I began to get tired of staying in one place so long. There was no longer satisfying variety in going down to Carson to report the proceedings of the legislature once a year, and horse-races and pumpkin-shows once in three months. . . . I wanted to see San Francisco. I wanted to go somewhere.

I wanted—I did not know *what* I wanted. I had the "spring fever" and wanted a change. (*Roughing It* 398; ital. in orig.)

Whatever vague thing Twain wanted, San Francisco probably provided it. He gave his first successful major public performance there—and he contemplated suicide. But even San Francisco eventually ceased to satisfy him, for he "wanted another change. The vagabond instinct was strong" (444). So Twain secured a commission to write a series of articles about the Sandwich Islands for the *Sacramento Union* and, both geographically and imaginatively, set off farther west.

Roughing It begins in the Missouri that was still the center of Twain's universe in 1861 and heads west. Less than a decade later, Twain would set out to explore the east in the journey that became *The Innocents Abroad*. In mythic terms, these first two important books chronicle the hero's journey out, the testing, just as the war in Ilium is the hero Odysseus's principal testing field in Homer's *Odyssey*. If *The Innocents Abroad* asserts the United States' cultural independence from and equality with the Old World, *Roughing It* claims that the American, even the unpolished westerner, can be a fit subject of interest. On a greater level, the two books signal the double focus of American culture in the immediate post–Civil War period: the recovery of the Old World by newly wealthy Americans and the vision of the New World in the still-open West. As Twain scholar Henry Nash Smith puts it, "The two books deal with the two poles of nineteenth-century American culture: the Europe from which the first colonists had come, and the beckoning West toward which for two centuries and more they and their descendants had been moving" (52). These were important journeys for Mark Twain and the United States to make.

But the inveterate world traveler's most meaningful journey was an odyssey home to Hannibal, Missouri, that he made in the spring of 1882 at the age of forty-six, after a twenty-nine-year absence. Twain returned to the Mississippi, from which he had also been away for more than twenty years, to conduct research for an expansion of "Old

Times on the Mississippi," a memoir of his brief career as a riverboat pilot in the late 1850s and early 1860s that he had written for the *Atlantic Monthly* at the behest of its editor and Twain's best literary friend, William Dean Howells. That 1875 series had been well received, and seven years later, Twain went back home to do further research, but mostly to summon up vivid memories of his years on the river with the intention of expanding "Old Times" into a book. It was published in 1883 as *Life on the Mississippi*.

Twain began his journey by retracing the course of the river he had known as a cub and then a pilot: the southern stretch from Saint Louis to New Orleans. But that river he remembered was gone. One of the themes of "Old Times" is that the river is a living thing, always changing and challenging pilots, who had to navigate as much by intuition and pluck as by any firm knowledge of the river's contours, since they would have changed, sometimes dramatically, since the last journey up or down. Still, Twain was stunned by how seemingly all the old landmarks had been washed away by the currents of time: "The river is so thoroughly changed that I can't bring it back to mind even when the changes have been pointed out to me. It is like a man pointing out to me a place in the sky where a cloud has been" (qtd. in Powers 459). Although he would eventually make his way to Saint Paul, Minnesota, nearer the river's headwaters, he saved for the last part of his southern trip a three-day visit to his hometown.

The old town had changed nearly as much as the river. Twain arrived on a sleepy Sunday morning. There was none of the bustle about the docks that he remembered from his youth; "everything was changed." Nevertheless, the memories began to flood back: "When I reached Third or Fourth street the tears burst forth, for I recognized the mud" (qtd. in Kaplan 246). Biographer Justin Kaplan explains that "despite his hostility to the South and to much of its culture, which he said was a feudalistic sham borrowed out of Walter Scott, it was still *his* South he had come back to" (245; ital. in orig.). It moved him deeply to see his old hometown, to visit with his childhood friends after so many years. The experience fueled two of his greatest works.

Life on the Mississippi is travel writing as epic. Just as novelist Herman Melville sought to create an epic of the whaling industry in *Moby-Dick* (1851), Twain aspired to write an epic of the steamboat industry and the great river on which heroic men plied the intricate craft of river piloting. This at least partially accounts for the structure of the book, which some readers consider to be uneven. Chapters 4 through 17 of *Life on the Mississippi* essentially reprint "Old Times on the Mississippi"; they are preceded by three chapters describing the history of the river and followed by forty-three chapters that might be characterized as miscellaneous. Four appendixes complete the book. There undoubtedly is some truth to writer Willie Morris's argument that the new material was added for "the purpose of doubling the length of the narrative for one of those bulky 'subscription' books of the day, which explains much of the extraneous padding of some of the chapters in the second half" (xxxiv). This is a commonly held opinion. Such subscription books, sold by door-to-door salesmen, normally had contract stipulations that demanded a minimum of 600 pages, and *Life on the Mississippi* comprises 624 pages, including appendixes, in its original edition. But another way to understand the overstuffed text is to think of it as aspiring to an encyclopedic quality that characterizes the epics of Melville, Homer, and virtually all other epic writers. This inclusiveness is central to the very idea of the epic as a genre. Just as Melville felt the need to justify the importance of the whaling industry—which in the first half of the nineteenth century was crucial to the existence of the United States but seemed to many Americans, if they thought of it at all, to be dirty, obscure, and remote—Twain wanted his readers to understand the Mississippi and the men who worked it as he understood them. *Life on the Mississippi* begins, "The Mississippi is well worth reading about. It is not a commonplace river, but on the contrary is in all ways remarkable" (21). The reader can understand much of the rest of the book, even and maybe especially those overstuffed chapters, as Twain's attempt to prove his initial thesis.

The riverboat pilot is the hero of this epic. Scholar Joseph L. Coulombe argues that Twain equates the pilot with a "new American hero: that is, a professionally successful man with the financial and physical power to back his judgment" (69). Indeed, Twain stresses the physicality and courage as well as the will necessary to be a successful pilot. He portrays the pilots as princes of the river, noting the high wages and resultant respect that they earned. Coulombe claims that in Twain's description of how he became a pilot, "his self-presentation unite[s] him to the national story of American material success" (69).

Biographer Ron Powers argues that with Twain's journey home to Hannibal, "a conversion . . . occurred"; Twain's original plan to mix personal reportage with factual information gleaned from other sources, as he had in other travel books, became "inadequate to the Homeric urgencies now building in [his] mind" (465). Powers is here discussing the ways in which *Life on the Mississippi* had been recast as an epic in Twain's imagination, but there was another work of even greater proportion that was also emerging and would appear shortly after the publication of *Life on the Mississippi*. In the summer of 1883, Twain toiled productively in his summer retreat, the little octagonal writing studio his sister-in-law, Sue Crane, had had built for him on a hillside in Elmira, New York. After seven years of fitful starts, Twain was driving his way toward the completion of *The Adventures of Huckleberry Finn*. In a sense, Twain was not in Elmira that summer; he was back home in Hannibal, his imagination fired by his journey of a year earlier.

Twain was able to find the old Hannibal he had known, despite the changes that had inevitably occurred in the town. His memories became palpable in his reunions with old friends. Revisiting the old haunts and reuniting with the ghosts of his youth were crucial, but most important for Twain was hearing those voices again. Powers explains:

As always, he homed in on the language around him. . . . He homed in on Southern culture as well. . . . Sometimes he heard in [the] speech a ripe hypocrisy. . . . Conversely, he was happy to reencounter the particular music of Southern Negro speech, and he filled several notebook pages with overheard conversations. . . . And then there was the speech of the pilots—speech that was fated soon to be a dead language. . . . He harvested a colorful inventory of their yarns, river lore, varieties of swearing, and jargon. (459–60)

In her groundbreaking *Was Huck Black? Mark Twain and African-American Voices* (1993), scholar Shelley Fisher Fishkin asserts that "Mark Twain helped open American literature to the multicultural polyphony that is its birthright and special strength. . . . He helped teach his countrymen new lessons about the lyrical and exuberant energy of vernacular speech" (5). He had always known of this energy, but the book that preceded *Life on the Mississippi* and *Huckleberry Finn* had been *The Prince and the Pauper* (1881), a book favored by his family and particularly by his favorite daughter, Susy, who thought it demonstrated her father's gentlemanly good taste better than his earlier books. That kind of taste is little in evidence in *Life on the Mississippi* and completely lacking in *Huckleberry Finn*, both of which are infused with that "exuberant energy of vernacular speech" that seems to have been reenergized by Twain's journey home. Indeed, the only time Twain speaks to the reader in his own voice and without irony in *Huckleberry Finn* is in the "Explanatory" that precedes the table of contents. His focus is on the centrality of language in the novel:

In this book a number of dialects are used, to wit: the Missouri negro dialect; the extremest form of the backwoods South-Western dialect; the ordinary "Pike-County" dialect; and four modified varieties of this last. The shadings have not been done in a haphazard fashion, or by guesswork; but painstakingly and with the trustworthy guidance and support of personal familiarity with these several forms of speech. (7)

One can almost hear the pride in those last words: "with the trustworthy guidance and support of personal familiarity with these several forms of speech."

In his biography of Twain, Powers points out that the writer "chose a good moment to step outside the pressurized world he'd been creating for himself. His prevailing anxieties had steamed toward rage since the year began. . . . His stocks were floundering. Copyright threats continued to bedevil him." A host of other financial pressures began to weigh him down, and he became convinced that the New York *Tribune* had begun a vendetta against him (456–57). The enormous wealth he had believed he was certain to reap from his investment in a new invention, the Paige typesetting machine, was perhaps beginning to look a bit less certain as his investment and the thousand little glitches that bedeviled the machine increased with each year. Eventually this investment would be the principal cause of Twain's financial ruin; already it was looking dubious. Scholar Edgar J. Burde further emphasizes Twain's anxiety as he prepared to set off for his journey home: "In preparation for the journey Twain was haunted by his personal recurring anxiety dream in which he, as a pilot, is completely befuddled as to his position on the river, thus risking a shipwreck" (886). Yes, the spring of 1882 was the time to light out from Hartford and his eastern commitments, time to light out for home. It was the right time to leave behind, as best he could, the seductive siren song of money, fame, and ambition. Given the pressures of a high-powered adult life newly fraught with gnawing financial anxieties, mixed with the deeply evocative homecoming of the native son, it is a wonder that Twain's trip home did not result in a work of honeyed nostalgia. Twain had shown and would show again that he could write that kind of book, but the particular chemistry of this experience led to something very different. Meeting with old friends and seeing old haunts unleashed a deluge of memories that allowed Twain to reset the course of his great novel after years of false starts and wrong turns. His journey home helped him to find his true course and, while the rich vernacular voices he heard in Hannibal were still ringing in his ears, find his authentic voice for the novel in his decision to let Huck tell his own story in his rough-hewn yet lyric dialect.

Twain wrote *Life on the Mississippi* in a rush of activity, but his work the next summer on the manuscript of *The Adventures of Huckleberry Finn* was even more driven. On July 20, 1883, Twain wrote to Howells:

> I haven't piled up MS [manuscript] so in years as I have done since we came here to the farm three weeks & a half ago. Why, it's like old times, to step straight into the study, damp from the breakfast table, & sail right in & sail right on, the whole day long, without thought of running short of stuff or words. I wrote 4000 words to-day & I touch 3000 & upwards pretty often, & don't fall below 2600 on any working day. (Twain and Howells 435)

A month later, on August 22, and near the end of his summer of writing, he again wrote to Howells:

> I've done two seasons work in one, & I haven't anything left to do, now, but revise. I've written eight or nine hundred MS pages in such a brief space of time that I mustn't name the number of days; I shouldn't believe it myself. . . . I used to restrict myself to 4 & 5 hours a day & 5 days in the week; but this time I've wrought from breakfast till 5:15 p.m. six days in the week; & once or twice I smouched a Sunday when the boss wasn't looking. Nothing is half so good as literature hooked on Sunday on the sly. (438)

One hears several things in these letters, first of all the sheer exuberance Twain felt in the act of writing. His language displays a buoyant playfulness: when he says that he has "wrought from breakfast till 5:15 p.m.," he may well have substituted "wrought" for "written" inadvertently, but more likely he enjoyed the fusion of the act of writing with the old-fashioned past participle of work and especially craftwork. Finally, Twain, writing in his own voice, betrays echoes of the voice of his young fictional narrator with whom he has been communing in this intense summer of remembrance and writing: "Nothing is half so good as literature hooked on Sunday on the sly."

The language of *Huckleberry Finn* is in itself a revelation and a delight, but language was also the key that allowed Twain to make further breakthroughs in the novel. Travel had always been about adventure for Twain. Travel was about learning, too, but in *The Adventures of Huckleberry Finn*, it also assumed a moral dimension. Twain had originally thought of *The Adventures of Huckleberry Finn* as a companion piece to his *Adventures of Tom Sawyer* (1876)—what twenty-first-century readers would call a sequel. That earlier novel was Twain's first venture into what was becoming a popular new genre: the boy book. In the wake of the deaths of three-quarters of a million boys and men in the Civil War, and in the spirit of the new interest in gender developing in the Victorian era, writers had begun to try to define what it meant to be an American boy, just as Louisa May Alcott and Henry James searched for the American girl in works such as *Little Women* (1868–69) and *Daisy Miller*. Such books were often written in the third person, usually in an adult voice and often with a healthy dose of nostalgia for a lost youth. *Tom Sawyer* was that kind of book, albeit a particularly fine example of the genre. Twain originally tried to adopt a similar narrative voice when he began to work on *Huckleberry Finn*, but after his sojourn to the Mississippi and his hometown, he realized that Huck Finn, naive and only semiliterate, must tell his own story. This naiveté, of course, allows Huck to discuss the contradictions and outright corruptions of his culture. It allows the reader to see how a culture's idiosyncrasies—its racism, for example, or its blood feuds, such as that practiced by the Grangerfords and Sheperdsons—can be assumed to be natural and universal when not considered critically. This in turn encourages readers to consider their own givens, all those things they may think of as natural and universal and invariable.

Twain grounds this moral element not only in Huck's naiveté but also in his very language. Twain took great care to capture and differentiate between various regional dialects of the time, as well as create speech patterns for his narrator that also represent Huck's particular concerns and personal conflicts. One powerful example is his adaptation of the use of the pause that he considered a significant element of the American humorous story. In the humorous story, told orally, the pause creates a small moment of dramatic tension before the snapper—the story's punch line. In Huck's narration, the pause may have a humorous effect, but it just as likely points to a moral dilemma. Huck's first words are:

> You don't know about me without you have read a book by the name of *The Adventures of Tom Sawyer*, but that ain't no matter. That book was made by Mr. Mark Twain, and he told the truth, [comma representing a pause] mainly. There was things which he stretched, but mainly he told the truth. That is nothing. I never seen anybody but lied, one time or another, [comma representing a pause] without it was Aunt Polly, or the widow, or maybe Mary. Aunt Polly—Tom's Aunt Polly, she is—and Mary, and the Widow Douglas is all told about in that book—which is mostly a true book; [semicolon representing a pause] with some stretchers, as I said before. (1)

Subtly and humorously, in the verbal constructions of his naive narrator, Twain raises the question of honesty, one of the novel's main moral concerns. The pauses reflect Huck's own ambivalence about truth telling. Huck lies repeatedly throughout the novel, sometimes in offhanded ways but often to protect Jim, the slave he helps escape from bondage. Ultimately, for all his fabrications, Huck possesses a rigorous commitment to an essential honesty, to following his heart, whatever the consequences.

An even more powerful example of the use of this pause occurs several times while Huck and Jim are together on the raft. In one of his notebooks, Twain describes *The Adventures of Huckleberry Finn* as a book in which "a sound heart and a deformed conscience come into collision and conscience suffers defeat" (qtd. in Kaplan 198). It is clear that Huck thinks of conscience as all that he has learned from people such as Aunt Polly and the Widow Douglas and her companion, Miss Watson. In reality, what Huck thinks of as conscience is the collective values of a particular culture—and Huck's culture practices slavery and tolerates blood feuds, cruelty to animals, and a host of other practices that twenty-first-century readers are unlikely to judge as good. When Huck refers to his "heart," however, he means his intuitive sense, what one might call his honest self, the true Huck. This struggle is made more poignant, of course, precisely because Huck believes that conscience is the actual moral voice and that his heart is evil. The readers know the opposite. The values of Huck's society, the society of the antebellum South, are deformed; Huck's heart, his instinctual self, is sound, good, and true. This conflict comes to a head several times in the novel, particularly in chapter 31, when Huck, after listening to his conscience and writing a letter to Miss Watson telling her how to reclaim her runaway slave, finally listens to his heart. He tears up the letter and declares, "All right, then, I'll *go* to hell," choosing to assist in Jim's escape from slavery (272; ital. in orig.).

Throughout the novel, in smaller ways, Twain uses the pause to suggest the powerful struggle between Huck's conscience and his heart. At one point, relatively early in their journey together, Jim describes his vulnerability as a runaway slave, saying that he knows Miss Watson will surely sell him down the river if he is ever returned to her. Huck has to concede him the point, telling the reader, "Well, he was right; he was most always right; he had an uncommon level head" (109). This is Huck's heart speaking, running counter to his culture's expectations of a slave, a black man, acknowledging instead that Jim is an intelligent and wise human being. However, Huck's thought does not end there. In full, he says, "Well, he was right; he was most always right; he had an uncommon level head, [comma representing a pause] for a nigger."

In this one short sentence the reader can see the powerful conflict between heart and conscience and how hard it is for the essentially good-hearted Huck to break completely from the corrupt prejudices of his culture. Statements such as this occur throughout the novel. Twain was a realist, and he understood that it takes a monumental effort to free people from the values of the culture that envelops them.

It is only at the very end of the novel that the reader might suspect that Huck really understands his—and the reader's—dilemma. He tells the reader, "I reckon I got to light out for the Territory ahead of the rest, because Aunt Sally she's going to adopt me and sivilize me and I can't stand it. I been there before" (366). Ostensibly he is banishing himself from his home; in fact, he is journeying home. Huck seeks a home in which civilization holds less sway, in which he can be his natural, true self in a natural place, the place where he belongs—in this case, the western wilderness. He has achieved this rough-hewn wisdom precisely because he left that other home, because he became an outlaw—as a runaway, but particularly in abetting a runaway slave—and because he was able to survive a number of trials of civilization at least as perilous as any faced by Odysseus on his journey home after the Trojan War. The most important counter to that civilized world was the outlaw life he and Jim shared on their little raft, alone, in the dark, and on the river.

Set in the antebellum South of the 1830s or 1840s, *The Adventures of Huckleberry Finn* was published and first read less than a decade after the end of Reconstruction and slightly more than a decade before the Supreme Court's ruling on *Plessy v. Ferguson*. The end of Reconstruction in 1877 marked the beginning of a widespread policy of segregation of the races by law, and the 1896 *Plessy v. Ferguson* decision gave federal sanction to the policy of segregation. By then, slavery was a remembered but no-longer-contemporary issue, no longer a present moral dilemma. But in the midst of a twenty-year period during which the United States rushed to become a brutally segregated society, Twain showed readers a white boy and a black man living together on a tiny raft and united in a common cause, emphasizing the powerfully transformative and liberating possibilities of such radical integration, of such a crucial journey.

If Huck found his true home by following his heart, Twain himself did something similar. By the 1880s, Twain was one of the most famous men in the United States and was rich by almost any standard, living in the toniest neighborhood of the richest city in the country. He was living an American myth. Part of that myth suggested that one should always move on and never look back. Twain had never really done that, but in the spring of 1882, he "came home" in a way that surprised even him. Revisiting the person he had once been and hearing the voices of his old neighbors, the music of that place that had been home, he found himself listening to a heart much like the one that inspired his character, Huck, to be his best and truest self. In writing *The Adventures of Huckleberry Finn*, Twain journeyed home to his own best and truest self and, in doing so, created his most enduring work.

Works Cited

Burde, Edgar J. "Mark Twain: The Writer as Pilot." *PMLA* 93.5 (1978): 878–92. Print.

Coulombe, Joseph L. *Mark Twain and the American West.* Columbia: U of Missouri P, 2003. Print.

Fishkin, Shelley Fisher, ed. *The Oxford Mark Twain.* 29 vols. Oxford: Oxford UP, 1996. Print.

___. *Was Huck Black? Mark Twain and African-American Voices.* Oxford: Oxford UP, 1994. Print.

Kaplan, Justin. *Mr. Clemens and Mark Twain: A Biography.* New York: Simon, 1966. Print.

McCloskey, John C. "Mark Twain as Critic in *The Innocents Abroad.*" *American Literature* 25.2 (1953): 139–51. Print.

Michelson, Bruce. "Mark Twain the Tourist: The Form of *The Innocents Abroad.*" *American Literature* 49.3 (1977): 385–98. Print.

Morris, Willie. Introduction. *Life on the Mississippi.* By Mark Twain. Oxford: Oxford UP, 1996. xxxi–xxxix. Print. Vol. 9 of Fishkin, *Oxford.*

Powers, Ron. *Mark Twain: A Life.* New York: Free, 2005. Print.

Smith, Henry Nash. *Mark Twain: The Development of a Writer.* Cambridge: Belknap, 1962. Print.

Twain, Mark. *The Adventures of Huckleberry Finn.* Oxford: Oxford UP, 1996. Print. Vol. 10 of Fishkin, *Oxford.*

___. *The Innocents Abroad*. Oxford: Oxford UP, 1996. Print. Vol. 2 of Fishkin, *Oxford*.

___. *Life on the Mississippi*. Oxford: Oxford UP, 1996. Print. Vol. 9 of Fishkin, *Oxford*.

___. *Roughing It*. Oxford: Oxford UP, 1996. Print. Vol. 3 of Fishkin, *Oxford*.

Twain, Mark, and William D. Howells. *Mark Twain–Howells Letters: The Correspondence of Samuel L. Clemens and William D. Howells, 1872–1910*. Ed. Henry Nash Smith and William M. Gibson. Cambridge: Belknap, 1960. Print.

CRITICAL READINGS

Paradoxes along the Beat Journey in Kerouac's *On the Road*

Dominic Ording

This essay examines Jack Kerouac's novel *On the Road* (1957) from a gender and sexuality studies perspective. It focuses on the tensions, paradoxes, and contradictions in the views of narrator Sal Paradise and his road buddy Dean Moriarty about friendship, masculinity, women, and sexuality. Perhaps the most profound trouble is that while they claim to reject the conformist and hypocritical moral code of the early post–World War II period, their insistence upon traditional rigid notions of masculinity (e.g., the imperative against appearing vulnerable) threatens their ability to sustain their own ideal of an intimate friendship with each other. As much of the novel takes place "on the move" on highways, the essay will also touch upon the crucial role of the Road as both a means toward spiritual fulfillment and an exhausting, demoralizing, and potentially destructive influence.

Kerouac's most famous book, published in 1957, makes a dramatic and self-conscious contribution to post–World War II fictional representations of masculinity and male intimacies. Moreover, it has a problematic and ambiguous relation to questions of homoeroticism and homophobia. In this novel, the male characters intuitively pursue and inhabit versions of masculinity and intimacy and ecstasy, only to reach crisis points brought about by a growing understanding that they cannot go on like this—that something has come between them; that something has fallen apart.

On the Road also raises questions about traditional notions of family and the pursuit of two goals that may be mutually exclusive: transgression against the reigning morality and the maintenance of and nostalgia for old-fashioned American heteronormativity. Kerouac's characters—torn and consumed with the balance between being on the road and settling down—seem out of control, wishing to relinquish

---

the responsibility of deliberative action, preferring instead to be swept away, at least until the end of the book, when Sal makes a decision.

Five of the main themes of *On the Road* concern me here:

1. The travels and togetherness of Sal and Dean as they pursue "kicks" and attempt to articulate their version of the American dream. At first glance, and as the public mythology of the book largely has it, they reject middle-class values and proprieties, replacing them with the wild abandon of drugs, booze, sex, and jazz.

2. Sal's nostalgia for a lost America of small-town innocence and family life, which he often describes in terms of lost fathers or his desire to find a wife and settle down.

3. Sal's descriptions of intimacies, whether between the main male characters, with women, or with strangers he meets along the way. At times, it appears he might achieve a sort of intimacy and "love" with hitchhiking mates he only knows for a few hours or less.

4. Sal's discussions of relations between the sexes. The narrative contains both misogyny and somewhat essentialist apologies explaining why men and women do not get along.

5. The apparent conclusion that even Sal and Dean, the best of buddy buddies, are unable to stay together or remain loyal, partly because of their inability to negotiate a sustainable form of masculine intimacy.

Indeed, while *On the Road* carries on the tradition in American letters of representing troubled, if at times pleasurable, masculinities, it marks a departure because of its treatment of characters obsessed with self-exploration and inwardness. (We can only speak with assurance about the first-person narrator, Sal, but dialogue from others suggests they are on similar spiritual quests.) At least a handful of the men in the book are conscious of and explicit about exploring the meaning and potential extent of their togetherness as they try to talk about intimacy and their possible relation to the godhead. Yet they still confront problems with gendered expectations, both with each other and in their relations with women.

Initial critical reception of *On the Road* was extremely polarized. Its first review in the *New York Times* hailed it as a tremendous success, calling it the beat generation's version of the lost generation's *The Sun Also Rises*, Hemingway's 1926 novel about expatriates and their antics in Paris and Pamplona. This single review, written by stand-in critic Gilbert Millstein, assured the book's immediate commercial success. On the other hand, conservative critics complained about the novel's literary shortcomings and, more disdainfully, about its embodiment of the moral decay of the young generation of the 1950s. Such mixed reception would follow Kerouac and most of the beat writers for years to come, with the moralizing tendency of the criticism almost always at the forefront.

Recent scholarship is generally kinder to the novel as a work of literature, including appreciations of its stylistic innovations and huge cultural influence, and much less critical of its purported moral degeneracy. After all, the beats in general, and Kerouac's *On the Road* and Allen Ginsberg's "Howl" (1956) in particular, were important participants in the incipient discourse of what have come to be called the sexual revolution and the counterculture of the postwar period, as Kerouac's narrator Sal will articulate as he describes Dean Moriarty's single-handedly bringing a new sexuality into being. The portrayal of promiscuity in *On the Road*, in both male-female heterosexual relations and the male same-sex relations simmering just under the surface of the published version, was quite unorthodox for the time, especially its portrayal of sexually active women. In *Make Love, Not War* (2001), David Allyn describes attitudes of the time toward sexual activity and the double standard, and even a curious double standard of sorts toward the double standard itself, as follows:

> In the 1950s, as Americans reveled in the "return to normalcy" after years of depression and war, the double standard was reaffirmed in books,

movies, television shows, and popular magazines. American males were told that if they were healthy they should hunger for sex, while young women were advised to resist forcefully and demand a ring. (14)

No matter what was really going on behind closed doors, those who publicly criticized the double standard could suffer severe consequences. As long as one championed sexual restraint *for both sexes*, there was no need to fear. But as soon as one advocated sexual freedom for women as well as men, the public responded with outrage. (16; emphasis added)

Scholars have also recently put readings of *On the Road* in the context of 1950s discourse about sexuality and gender categories. In *Homosexuality in Cold War America* (1997), Robert J. Corber discusses Sal Paradise's problems with gender in the context of white men in the era mourning the loss of the "pioneer spirit" and their attempts to recover it. In part, it is an issue of class, according to Corber:

One way of reading Sal Paradise's travels on the road is as his search for a masculinity that is commensurate with his fantasies and desires. By taking to the road, he hopes to recover the form of male identity displaced by the rise of the white-collar worker. . . . [He] constantly questions whether he is sufficiently masculine. . . . Sal does not want to possess the cowboy sexually so much as to inhabit his body, to experience his masculinity as though it were his own. Sal clearly thinks that the cowboy is more of a man than he is. Despite his working-class background, Sal has been pampered by comparison to the cowboy, whose life has been "raw" and austere. (50–51)

If we take seriously the premise that considerations of gender often subsume or at least widely overlap those of sexuality, then the distinction between the desire "to possess the cowboy sexually" and the desire "to inhabit his body" and "experience his masculinity" is not self-evident. To inhabit him would be a form of sexual possession. The more important point is that Sal is attracted to the idea of becoming more masculine than he perceives himself to be. He wants to be a cowboy—and black and Mexican and a hobo, as well as a lot of things other than what he is, all of which indicate his association of untainted masculinity and freedom with the Other, as opposed to the conformist, bourgeois white American value system of the time.

Another critic who notes the significance of the beats and *On the Road* in postwar American literature and discussions of gender, sexuality, and race is David Savran. In *Taking It like a Man* (1998), Savran describes his own book as an examination of what he calls the fear of the "feminization of the male subject" (33), as well as the appearance of "the fantasy of the white male as victim" (4) in the 1950s. He also makes an important claim about the similarities between white masculinities, arguing that gender concerns subsume differences between categories of identity based on sexual preference:

> [This book] also attempts to interrogate the relationship between ostensibly heterosexual and ostensibly homosexual white masculinities in U.S. culture, arguing that they are far more alike than they might at first appear to be. Reacting in remarkably similar ways to anxieties over what they fantasize to be an encroaching feminization of the male subject (and of U.S. culture), they are sometimes almost indistinguishable. (Savran 33)

Savran's claim seems to presuppose an essential white masculinity that ostensibly gay and straight men could share. It also raises the question of the extent to which claims about gender are made by an outsider observing a performance, rather than by a gendered subject describing how it feels to be anxiety ridden about gender.

As for the beats, Savran sees them as being willing to embrace aspects of the feminine—in contrast, for instance, to the so-called organization man, "who was expected to subordinate his personal ambitions for the good of the corporation and develop those interpersonal skills that were becoming an increasingly important part of the business world" (Savran 47)—but only on the condition that they can become "real men" again at will when the feminine becomes uncomfortable. This retreat is exemplified by Sal Paradise's homophobic outbursts in the narrative of *On the Road*. According to Savran,

> The Beats negotiated the treacherous binarism of sexual difference during an era in which both gender and sexual deviance were, to say the least, subject to extraordinary negative pressure. In what passes for American literature, the Beats were the first explicitly to embrace a feminized position—but only on condition that they could beat a hasty and horrified retreat from it. (67)

The book is very much about men falling in love, especially Sal with Dean, and wondering what it means and how best to deal with it in the context of an ostensibly heterosexual milieu. On the second page, this is a condensed version of what will remain a trinity of Sal's descriptions of Dean: his body, his language, and his soul. It is clearly love at first sight: "I went to the cold-water flat with the boys, and Dean came to the door in his shorts. . . . To him sex was the one and only holy and important thing in life, although he had to sweat and curse to make a living and so on" (Kerouac 2). The descriptions of the body are often quite heroic, adoring, and steamy. One thinks forward here to the Dustin Hoffman character upon seeing the Jon Voight character in the film *Midnight Cowboy* (1969). This is a striking example of the resonance of representations in *On the Road* through the 1960s, the Stonewall gay-rights uprising, and beyond. The relationship in the film also goes back to this novel to register a sense of suspicion from the start—that the rush of the immediate sense of connection cannot last, that the object of adoration is too good to be true, the over-the-top cowboy masculine posture somehow dangerous. But in each, the sense of excitement and attraction far exceeds any concerns. The difference is that in the film, the cowboy learns to con from Ratso Rizzo (Hoffmann). In this novel, though Dean approaches Sal under the pretext of wanting to learn how to write, it is Sal who learns from con man Dean about the joys and perils of unbridled masculine energy:

> He was conning me and I knew it (for room and board and "how-to-write," etc.), and he knew I knew (this has been the basis of our relationship), but I didn't care and we got along fine—no pestering, no catering; we tiptoed around each other like heartbreaking new friends. I began to learn from him as much as he probably learned from me. (4)

Here we see the basis for a possible ideal of intimacy: compromise and tiptoeing, no pestering, a sense of heartbreak at least on one side, and learning from one another. There is also a sense between them of mutual support and excitement about common interests (in this case, literary artistry and intensity of experience) and of sharing something unique in the world, at least an unconventional perspective (a sort of us-against-the-world sharing, a sharing of secrets), and most definitely not being "hung-up."

Then Dean meets Carlo Marx, and, in a widely quoted passage, Sal watches as two others embark on a form of intimacy he is unable to share, however much he might want to. This is one place where explicit reference to their homoerotic and homosexual relationship was removed from the final draft of the novel: "A tremendous thing happened when Dean met Carlo Marx. . . . Their energies met head-on, I was a lout compared, I couldn't keep up with them" (Kerouac 5). Sal the narrator perhaps deceives himself about his feelings here, especially since the narrative is structured to be looking back in hindsight, back to a time before things had gone sour between him and Dean. Surely he was more than a little sorry to have been replaced as the object of affection and con job of the "amorous soul" (6) of Dean. And he will later discover that it is not, as he maintains, only mad people whom he adores. They become too much for him, and he comes to prefer mellower, gentler, perhaps even more stable and predictable company, at least as an ideal. Indeed, much of the action in the novel has Sal settling down to serious work, relieved to be home again off the road, only to be swept away again the next time Dean comes courting for kicks.

Indeed, even early on in the novel, Sal seems to realize potentially irreconcilable differences between himself and Dean but nonetheless finds Dean irresistible:

> he reminded me of some long-lost brother; the sight of his suffering bony face with the long sideburns and his straining muscular sweating neck made me remember my boyhood in those dye-dumps and swim-holes and riversides of Paterson and the Passaic. His dirty workclothes clung to him so gracefully, as though you couldn't buy a better fit from a custom tailor but only earn it from the Natural Tailor of Natural Joy, as Dean had, in his stresses. (Kerouac 7)

Clearly the desire for and ideal of adult male friendship and intimacy here is deeply connected to nostalgia for boyhood pals and homosociality, including a large component of bodily sensuality—it is a sensory nostalgia more than a rational or conceptual one. Its strong emotionality is much more physical than linguistic; it is not the words spoken by the boys but the sounds of their voices and their manner of speaking that are brought back.

Later, while hitchhiking, Sal loves some fellow riders. He appreciates their tenderness and care, their unconditional affection, and his own sense of altruism. In Sal's view of intimacy, a combination of passion and compassion seems necessary. Throughout the book, he describes such feelings of bonding with strangers: "Meanwhile the blond young fugitive sat the same way; every now and then Gene leaned out of his Buddhistic trance over the rushing dark plains and said something tenderly in the boy's ear. The boy nodded. Gene was taking care of him, of his moods and his fears" (Kerouac 28). This sort of spontaneous, unselfconscious intimacy happens almost exclusively with males. With females, he mainly describes them primarily as objects of his desire, focusing on sexual energy and his desire to have sex with them. Males most often receive the anointment of subjecthood. There appears to be a cultural understanding between men of a preexistent male-to-male code of buddy-buddy behavior.

Sal then hangs out with Slim, another fellow rider. In an encounter with women in which there is no talk of tender feelings or nostalgia and no emotional experience whatsoever, Sal reports having a momentary sense of his "whole being and purpose." Yet it rings shallow and inadequate as an example of what ideal contentment, happiness, and intimacy might mean for him:

> We picked up two girls, a pretty young blonde and a fat brunette. They were dumb and sullen, but we wanted to make them. We took them to a rickety nightclub that was already closing, and there I spent all but two dollars on Scotches for them and beer for us. I was getting drunk and didn't care; everything was fine. My whole being and purpose was pointed at the little blonde. I wanted to go in there with all my strength. I hugged her and wanted to tell her. (Kerouac 33)

But of course he tells her nothing. No talking is necessary, just to "go in there with . . . strength." He never really has conversations with women, at least not as he does with men. Women may have souls for Sal and capture his sentimental pining away at the sadness of the universe on occasion, but they do not seem to have minds or agency.

Another example of this disquietude surrounding gender relations, sentiment, and sex comes when Sal gets together with a woman named Rita. They have unsatisfactory sex (he is "too impatient" to prove to her how good it can be) and afterward stare at the ceiling, "wondering what God had wrought when He made life so sad" (Kerouac 58). Sal later reflects,

> I wanted to go and get Rita and tell her a lot more things, and really make love to her this time, and calm her fears about men. Boys and girls in America have such a sad time together; sophistication demands that they

submit to sex immediately without proper preliminary talk. Not courting talk—real straight talk about souls, for life is holy and every moment is precious. I heard the Denver and Rio Grande locomotive howling off to the mountains. I wanted to pursue my star further. (58)

Sal thus offers an unconscious apology for his behavior or asserts a genuine wish that things were different between "boys and girls." He gets weepy and sentimental when it comes to men and women together. Yet he does not get back in touch with Rita; it is the talk of the hobos that is warm and soft. He does not talk to girls about souls, but he does with boys. Yet no matter how much he adores and rhapsodizes about males' spiritual and physical manhood, the idea of men who might have sex with other men is highly discomfiting. A little later on comes a scene that disturbs Sal himself, when he remembers a moment in the restroom of a bar in San Francisco as a man he assumes is homosexual approaches him. He takes out a gun and threatens the "queer." Then Sal, as contemporary narrator, adds apologetically, "I've never understood why I did that; I knew queers all over the country" (73).

The narrative moves from a failure with a woman to a homophobic crisis to Sal's reunion with his buddies, who, at least according to Savran, are capable of embracing or retreating from the feminine—and hence the potentially homoerotic—at will. It would seem that one cannot be a man without negating the non-man, that one cannot imagine male-to-male intimacy, that is, masculine intimacy, without first excluding some so-called lesser, perverted form of desire and desiring subjects.

Shortly thereafter, Sal describes Dean's change into the mad angel he will be until the end. The cause of Dean's madness is never made clear, but the reader gathers that it must come from some combination of drugs and sheer overexertion:

He had become absolutely mad in his movements; he seemed to be doing everything at the same time. It was a shaking of the head, up and down, sideways; jerky, vigorous hands; quick walking, sitting, crossing the legs, uncrossing, getting up, rubbing the hands, rubbing his fly, hitching his pants, looking up and saying "Am" and sudden slitting of the eyes to see everywhere; and all the time he was grabbing me by the ribs and talking, talking. (Kerouac 114)

Thus, Sal has once more been overtaken by his attraction (and loyalty?) to Dean, even though it is now mainly Dean the body he must accompany; later in the book, Dean can no longer even talk coherently. But in this scene, at least, the road and the high energy it promises have won out over the family Christmas in the country. Even though Sal and Dean can no longer communicate verbally about soul things, the images of Dean's sexuality so openly and excitedly—and naturally, at least for Dean—displayed and expressed are enough to take Sal away from homelife and work.

Soon after being back on the road, however, Sal has another crisis of the conflict between the wildness and the quiet life:

It was a completely meaningless set of circumstances that made Dean come, and similarly I went off with him for no reason. . . . All these years I was looking for the woman I wanted to marry. . . . "I want to marry a girl," I told them, "so I can rest my soul with her till we both get old. This can't go on all the time—all this franticness and jumping around. We've got to go someplace, find something." (Kerouac 116–17)

This conflict between the desires for the new and for the normal, the road and the home hearth, is a constant presence in representations of the struggle for people to narrate liberatory experiences and construct liberated identities throughout American literature in the twentieth century. This is an example of where the Road becomes a great obstacle for Sal Paradise. He is magnetized by Dean but knows that the constant turmoil, and expending such physical and emotional energy, is not his own wisest path toward contentment and salvation. In fact, the domestic scenes and their inhabitants at whom he so long-ingly glances as he and Dean dash from coast to coast have little to do with the Road. It disturbs the tranquility of these ideals and renders them less attractive. So the highway and the heartland may be at cross-purposes in many cases.

Later, Sal and Dean are alone in a car, their first chance to talk alone in years, according to Dean. They talk about God, and Sal admits that Dean's talk is incomprehensible but that he has become a mystic. They discuss gender roles in America. The temptation is to find an essential gender to place blame on for the difficulties men and women face. The difficulty for some men may be to accept any responsibility:

> "I've pleaded and pleaded with Marylou for a peaceful sweet understand-ing of pure love between us forever with all hassles thrown out—she un-derstands; her mind is bent on something else—she's after me; she won't understand how much I love her, she's knitting my doom."
>
> "The truth of the matter is we don't understand our women; we blame on them and it's all our fault," I said.
>
> "But it isn't as simple as that," warned Dean. "Peace will come sud-denly, we won't understand it when it does—see, man?" (Kerouac 122)

Throughout the book, when they pause to consider such questions, Dean and especially Sal try to imagine and occasionally to negoti-ate arrangements between themselves and women that would allow for mutual understanding. Dean, when he speaks, tends in large part to blame the women. Sal does his best to take more responsibility, in words if not actions. But what is the peace that Dean predicts in this passage and why is it not so simple, but somehow deeply intertwined with gender and sexual relations—a day when there will be no "has-sles"?

Dean's more immediate proposal is that they continue their journey in the nude. He convinces Sal and Marylou to take off all their clothes. They comply and sit all together in the front seat. She applies cold cream to the men "just for kicks" (Kerouac 161). They are seen, first by truckers and then, when they get out to look at an old Indian ruin (Sal and Marylou don overcoats—Dean does not), by disbelieving tourists. For Dean, the whole scene is quite an unconscious expression of his desire; there is no deliberate intent to shock, nor a care in the world for others' reactions. But Sal must become "unfuddyduddied" (161) first and does notice who sees them. Such are the imaginable narrative options for scenes that depict the attempt at free, and even potentially public, sexual expression and one form of intimacy in the postwar period. This raises the question of what attitude would be more likely to lead to ultimately satisfactory intimacy—fud or unfud, Sal's or Dean's psyche? For truly liberated intimacy, is one better off with free love, a version of which might be called full-throttle promiscuity, or with a more confined, more easily defined and settled context for relationships?

The choice of radical freedom may have its costs; it implies a potential denial of traditional two-mate relationships and the conscious acceptance of more transient, fleeting possibilities for promiscuity without promises, liaisons that may or may not be impersonal and superficial. Both Sal and Marylou soon express concerns that Dean has crossed some line of acceptability in their minds. Marylou's love for him is described as

a love she knew would never bear fruit because when she looked at his hangjawed bony face with its male self-containment and absentmindedness she knew he was too mad. Dean was convinced Marylou was a whore; he confided in me that she was a pathological liar. But when she watched him like this it was love too; and when Dean noticed he always turned with his big false flirtatious smile, with eyelashes fluttering and the teeth pearly white, while a moment ago he was only dreaming in his eternity. (Kerouac 163)

This passage is extremely telling in several ways. In an obvious way, it shows the double standard of whoredom and liarhood. Both Dean and Sal call Marylou a "whore," meaning that she sleeps with someone other than the two of them, while they get as many kicks as they can. And Dean is surely as big a liar as anyone.

The more subtle and important point to note, though, is that Sal identifies completely with Marylou's view of Dean. It is Sal who provides the diagnosis of a particularly male "self-containment and absentmindedness," qualities that make the love bestowed by the adoring party destined to fail, or at least go largely unrequited in kind. The qualities of self-containment and absentmindedness, perhaps more precisely denoted as self-concernedness and unawareness, are characteristics often ascribed to the category *masculinity*. In fact, Sal has a similar set of revelations about Dean throughout the rest of the book. That is why their friendship is unsustainable in the end. Perhaps it is Sal who wants Dean's head in his closet (as narrator Sal assumes Marylou might), to be able to gaze on with memories and adoration, without having to weather the abuse, betrayal, and madness any longer. For in the end, even Sal has learned that the flirtatious smile must be false, as it accompanies Dean's ultimate selfishness. An example soon hereafter is Dean leaving Sal and Marylou stuck in San Francisco with no money, no roof, and no plan. In a sense, Sal distances himself not only from being a whore and a liar but also from this portrait of maleness. This distance may provide an insight into what he wants out of intimacy and why he cannot find it with either men or women, and certainly not with Dean Moriarty. He confesses that he has lost faith in Dean (Kerouac 171).

After going back east to get his life in order, Sal is once again captured—stung—by the bug of the road and wondering about Dean. He returns to find the women "chatting about the madness of men" (Kerouac 187). Dean has a broken, infected thumb (an injury incurred from beating a girlfriend), which the narrator gives significant attention, calling it a symbol:

That thumb became the symbol of Dean's final development. He no longer cared about anything (as before) but now he also *cared about everything in principle*; that is to say, it was all the same to him and he belonged to the world and there was nothing he could do about it. . . .

I was glad I had come, he needed me now. (188–89; ital. in orig.)

As Dean sinks further into what Sal calls madness, surely at least an even greater obliviousness to the feelings of those around him, Sal offers to pay for a trip for the two of them to Italy. It is a huge gesture of loyal friendship, given what has happened between them. This is a fine representation of their true love for each other, taken to new lengths after having been strained by intense challenges. Sal invites him; Dean responds. This is one of the most striking examples of their attempts at acknowledging their mutual desire for sustainable intimacy on their own modest, humble, and apologetic terms:

Resolutely and firmly I repeated what I said—"Come to New York with me; I've got the money." I looked at him; my eyes were watering with embarrassment and tears. Still he stared at me. Now his eyes were blank and looking through me. It was probably the pivotal point of our friendship when he realized I had actually spent some hours thinking about him and his troubles, and he was trying to place that in his tremendously involved and tormented mental categories. (190)

Sal as narrator describes Dean's "mental categories" as being "tremendously involved and tormented," though not his own, which are obviously also significantly troubled.

Sal names it a pivotal moment—a moment of commitment. He blushes. Sal is brought, brings himself, to tears; Dean looks through him, as though looking at him would place too much at stake, might make one or both of them too cognizant of their respective vulnerability. Not only is Dean bewildered and moved by the notion that a friend has spent hours thinking about his welfare, but Sal himself realizes something about his own capacity for care, generosity, and commitment. Can they handle the task of exploring such unknown territory in the domain of their mutual notions of masculinity? According to Sal, they find differing solutions to the problem: Dean immediately becomes "extremely joyful and [says] everything [is] settled" (Kerouac 190). Sal, as the narrator looking back in hindsight, already foresees that their relationship cannot bear the burden of the vast differences between their temperaments and ultimate desires (and mentions "that look" and the elliptical "what Dean did afterward") (190).

For the moment, though, they are back together, trying to cement a fragile peace, the ramifications of which Sal does not quite comprehend and the complexities of which Dean is portrayed as incapable of articulating. "That look," and the *something* they are uncertain of, remain undefined through the text—after all, *On the Road* is an exemplary and explicit chronicle of the search for what the characters describe as "IT," *the* IT. These passages make it clear that IT is at least in part a quest for a new form of intimacy. Indeed, an examination of representations of the IT in American literature would be a most worthy and welcome critical project. As I imagine potential understandings of the vague concept, IT may mean the elusive nature of satisfactory human connection. Dean and Sal appear to have different definitions, and these may change over time. What Sal means by "what Dean did afterward" is open to multiple interpretations. My current one is that it refers to a later moment of selfishness and betrayal in Mexico. Sal attempts to bolster his standing as the good guy, choosing devotion; Dean continues to follow whims. In the end, though, it is Sal who decides that their intimacy has become unbearable.

In any case, they embark on a journey together, only to be thwarted again. Here, they make the sort of pledges that we remember so fondly and painfully from our youth, if we were fortunate or cursed enough to have been through such happenings: "Yes, it was agreed; we were going to do everything we'd never done and had been too silly to do in the past" (Kerouac 191). Once again, Sal the lover-narrator treads on unstable epistemological ground, presuming to know what Dean thinks and longs for. Nonetheless, some sort of pact has been made, regardless whether either party can articulate it. They will do everything together they have not yet done.

In the next passages quoted here, Sal the narrator retreats from omniscience to wonder what exactly Dean "is knowing"; Dean tries to tell him. However, Sal, or perhaps Kerouac, goes on to make rather grand claims about Dean's life and sexuality. Not only does Dean have (male) disciples, he has brought a new sexuality and life into being. Indeed, Dean's proclivities, his purported prowess, and his oft-referenced penis make an enormous contribution to discourses about sex that resonate still. Dean is the definition of "BEAT," with only "pure being" ahead on his journey:

> Now his disciples were married and the wives of his disciples had him on the carpet for the sexuality and the life he had helped bring into being. I listened further. (Kerouac 194)

> He was BEAT—the root, the soul of Beatific. What was he knowing? He tried in all his power to tell me what he was knowing, and they envied that about me, my position at his side, defending him and drinking him in as they once tried to do. . . . Bitterness, recriminations, advice, morality, sadness—everything was behind him, and ahead of him was the ragged and ecstatic joy of pure being. (195)

This is one of the most crucial places in the novel, both as a dramatic moment in the narrative and as evidence for how important their shenanigans and Kerouac's record of them have been to US and world cultural history. Sal will defend Dean to the end for whatever "IT" he has brought to people's lives that they have found so irresistibly attractive. Further, the whole populace is somehow now freer because of the search for kicks of this singularly sensational man who spent much of his youth in juvenile detention centers. According to this moment in Sal's thinking, Dean, amidst his incredible selfishness and ultimate madness, has managed to change many people's lives in ways they cannot yet begin to fathom.

As Sal and Dean plan and begin to go toward their Italian dream, their friendship reaches another crisis point, just after they try to "work" a "fag" at a hotel (Kerouac 210). This is another scene that was revised by Kerouac before publication, taking out the sexual activity between Dean and the man, with Sal listening. The man has picked them up hitchhiking, and they stop for the night. He begins to proposition them. Dean asks about money. He gets nervous, and that is the end of the published version of the scene. But its significance lies in the crisis it apparently provokes between Dean and Sal.

The crisis occurs when they stop for food at a restaurant, where Sal shows Dean a little dick game of pissing into one urinal, then holding it in, and then continuing at another, which Dean says will be bad for Sal's kidneys and make him age more quickly. Sal freaks and yells at Dean not to make jokes about his age or manliness. Dean sulks away. Upon his return, Sal continues with a macho angry tone. Dean says that he had been crying. Then there is an extremely moving section in which Sal apologizes for being, in essence, a lousy friend—and violating their relationship by not believing, or allowing, Dean to be so emotional and forthcoming.

From out of the blue comes Sal's mention of his brother, whose purported purity he contrasts with his own ugliness and "impure psychologies" (Kerouac 214). Many of the most reflective passages and moral quandaries in the novel are accompanied by teary eyes or contemplations of the sadness of life. The relation of crying to masculinity is especially complicated here. On the one hand, Sal seems to accuse Dean of not being man enough to cry. On the other hand, his accusation implies that a recognition that Dean had cried over their relationship would threaten their mutual masculinity by admitting vulnerability. Dean is adamant. The admissions on Sal's part that he is wrong, that he does not have close relationships "anymore," and that nothing in "this lousy world" is his fault are startling (214). They are vivid indications of his struggle to come to grips with the unlikelihood of the possibility of intimacy within the confines of masculinity. Admitting being wrong is perhaps a fairly simple, generous gesture. The candid assertion about close relationships would only be made to an intimate of some sort. The indictment of the "lousy world" in this context may be interpreted in part as a desire for intimacies between people of whichever gender, outside the conventions of locker-room banter or prefabricated social niceties.

Toward the end of the book, in Mexico City, Dean abandons Sal, who is sick, to go be with his latest woman. This is the explicit articulation of Sal's ultimate evaluation of Dean, which started at the beginning of the novel. It cannot, though, be a final resolution quite yet: "When I got better I realized what a rat he was, but then I had to understand the impossible complexity of his life, how he had to leave me there, sick, to get on with his wives and woes. 'Okay, old Dean, I'll say nothing'" (Kerouac 302).

Dean at last visits Sal in New York, where Sal is finally meeting the woman he has been searching for all along to settle down with. They are headed for a Duke Ellington concert at the Metropolitan Opera. Dean asks for a ride to Fortieth Street. One of Sal's other male friends, the driver in charge, refuses absolutely. Dean walks off in a moth-eaten overcoat. Sal merely waves from the Cadillac. Laura, Sal's girlfriend, protests and almost cries. While Sal has no doubt told her something about Dean, she seems to intuit much more about the importance of the intense and intimate relationship that Sal has finally decided to reject. In the end, he feels forced to choose between the relentless instabilities of the road and settled heteronormativity; he chooses the girlfriend and the Met.

The cultural weight of *On the Road* cannot be overestimated, not just because of its continued popularity, but also because of the space it opens up for diverse imagined possibilities for intimacies and masculinities, both potentially liberated and frustrated. First conceived and drafted in the late 1940s and finally published in 1957, it makes a significant contribution to the discourse about the complexities involved in men trying to be intimate with men and women, a discourse that has become even more self-conscious, articulate, and complex in the time since the book first made such a splash.

Works Cited

Allyn, David. *Make Love, Not War: The Sexual Revolution; An Unfettered History*. New York: Routledge, 2001. Print.

Amburn, Ellis. *Subterranean Kerouac: The Hidden Life of Jack Kerouac*. New York: St. Martin's, 1998. Print.

Campbell, James. *This Is the Beat Generation: New York, San Francisco, Paris*. Berkeley: U of California P, 2001. Print.

Corber, Robert J. *Homosexuality in Cold War America: Resistance and the Crisis of Masculinity*. Durham: Duke UP, 1997. Print.

Fiedler, Leslie A. *Waiting for the End: The Crisis in American Culture and a Portrait of Twentieth Century American Literature*. New York: Delta, 1965. Print.

George-Warren, Holly, ed. *Rolling Stone Book of the Beats: The Beat Generation and American Culture*. New York: Hyperion, 1999. Print.

Kerouac, Jack. *On the Road*. New York: Penguin, 1991. Print.

Leland, John. *Why Kerouac Matters: The Lessons of* On the Road (*They're Not What You Think*). New York: Viking, 2007. Print.

Nicosia, Gerald. *Memory Babe: A Critical Biography of Jack Kerouac*. Berkeley: U of California P, 1994. Print.

Savran, David. *Taking It like a Man: White Masculinity, Masochism, and Contemporary American Culture*. Princeton: Princeton UP, 1998. Print.

Sinclair Lewis's *Free Air* and the "Voyage into Democracy"

Ann Brigham

Sinclair Lewis's 1919 novel *Free Air* begins with its female protagonist, Claire Boltwood, stuck in the mud. That may not seem so unusual for a writer like Lewis, who, in novels such as *Babbitt* (1922), *Dodsworth* (1929), and *Main Street* (1920), tells stories of those who are stuck—in small towns, bad marriages, unfulfilling jobs, sanctimonious social circles, and numbing lives. What is different about Claire is that, for her, being stuck is actually a mark of her freedom. Her submerged car, thick in the "gumbo" in the middle of nowhere, represents a clear, albeit dirty, sign of a newfound mobility.

Taking a road trip with her father as a cure for his nervous exhaustion, Claire represents the increasingly mobile New Woman who questions her upcoming marriage and leaves home to find herself. But Claire is not the only protagonist of *Free Air*, the expansion of a serial originally published in the *Saturday Evening Post* and a popular novel in its time. She is joined by Milt Daggett, a midwestern mechanic who comes along to rescue her from the mud. The novel focuses on the cross-class romance between Claire, a New York socialite, and Milt—two plucky individuals who undertake independent but intersecting transcontinental auto trips. Rugged and independent, as well as an orphan, Milt is introduced as the self-made man. Although he owns his own garage, he signifies the provincial working class, thus providing the contrast to Claire's urbanity. He is immediately infatuated with Claire when she patronizes his garage, and she becomes the inspiration for him to hit the road and seek bigger successes in unfamiliar places. As they travel west across the country, their respective class and regional differences figure as both attraction and deterrent, creating a tension about whether their love match can overcome—or accommodate—their differences.

Focusing on the course of star-crossed lovers from different economic and ethnic groups, this novel represents automobility as the democratic forging of intimacies across the yawning gap of social difference. In doing so, it epitomizes the early twentieth-century understanding of the cross-country auto trip as "a voyage into democracy" (Lewis 45).

But *Free Air* shows that, while the attraction of the road might be plotted as the romance of mingling classes, this mixing is plagued by concerns about the proximity between an Anglo-American upper (or upper-middle) class and a range of enterprising immigrants, foreigners, vagrants, and working-class folk. Produced at a time when discussions of the processes and very possibility of creating an integrated nation were paramount, the novel's focus on courtship articulates a prevalent tension between individualism and cultural assimilation in which the ideal and the problem appear to be the same: mobility promises to incorporate the outsider.

It is this relationship between mobility and incorporation that this essay examines, analyzing the pleasures and pitfalls of the cross-country courtship as a story about the tensions surrounding the incorporation of difference. In what follows, I argue that for Claire, Milt, and other motor tourists in the 1910s, cross-country auto travel does not enact the free-spirited *expression* of self, a claim so often made about mobility in all American road narratives. Instead, mobility takes shape as the gradual *education* of the self, which is realized through a series of geographical and social dislocations that function not as a mode of detachment or escape but rather as a method of entry and incorporation into the larger nation.

Geographer Tim Cresswell has identified the primary role that mobility has played in the construction of an American national identity and imaginary. Pointing to a history created by Anglo-Americans, he explains:

Mobility has often been portrayed as the central geographical fact of American life, one that distinguishes Euro-Americans from their European ancestors. . . . While Europe had developed through time and in a limited space and had thus become overcrowded and despotic, America could simply keep expanding west. (19)

In short, "the United States was different from Europe, it was claimed, because its people were *less rooted* in space and time" (Cresswell 19; emphasis added). Mobility occurred across scales, as a "new American spirit was forged in the movement of people from other parts of the world and within the emerging nation" (20). In this context, and in countless narratives, mobility came to epitomize "a uniquely American geographical and historical experience guaranteeing freedom, opportunity and independence" (21).

However, Cresswell further argues that there exists a tension between this understanding of mobility and one in which mobility is a threat to the "rooted and moral existence of place" (21). "Place," writes Cresswell, "in its ideal form, is seen as a moral world, as an ensurer of authentic existence and as a centre of meaning for people" (14). From this viewpoint, intrusions by those deemed inappropriately, excessively, or unpredictably—that is, *too*—mobile, figures such as such as tramps, gypsies, (im)migrants, and undocumented workers, jeopardize the "cosy familiarity of place-based communities and neighbourhoods" (14). Furthermore, persons considered too racially, ethnically, or gender mobile are also determined to be out of place and a threat to social order.

Cresswell's foundational argument productively asserts competing definitions of mobility. He defines mobility and the promise of it as integral to the American national imaginary and yet contends that its meaning is not one-dimensional, ahistorical, or fixed. Using Cresswell's two-pronged formulation of a contradictory American mobility as a point of departure, I examine *Free Air* as one example to argue that road narratives show how mobility is not only tension filled but also a mode of engaging with tensions. This reading stands in contrast to road scholars' prevalent conceptualization of mobility as an escape from tensions, where going on the road is defined as a move beyond society and to a space outside of its reach.

This essay demonstrates that road narratives have much to tell us about how mobility thrives on, articulates, and attempts to manage larger social and cultural tensions, especially as these tensions concern issues of incorporation. Mobility introduces an otherness that is both spatial and social, and road narratives emphasize the working out of difference as the traveler seeks or fails to be incorporated with a different space or identity. In this novel, the tensions of mobility occur around the joining and merging of one thing to, with, or into another. The romantic union between dissimilar figures symbolizes the era's larger concerns about union making. Issues such as regional sectionalism, large-scale immigration, and an increasingly mobile working class prompted conversations about Americanization and questions about how to create a national union through the merger of its disparate components. Taking place as they travel across the country, Claire and Milt's courtship develops in the context of discovering America. Thus, the story of their union making merges with a national one, and it suggests that the prerogatives of incorporation require that their union, like that of the nation itself, transcend the sum of its parts.

Cross-Country Motoring and the Promise of National Unity

To understand how and why the road narrative becomes a site for these issues to appear, I want to examine more closely the beginnings of the phenomenon of automobile touring. In the early twentieth-century United States, the cross-country motor trip emerged as a mode of national unification. But it was not the first tourist enterprise considered capable of creating a national citizenry. The idea that "true Americans would emerge through travel to places increasingly coded as 'national'" (Freeman 147–48) goes back to the nineteenth century, when writers urged Americans to visit quintessentially American places such as Niagara Falls and Yellowstone National Park. But while these accounts touted exceptional destinations as representatively American, motor travel spatially democratized the process of nationalization, extending it to the whole country, thus contending that "true Americans" emerge in ordinary, rather than extraordinary, locales. As Frederic F. Van de Water puts it in his 1927 cross-country nonfiction road narrative, *The Family Flivvers to Frisco*, "We know America and Americans as only those who go motor camping can learn to know them. We have discovered a people and a land whose existence the average New Yorker never even suspects" (240). Based on this discovery, Van de Water claims that motor touring helped "to drive out sectionalism and to knit the American people into a more cohesive, more sympathetic union" (242). Van de Water's "knitting" emphasizes that it is the joining and incorporation of the parts, not the extolling of one part as representative, that defines national identity. Or, in his words, he and his traveling companions are "no longer New Yorkers, but Americans" (5).

In an article written for *Travel* magazine in 1915, Newton A. Fuessle argues that the Lincoln Highway, as a *national* road, is uniquely capable of uniting disparate parts and enacting patriotism:

> America's amazing Highway is at once a road to yesterday and a road to to-morrow. Teaching patriotism, sewing up the remaining ragged edges of sectionalism, revealing and interpreting America to its people, giving swifter feet to commerce . . . it is quickening American neighborliness, democracy, progress and civilization. (26)

These proclamations of unification appear to respond to a number of intersecting social issues, including those of urbanization, sectionalism, and immigration. The one-on-one encounters made possible by motor travel countered the "isolating, insulating qualities of mass society" (Belasco 24). Large-scale immigration, along with the influx of people from rural backgrounds to the urban industrial workforce, caused an "unprecedented confrontation of social groups and ways of life" (Marston 178). Travelers like Van de Water recounted positive encounters with a diverse group of foreign-born, rural, and working-class Americans on the road. At the same time, such encounters with heterogeneous populations prompted calls for a unifying scale of identity. In 1925, motorists such as Harriett Geithmann perceived cross-country automobile travel not only as a form of recreation but also as one of re-creation, crediting it with "transforming the provincial-minded man into a national-minded one" (qtd. in Belasco 93).

Concerns about creating a national citizenry intersected with those of developing class fractions. Capitalism represented the economic system of democracy, but the increased focus on consumption, in which the automobile played a large part, also could create serious social rifts that would undermine the principles of a democracy. Woodrow Wilson articulated such a concern in 1907, worrying that the automobile was "a picture of the arrogance of wealth, with all its independence and carelessness," that would "spread socialistic feeling" among those of the lower classes who, unable to afford such luxuries, resented such displays of wealth and would consequently reject capitalism as unjust (qtd. in Dulles 313–14). Wilson's concerns were not unfounded: in 1910, the cheapest car sold for $400, while the average American worker earned about $574 annually (Jakle 101). However, this picture changed rapidly with Henry Ford's implementation of the moving assembly line in 1913. Mass production reduced manufacturing costs and increased production, resulting in lower prices. In 1916, a Model T cost $360, down from $850 in 1908 (Scharff 56). While 458,000 cars were privately owned in 1910, by 1920, that number had reached 8 million (Flink 191).

These changes affected the car's cultural status, transforming it into a symbol of the lives, aspirations, and mobility of the Everyman. Mass production of the Model T also made motor touring much more accessible to all classes. Although only a dozen or so motorists managed to drive across country in 1912, by 1921, some twenty thousand such trips were made (Havlick 20). Large numbers of people mingling on the road, and at tourist camps and roadside restaurants, challenged traditional social demarcations. Describing her first motor-camp trip in 1925, Norine H. Morton reported, "It is not unusual to see the man with a Packard sitting around with the proud possessor of a Ford" (533).

But while motor travel may have been "sewing up the remaining ragged edges of sectionalism" (Fuessle 26), the picture is not a seamless one. Some traveled leisurely, while others searched for work or moved for health reasons. And so, at the same time that many travelers lauded the pleasures of campsite camaraderie, members of the upper class squirmed uncomfortably camping next to migrant workers at free campgrounds, while the figures of real hoboes belied the elite's romanticized versions of "roughing it." Less concerned that the automobile might exacerbate inequity between the classes, some commentators feared instead that the phenomenon of automobility might level class differences in dangerous ways. Providing a new space of privacy free from the watchful eye of the chaperone, the car "might lead to disorderly and dangerous cross-class familiarities, particularly between [female] passenger-owners and their [male] chauffeurs" (Scharff 18)—or, in the case of *Free Air*, their mechanics.

Close Encounters in *Free Air*

Free Air addresses class conflict with its questioning of a rigid social order and its understanding of the couple as a consummation of differences that promises a transformative new union: a middle-class ideal. The novel works from the premise that the superiority of the upper class derives from presumption, rather than merit, and uses a story of physical mobility to suggest the ways in which members of this class must relocate their priorities.

In this scenario, Claire Boltwood represents a feminized upper class that comes under suspicion as too effete. But unlike the men of that class, especially her fiancé, Geoffrey Saxton (note the closeness to *Saxon*), Claire shows an awareness of the upper class's constraints and deficiencies, struggling against an insularity and suffocation that enervates men and women alike—recall that it is her father's nervous exhaustion that instigates the road trip. In a female version of Teddy Roosevelt's strenuous life, Claire takes to the open road with nerve and determination. In search of new and different experiences, she is the independent New Woman, demonstrating, like the heroines of an early twentieth-century girls' automobile series, "courage, stamina, physical strength, independence, and leadership qualities" in a variety of "dangerous, alien, and challenging situations" (Romalov 76). Experiencing early on the "pleasure in being defiantly dirty" (Lewis 15), she discovers a desire to "conquer new roads" and have "something to struggle against" (45).

With the woman as the subject on the move, rather than the object of pursuit, the novel suggests that access to new territory may transform not just the individual but gender roles and relations. For the new woman represented in early road narratives, automobility represents an escape from domestic life in favor of the pursuit of individual adventure. The woman is in the driver's seat, but her independence and liberated desire, perhaps not surprisingly, are achieved through selection of husband rather than rejection of marriage. On the road, Claire undergoes a transformation of individuality, feeling that "she [is] a woman, not a dependent girl" (Lewis 45), a statement that comments on her engagement to the much older Uncle Jeff, who hovers over her as another paternalistic figure. Though a marriage may be imminent, the process of incorporation for such a union is what is at stake. As Nancy Cott has argued, in the early twentieth-century United States, the differences between an arranged marriage and a love match came to "stand for the difference between the Old World and the New, between outdated tradition and modernity, between falsity and truth, tyranny and freedom" (151). Romantic love exemplified a form of consent that paralleled the "voluntary allegiance" central to democratic citizenship (Cott 151). Therefore, Claire's choice of suitor seems to be doubly mobilizing as a statement of democratic incorporation and a demonstration of gender equality.

But not quite. Milt's courtship strategies involve the thought of kidnapping Claire, making the car yet another space of captivity for women and introducing a male rescue narrative, which supersedes the story of the mobile new woman by literally immobilizing her. However, with a chapter entitled "The Free Woman," Lewis seems to reject this masculine plot. Fearing Claire will forget him when she arrives at her relatives' home in Seattle, Milt tells Claire he wishes he could kidnap her. Claire responds:

> You have been reading fiction, about this man—sometimes he's a lumberjack, and sometimes a trapper or a miner, but always he's frightfully hairy—and he sees a charming woman in the city, and kidnaps her, and shuts her up in some unspeakable shanty, and makes her eat nice cold boiled potatoes, and so naturally, she simply adores him! A hundred men have written that story, and it's an example of their insane masculine conceit, which I, as a woman, resent. (Lewis 214–15)

As the new woman, Claire rejects men's fantasies of romance and domestication. And yet, by the time she gets to Seattle, Claire wishes only "to be out on the road . . . an independent human being—with Milt not too far behind" (281). She has become an object of pursuit. When Milt proposes to her at the novel's end, she responds, "Oh! Milt! Life is fun! I never knew it till you kidnapped me" (368). The new woman's mobility becomes a process of voluntary incorporation. In other words, she leaves home only to be "freely" maneuvered back into place, suggesting that her transformation consists of a shift from initially viewing domestic life as a trap to now accepting it as a place she desires.

For Lewis, who seems to undercut the independence of his female heroine, the heterosexual romance figures primarily as a way to examine class conflict. Claire's notion of domestic captivity is shaped by class differences. To her, the captors are working-class rural men, unkempt and crude, whom she calls "brute[s]" and "cavemen" (Lewis 215). Milt, however, believes that the luxuries of class privilege, not the fantasies of men, squelch female independence. He thinks her "smart set" is the "boorish" one (217), and though he admits Claire has courage, he thinks she would "have still more, if [she] bucked the wilds!" (215). To him, kidnapping Claire means freeing her from the insularity and moral stinginess of her social class.

The novel sets up this class conflict to develop a story of national vitality shaped by the search for a representative class location that could accommodate characters of seemingly incompatible origins. For all their differences, Claire and Milt represent figures of mobility. She may be part of an East Coast, feminized upper class, but she shows verve. He may exemplify the rural, overly masculinized working class, but he demonstrates skills of cultivation. It is fitting, then, that the story of these two mobile characters begins not in a place of origin or residency but on the road, with Claire stuck in the mud.

This physical struggle quickly develops into a human one, focusing on enterprising locals who take advantage of unsuspecting and gullible city drivers. In this case, a German immigrant farmer creates a scam to tow the Boltwoods' car out of a mud pit that he manufactured. Milt arrives just in time to save Claire, dealing with the farmer in the only terms he will understand: "pidgin German" and "swear[s] and holler[s]" (Lewis 22–23).

Allowing for new kinds of access and intimacy, early automobility reveals social tensions as encounters on the road enunciate the collision and gulf between different social worlds. In this opening scene, not only are the father and daughter unable to reason with the farmer but they also do not know how to negotiate with their savior. Lewis's narrator reports, with a wink:

Now of all the cosmic problems yet unsolved, not cancer nor the future of poverty are the flustering questions, but these twain: Which is worse, not to wear evening clothes at a party at which you find every one else dressed, or to come in evening clothes to a house where, it proves, they are never worn? And: Which is worse, not to tip when a tip has been expected; or to tip, when the tip is an insult? (26)

The Boltwoods' dilemma about whether to pay Milt for his roadside assistance shows just how far the Brooklyn pair has traveled outside of their familiar social space. Milt's ability to negotiate with the farmer and the New Yorkers presents the novel's central—and most entertaining—dilemma: how to forge social relations between individuals rather than between types. Although Claire surmises that Milt would be offended by a tip since he seems like such "an awfully independent person" (Lewis 26), her father's interactions "with young men in cheap raincoats [are] entirely monetary." Dismissing Milt as representative of a class, Mr. Boltwood finds that after being paid, such men "[cease] to be" (27). For Mr. Boltwood, cash transactions represent his only awareness of the existence of a class outside his own. But the road, physically and socially, is a work in progress: its open-ended and unfinished state shapes the quality of social relations that take place, challenging the clipped finality that Mr. Boltwood epitomizes.

The novel represents the road as a place that creates new encounters that unsettle class relations, thus requiring negotiations of those relations. When Mr. Boltwood, for instance, learns that Claire and Milt are calling each other by their first names, he wants to talk to her about this "social problem." Adding new meaning to the observations of motor-touring enthusiasts, he asks, "Do you think you ought to be too intimate with him?" (Lewis 152). Epitomized by his dual role as upper-class father and railroad executive, Mr. Boltwood embodies an attitude of insularity and detachment, voicing concerns about the larger repercussions of mixing with outsiders.

As the novel develops, the Boltwoods' worldview becomes the largest problem. Early in their travels, at a hotel in provincial Gopher Prairie, various employees and guests remark to Claire and her father that they are "quite a ways from home" (Lewis 40). Claire takes offense, interpreting their remarks as hints that she and her father are unwelcome and out of place. Finally, realizing that people just mean to be friendly, she exclaims to her father, "There's people in the world who want to know us without having looked us up in the Social Register!" (46). Claire's mistake, which stems from her inability to understand the regional dialect, points to the novel's inquiry into whether there might be a common language that can unite strangers. In other words, unification requires a shared set of ideals.

The novel opens with a demonstration of the problem to be addressed. Zolzac, the scheming farmer who takes advantage of the Boltwoods, shows the failure of unification when an individual does not consent to the right ideals. He is a German immigrant who pursues self-interest—getting rich off unassuming travelers—with no regard for the common good. This behavior is quickly and explicitly deemed un-American. Significantly, it also prohibits his family's social mobility. As his wife laments to Claire: "Oh, I vant man lets me luff America," but her husband stands in the way: "You got the money, he says, nobody should care if you are American or Old Country people. I should vish I could ride once in an automobile!" (Lewis 19). Zolzac's disdain for America and Americanization is signified by two things: his blind pursuit of money and his contempt for the automobile, the novel's symbol of physical and social mobility. His love of the dollar and refusal to become part of America sets up a cautionary tale: Claire learns that having money and social status is not enough to claim a worthwhile identity. Not unlike Zolzac, she, too, needs to learn to be American. Driving across country offers the immersion necessary for her to become part of something bigger. She begins to listen to people, to understand their ways, and to adopt their ways of speaking. Energized by her new encounters, the socialite embraces her trip as a "voyage into democracy" (45, 47) through which she has "discovered America" (67). Exposed to an alien environment, she no longer adopts a position of superiority in relation to "a race she had been trained to call 'common people'" (67). Instead, she now "experience[s] a new sensation of common humanness" (68), trading in a perspective of derision for one of shared humanity.

Discovering the Representative American: Mobility, Individuality, and Adaptability

Claire's embrace of diversity drives the plot for unification, which unfolds as the story of her education and self-transformation. And she looks to Milt as the key to that transformation, pleading, "Make me become real! A real woman!" (Lewis 239). This appeal suggests that class privilege has shaped her into a mouthpiece for social convention and type, out of touch with anything genuine. As in other motoring accounts from the 1910s and 1920s, the cross-country journey teaches (largely northeastern) travelers to view strange scenes and locals not as objects of scorn but as candidates for the authentic and representative America(n). And Milt steps into this role.

Milt's candidacy for the representative American resides in his authenticity as the rural working-class mechanic who provides an antidote to the urban feminized upper class. He is also a self-made man whose success is rooted in self-reliance: introduced as an orphan, he is the hardworking small-town mechanic who, by owning his own garage, has already made a start for himself as an entrepreneur. By the end of the story, Milt has enrolled at the university, pursuing his dream to be an engineer. Such self-reliance will ensure his social mobility and incorporation of his otherness into a new social class.

But Milt's mobility also develops in ways that deemphasize his original authenticity. He appeals to Claire because, with his honest and ethical nature, he exemplifies the working-class exception rather than the rule. As comically romantic as the novel might be, it emphasizes the social differences that characterized the nation at the beginning of the twentieth century, represented by a growing population of immigrants, the increasingly mobile middle and working classes, and the wildness of the West—all of which register as decidedly unincorporable elements. Indeed, Claire's close-up encounters with most working-class figures emphasize rather than mitigate class and ethnic differences.

The working-class or "real" America, defined by hotel operators, chauffeurs, cooks, and hoboes, overwhelmingly comes into view in the form of eclectic, uprooted, and often dangerous individuals. Though they personify Claire's "voyage into democracy," these individuals represent not a national emblem of rugged individualism or self-reliance but a roving menace. And so the story of the mobility of the individual is also the story of anxieties about persons who may be too mobile. Scammed by unethical farmers, innkeepers, and restaurateurs throughout *Free Air*, Claire repeatedly finds herself at the mercy of a rising rank of working-class entrepreneurs upon whom upper-class travelers must depend. As the novel suggests that the upper class must learn to mingle with those outside its purview, thus creating new social relations, it simultaneously points to a discomfiting social mobility. The indiscriminate spread of free enterprise appears especially problematic because it often includes other kinds of "free" associations. First, a drunk, leering proprietor accosts Claire in her hotel room; later, a hitchhiking hobo grabs the steering wheel from her and threatens, at gunpoint, to help himself to the Boltwoods' money and Claire. In both cases, Milt saves the distressed heroine. As with his dealings with Zolzac, Milt's feats of rescue show him to be a singular individual. But his acts of individuality also directly oppose the behavior of other working-class and socially mobile characters, so that he stands out, not as a representative figure of that class, but as an uncharacteristic one.

Although commentary on *Free Air* remains sparse, published accounts share the view that Lewis shows an alternative social order with his representation of Milt's social mobility. Robert E. Fleming praises the novel for "its emphasis on the merit of the individual rather than his or her social class or family background" (vi), suggesting that Milt succeeds because of an innate individuality that transcends social and economic definition. Marguerite S. Shaffer argues that, on the road,

Milt becomes "an individual unfettered by his social background, his small-town roots, his high school education, and his provincial manners. He could rely on his own skill and intelligence to solve the problems that confronted him." Expressing a view common among road scholars, she views the road as a space outside of social structures: "a place beyond the restrictions of work and home—where one was freed from the confines of occupation, social class, and family background, a place where one could actualize, if only temporarily, the American dream" (*See* 242).

Such analyses suggest that Milt's individuality and mobility signify classlessness. Shaffer proposes that the road offered a space "where one could discard the social self and actualize the personal self" ("Seeing" 178). Yet Lewis's novel presents the road not as asocial but as a site of struggle between social conventions, which may or may not result in liberation from them. The self may be refashioned, but there is no personal self that transcends a social one. In fact, the novel suggests quite the opposite, especially since the skills Milt displays on the road, above all mechanical ones, are pointedly class specific.

The negotiation that the road creates and requires is, finally, deeply rooted in the recognition and acceptance of class conventions, which surface during the stages of Milt and Claire's courtship. What constitutes Claire's initial attraction to this stranger? Although Milt may appear "unfettered by [a working-class] social background" (Shaffer, *See* 242), upon closer scrutiny, his distinguishing merits bear the marks of a particular social class. Detecting a "rather fine forehead" above his dirty raincoat (Lewis 23), Claire finds out that, like hers, Milt's family is from Maine. They moved to the Midwest so his father could open a medical practice. Except for the displacement caused by that parent's pioneering spirit, Milt might have been a respectable, even new-moneyed, New Englander. Moreover, Milt reveals how he came to be such an individualist, explaining that, as a kid, he wanted to play Robin Hood, "but none of the other kids—so many of them were German; they didn't know about Robin Hood; so I used to scout off alone"

(147). As the syntax suggests, the foreigners interrupt and forestall Milt's desire to be an integrated, assimilated American. His individuality results from the marginality imposed upon him by a geographically and socially foreign environment.

It is not just Milt's visage that undermines the idea of a world of unfettered and mobile individuals, immune from social classification. Plotted as a narrative of seeing America, this novel is also invested in other kinds of observation. Seemingly the object of the tourist gaze, Milt himself appears as a relentless voyeur. He constantly spies on Claire in scenes that repeatedly emphasize her upper-class status—and his attraction to those class markers. When she pulls into his gas station, it is his "first time seeing a smart woman" (Lewis 58). Claire is a "nice-lookin' girl, kind of" (59), but there is no hesitation about her dress: "Nice clothes she's got, though" (59). Milt details not Claire's bodily features but the wardrobe markers of her class: the "closely-belted, gray suit, her small black Glengarry cocked on one side of her smooth hair, her little kid gloves, her veil" (58–59). Later, peeping into a hotel window, he notes her "blue silky dress—that funny long line of buttons, and her throat'" (95).

Instantly infatuated, and overhearing her plans to drive to Seattle, Milt leaves his successful garage and doggedly tracks her across the country. He monitors his speed so "he might always be from three to five miles behind Claire—distant enough to be unnoticed, near enough to help in case of need" (Lewis 94). At Yellowstone National Park, he spies on her as she dines with "her own kind of folks" in the lodge (131–32). After the two travelers arrive separately in Seattle, Milt sneaks onto the property of Claire's cousins, "prowl[ing] toward the house" and "star[ing] up at the great squares of the clear windows" (260). When caught by Claire, he longs to, as he says, "sneak in one more glimpse of her to take back with me where I belong" (99). Even after Milt has won Claire's heart, he does not give up his spying ways. On a picnic with her family, Claire finds herself "looking at a bristle of rope-colored hair and a grin projected from the shelter of a manzanita bush" (362).

These scenes of Milt spying from the margins thrive on the tensions of social difference and yet manage them by creating an insider/outsider dynamic that reemphasizes the rigidity of social relations and boundaries. With Milt on the outside looking in, no wonder the novel ends with the two lovers traveling in his car; it cannot yet imagine a space where both would belong. Yet these scenes of spying, which seem to point to two different worlds of social class, also define the desires of the voyeur as a longing to be part of the scene on which he is spying. They repeatedly emphasize Claire's upper-class identity and Milt's attempts to get closer to her by schooling himself in the ways of her kind. On the road, he buys five pairs of expensive "silk and lisle socks," pleased that "what they [lose] in suitability to touring . . . they [gain] as symbols" (Lewis 89–90). He watches films "in which the leading men [wear] evening clothes" and are "assisted by a 'man'" (86). He consumes visually—again the spy—every detail of the stylish traveling salesmen because these "pioneers in spats" (87) have successfully settled in the upper echelons; he would be horrified to know Claire associates them with "gray greasiness" (86). Desperate to be acceptable to Claire, he examines silverware "as he had once studied carburetors" (88).

Although Lewis presents many of the scenes comically, Milt's voyeuristic and fetishistic adulation of the upper class undermines the socialite's designation of the working class as the pinnacle of authenticity and admiration. That is, if the working class always has its eye on the upper class, then the upper class seems attracted to a vision of itself as attractive. As Claire puts it, she finds Milt to be a "real person . . . [who] had found her worthy of worship" (Lewis 123).

One could argue that Milt's voyeuristic admiration of the upper class and Claire's reciprocal acceptance of his attention create an ideal middle-class space—the merger, and thus transformation, of features from both characters' class-specific backgrounds. Milt's characterization, a combination of working-class industriousness and latent refinement, suggests this direction because his cross-class profile positions him as the mediator between Claire and the folk of middle America. But although the novel lauds Milt as an individualist, it also frames him with a story in which the title *Free Air* refers not to the open road but to a gratuitous roadside service for travelers to consume. On the road, Milt too becomes a free resource at others' disposal. Robert E. Fleming claims that Milt's "skills as a traveler, a pathfinder, and a mechanic overshadow his lack of social acceptability" (ix); I would argue that those skills do not oppose but serve, quite literally, his social acceptability. Though his unique mechanical and trailblazing talents ostensibly make him socially mobile, they appear in scenarios that cater to class privilege. As Milt uses his skills to run off bad guys and sniff out scams, his acts of independence ultimately appear as indistinguishable from gestures of servitude to Claire and her father. That is, his seemingly independent actions repeatedly occur as responses to situations happening to the Boltwoods. Milt's actions emphasize accommodation, which becomes his form of incorporation and Americanization. As Claire pronounces, "He's the real American. He has imagination and *adaptability*" (Lewis 125; emphasis added). She subsequently expresses her interest in Milt as one that "any creator [would have] in a new outlet for his power" (163), a comment that asserts a telling sense of power and privilege.

Driving off with Claire at the end of the novel, Milt declares, "There's just you and me—you and I—and if we stick together, then we have all society, we *are* all society!'" (Lewis 359; ital. in orig.). As his pronoun correction suggests, he even accommodates himself grammatically to Claire's position. She responds with hesitation: "Ye-es, but, Milt dear, I don't want to be an outcast" (359). To her future husband, she declares, "You can't have any idea how strong social distinctions are. Don't despise them just because you don't know them" (360). As the new woman who recognizes the limitations that established conventions impose upon her, but also benefits from them, Claire is both attracted to and fearful of the possibility of new arrangements. Furthermore, she suggests that for all of his imagination and adaptability, Milt lacks knowledge, something she clearly claims as the province of her class. Milt's mobility allows him to be incorporated into a union, but it is not one that transcends the sum of its parts.

Over the course of the novel, Claire's education takes the form of a growing awareness that she exists as part of a distinct class among other classes. Before her journey, the world was defined solely by her kind; outside of that, there was nothing. Her encounters with strangers reveal the artifice that structures her own life—namely, her unfounded snobbery and privileging of the superficial. But as her concluding comments suggest, ultimately Claire discovers what she already knew: class distinctions matter. As for Milt, his individuality is at odds with his authenticity; while the former sets him apart from the working class, his working-class affiliation guarantees his authenticity, which is his desirability. As the emphasis on his adaptability shows, the novel wants it both ways: for Milt to be a genuine individual and for him to show he is already like everyone else.

With its cross-country road trip, *Free Air* explores questions about who counts as an American and how to define Americanness in a time of large-scale change. The novel also raises questions about the costs of belonging, asking whether, in the process of becoming a part of a larger union, one forfeits individuality. Revealing a conflict between two visions of the representative American, the novel prompts us to consider whether the individualist American and the assimilated American can ever be united.

All of these questions are explored through the text's emphasis on the incorporation of the outsider. But there are no easy answers. With its nationwide courtship, this early road novel simultaneously juxtaposes and conflates the desires to differentiate and to assimilate. Characters are attracted to the very thing they want the object of their attraction to give up—that is, their difference. Milt is drawn to the same scenes of wealth that he wants Claire to denounce as trivial; Claire admires Milt's refreshing sense of individualism, but not when it abandons social order. The characters represent a desire to see America and become intimate with its vast foreignness, but at the same time, much of the country reveals itself as too alien. The novel remains ambivalent about whether a representative America is one of assimilation or one of difference. With its orphan-protagonist and new woman, Lewis's road novel expresses an appreciation for the self-made individual who is not tethered to an ancestral past or social order that might predetermine—or immobilize—the future. And yet, while *Free Air* plots the desire for custom-made individualized routes, it overwhelmingly positions assimilation not only as the destination but as the logic of independence.

Works Cited

Belasco, Warren James. *Americans on the Road: From Autocamp to Motel, 1910-1945*. Baltimore: Johns Hopkins UP, 1997. Print.

Cott, Nancy. *Public Vows: A History of Marriage and the Nation*. Cambridge: Harvard UP, 2002. Print.

Cresswell, Tim. *The Tramp in America*. London: Reaktion, 2001. Print.

Dulles, Foster Rhea. *America Learns to Play: A History of Popular Recreation, 1607-1940*. New York: Appleton, 1940. Print.

Fleming, Robert E. Introduction. *Free Air*. By Sinclair Lewis. Lincoln: U of Nebraska P, 1993. v–x. Print.

Flink, James J. *The Car Culture*. Cambridge: MIT P, 1975. Print.

Freeman, Elizabeth. *The Wedding Complex: Forms of Belonging in Modern American Culture*. Durham: Duke UP, 2002. Print.

Fuessle, Newton A. "The Lincoln Highway: A National Road." *Travel* Feb. 1915: 26–29. Print.

Geithmann, Harriet. "Our Camping Neighbors: A Cosmopolitan Group." *Motor Camper & Tourist* Nov. 1925: 432+. Print.

Havlick, David G. *No Place Distant: Roads and Motorized Recreation on America's Public Lands*. Washington: Island, 2002. Print.

Jakle, John A. *The Tourist: Travel in Twentieth-Century North America*. Lincoln: U of Nebraska P, 1985. Print.

Lewis, Sinclair. *Free Air*. Lincoln: U of Nebraska P, 1993. Print.

Marston, Sallie. "A Long Way from Home: Domesticating the Social Production of Scale." *Scale and Geographic Inquiry: Nature, Society, and Method*. Ed. Eric Sheppard and Robert B. McMaster. Malden: Blackwell, 2004. 170–91. Print.

Morton, Norine H. "Motor Camping, My First Real Vacation." *Motor Camper & Tourist* Feb. 1925: 532–33. Print.

Romalov, Nancy Tillman. "Mobile and Modern Heroines: Early Twentieth-Century Girls' Automobile Series." *Nancy Drew® and Company: Culture, Gender, and*

Girls' Series. Ed. Sherrie A. Inness. Bowling Green: Bowling Green State U Popular P, 1997. 75–88. Print.

Scharff, Virginia. *Taking the Wheel: Women and the Coming of the Motor Age*. Albuquerque: U of New Mexico P, 1991. Print.

Shaffer, Marguerite S. *See America First: Tourism and National Identity, 1880–1940*. Washington: Smithsonian, 2001. Print.

___. "Seeing America First: The Search for Identity in the Tourist Landscape." *Seeing and Being Seen: Tourism in the American West*. Ed. David M. Wrobel and Patrick T. Long. Lawrence: U of Kansas P, 2001. 165–93. Print.

Van de Water, Frederic F. *The Family Flivvers to Frisco*. New York: Appleton, 1927. Print.

Means and Ends of the Road in the Works of Wright Morris

Joseph J. Wydeven

In his introduction to Sherwood Anderson's *Windy McPherson's Son* (1916), Wright Morris claims that "the proper unit of measure" in "space and time" for Anderson is "the *walk*": "Both Winesburg and Sherwood Anderson are *back* when a man went for a walk, rather than a ride" (vii; ital. in orig.). In the same essay, Morris speaks of his father's experience: "It is just fifty years since Anderson sat brooding over the pages of *Windy McPherson*, and my father drove his first horseless carriage from Omaha to Central City" (viii). That automobile was the first of many that marked for Morris a new era in American culture.

Morris found himself intrigued by the new and transformative invention—and although he himself *walked* through the many towns of his childhood, by the age of fourteen or fifteen, he was already an experienced driver with a basic working knowledge of mechanical and pneumatic functions. If he understood his itinerant father at all, it was primarily through the automobile; the chosen circumstances of Morris's life as a photographer made the automobile essential to what he wanted to do, the spaces he wanted to traverse.

Morris was a slow developer, as he himself admitted, and it was not until his early thirties that he began his remarkable publishing career, first as a photographer and maker of photo-texts and only slightly later as a novelist. The automobile proved crucial to both careers, both as means of essential transport and, later, as subject matter for some of his fiction. His autobiographical writings—including two of his three memoirs, *Will's Boy* (1981) and *A Cloak of Light: Writing My Life* (1985), as well as several essays, including "The Cars in My Life"—are replete with references to life on the road. His collection *Photographs and Words* (1982) details much of his activity, especially what he called his "photo safari," focusing his camera on examples of vernacular American architecture. Most immediately important for his career as a road novelist are three of Morris's short novels: *My Uncle Dudley* (1942), *Fire Sermon* (1971), and *A Life* (1973).

I

Three important foundations of Wright Morris's career as a novelist are his involvement with photography, his interest in American vernacular architecture, and the roads on which he traveled to bring his camera to the structures he was compelled to photograph. But all this came later in his life, when Morris was in his late twenties and early thirties, after much reflection upon his aspirations and goals. First came a grounding in the automobile as a mechanical wonder and a vehicle capable of moving rapidly through space. Much of this came from Morris's father, Will, who, it seems, was incapable of staying put and who first introduced Wright to the inducements of long-distance travel.

Will Morris apparently turned into something of a nomad after the death of his wife, Grace, just a few days after she gave birth to Wright on January 6, 1910. Always an indifferent father, Will often left Wright with neighbors and took off for places unknown. When he returned to Wright's life from these places, he did so by way of a variety of different automobiles. He liked the glitz but was not very knowledgeable about the intricacies of automobile systems. Wright, in contrast, learned basic mechanical functions early, as well as some of the tricks car salesmen used to disguise mechanical idiosyncrasies in problematic cars on their lots.

At thirteen, Wright lived with his father in Omaha, and he often drove his father around the countryside—especially when Will was trying to convince his brother, Uncle Verne, to go into his egg-and-chicken business with him. Wright got this experience as a driver because his father "found it hard to drive and talk business at the same time" (*Will's* 76). Two years later, in 1925, when Wright was fifteen, he "swiped a roll of black tape without any use for it, just to swipe it" and was incarcerated in a detention home (87). When his father came to rescue him, he drove up in a Big Six Studebaker, and the two of them left immediately for a new life in Chicago. As usual, Wright was the chauffeur. It was a major experience for him. Driving on unpaved roads, it took them several days to make the trip.

> Arriving in Chicago, driving through the lights, and finally coming out on Michigan Boulevard, along the lakefront, a street so wide I was afraid to cross it, was like nothing that had ever happened to me. . . . My father was asleep behind the side curtains in the back seat. Only someone who has done it the way I did it, driving from Omaha and coming in after midnight, going north on Michigan toward the Wrigley Tower, the waterworks building and the Drake Hotel, will understand what it was like to reach Lincoln Park and know the lake was there and not be able to see it, just hear the boats honk. (91–93).

Further fruits of the Morrises' travels together appear to have been several trips from Chicago to Los Angeles and back, for which Wright's father pulled him out of school and away from his employment at the Larrabee YMCA. To finance these trips, Will sold passage to strangers, transforming what might have been intimate voyages into crowded cross-country treks—as presented in fictional form, for example, in Morris's first novel, *My Uncle Dudley*. Obviously, the automobile provided a sense of adventure, freedom, and release in a period not far removed from horse-and-buggy days. It should be remembered that by 1925, about the time that Morris and his father made their trips west, "half the families in America owned cars"; in 1924, Chevrolet estimated that there were fourteen million automobiles in America (Patton 55, 61).

Morris's memoirs recount various automobile trips—from California to Ohio or Nebraska, travels in the East, even two trips to Mexico. In addition to the memoirs, a third source on Morris's unrestrained appreciation of the automobile in American culture is found in "The Cars in My Life," one of a series of travel articles he wrote for *Holiday* magazine following the success of his novels *The Field of Vision*

(1956) and *Love among the Cannibals* (1957). From this article, the reader gets a strong sense of the automobile culture of the 1920s and 1930s, when American roads had not yet caught up to the ingenuity of automobile technology. Morris's exuberance about the sheer variety of automobile types is evident: "Things change, and so do cars. You can count off the changes by ticking off the models: Model T, Model A, the E.M.F. (Every Morning Fixit), the Big Six, the Super Six, the Twin Six, the Bearcat and the Whippet, the Flying Cloud and the Apperson Jack Rabbit were mechanical marvels of those good old days." In addition, there were the "air-cooled Franklin," the 1920 "liver-colored" Pierce-Arrow, the 1919 Willys-Knight touring car, the 1916 Packard, the 1921 Buick, the 1924 Essex Coach, and the Marmon (45–49). It was a Model T Ford touring car that Morris rode in to deliver eggs with his Uncle Harry; a Willys-Knight that his father purchased as his first car, driving home from the dealer in Columbus, Nebraska, in second gear because he did not know how to shift (nor how to employ reverse); and a 1924 Reo Flying Cloud that Morris's father chose for his and Wright's flight to California with cash-paying passengers, luring the latter in with ads suggesting they "See America First" (45–47)—a phrase first associated with the development of the Lincoln Highway as early as 1914 (Patton 39).

Morris's most important trip was the project he called his photo safari, undertaken in 1940 and 1941; this trip was planned after he had become a photographer and had conceived expansive plans to document vernacular architecture and ways of ordinary life in various sections of the country. Morris had been experimenting with what he called photo-texts: photographs on one page, poetic prose passages on separate pages across from them. His vehicle of choice was a "'34 Ford coupe, with a rebuilt motor, the seat wide enough for me to curl up in, . . . fitted out with recapped tires and a South Wind heater" (*Photographs* 20). Morris's plans to travel from New York were ambitious:

I planned a trip of some eight or ten thousand miles . . . going south to Georgia, west to Mississippi, north along the river to Nebraska, then southwest through Kansas, New Mexico, and Arizona, to California, where I would spend the winter. In early spring I would head east, though Nevada, Utah, Idaho, and Wyoming, crossing the plains while the trees were still barren, following the back roads through the farms of Iowa, Indiana, and Illinois.

He planned to take a thousand photographs of representative American architectural structures under threat of dissolution or disappearance; he wanted to publish them, with prose commentary, in a series of books on the cultural and social state of the nation (20). Beyond *The Inhabitants* (1946), however, these books were not written, though many of his memorable photographs followed Morris throughout his career as a photographer and novelist.

In New Jersey, Morris took his first photograph, of "a church as white and pure as Ivory soap"; near Washington, DC, he found "the narrow highway . . . lined with used-car lots and fields of wrecked cars," the detritus of the automobile age. He describes places he photographed and the road where he slept in his car in Virginia. He was obviously elated: "To be free in this manner, free in my mind and on wheels, yet captive of an abiding and pleasurable enthusiasm that demanded realization—this seemed to me one of the best of possible worlds" (*Cloak* 51–53).

The high points—and perhaps an equally low one—were found in the South, where Morris observed the inhabitants with much interest and empathy. "The soul of the South, as I was privileged to perceive it, seemed to me more complex, and bizarre, than the reports I had read about it. More incredible to me, I found its strangeness wondrous and life-enhancing, rather than merely monstrous and grotesque" (*Cloak* 65). Nevertheless, he saw himself being perceived as "a Northern snooper out to discredit the troubled, dilapidated Southern self-image" (56).

Morris was careful in North Carolina when he tried unobtrusively and empathetically to observe poor whites, "a real 'tribe' of people. . . . How was it that I, a native of the plains, should feel that here I was at long last among my own people?" (*Cloak* 58). He was fearful in South Carolina when a giant black man approached him in a field on private property, where he was photographing a clapboard house. But in Greenville, South Carolina, things came to a head. He was picked up, more or less gleefully, by the police "as a vagrant, and charged with being a possible spy." Morris writes, "My camera, at the ready, was there beside me in the seat, and I had obviously been taking pictures. Of what? Of critical installations, surely." He spent about a week in a cell "with a motley crew of bums, ne'er-do-wells and poor whites" before he was released, having had sufficient time to collect an assortment of vermin in his clothing (58–61).

The account of the journey continues at some length. Morris's experience in Georgia, observing characters seemingly straight out of the works of writer Erskine Caldwell, helped him discover "the emotion that finds its fulfillment and release in the ballad" and later helped him "appreciate" James Agee and Walker Evans's *Let Us Now Praise Famous Men* (1941). In Alabama, Morris was warned off by a shotgun blast fired by someone who took offense at his camera and tripod. He stayed with friends in New Orleans. In Mississippi, he visited with author Eudora Welty and, too shy to intrude on the famed William Faulkner, went instead to Faulkner's lawyer friend Phil Stone, who allowed him to sleep in his car in the driveway and observe at first hand the subservience of the white "masters" to their black servants, a household "drama of the slaves who were now the masters, and seemed even more fawning in their service" (Morris, *Cloak* 63–66).

From there, Morris traveled on to Kansas, Colorado, and New Mexico, where he visited pueblos, "watched Maria Martinez shape and fire her pottery, and bargained with Fred Kabotie for one of his paintings" (*Cloak* 68–69). Soon he was back in California, where he stayed the winter in Los Angeles and wrote most of *My Uncle Dudley*. Back on the road in March, he traveled through several other states, including Nevada, where he took memorable photographs in Virginia City, and Idaho. By the end of March, he was back with his wife in Cleveland Heights, Ohio.

Finally, two more instances of Morris's wanderlust should be briefly noted: his two trips into Mexico. Readers can get some idea of the richness of Mexico for tourists in "Mexican Journey," another of the articles he wrote for *Holiday*. Morris does not reveal much of himself here, nor of his automobiles, but his appreciation for Mexico is clear in his observations of the Mexican women, the ruins and murals, the livestock on the highway, and the wonderful place names—Culiacán, Mazatlán, Guadalajara, Pátzcuaro, Querétaro, Guanajuato—that offer such flavor and history, hinting broadly at the underlying culture embedded in them.

The first trip to Mexico occurred in July 1940, after his friend Magdalene Schindelin, nicknamed Schindy, suggested that Morris and his wife, Mary Ellen, take a trip with her into Mexico. Although he was already anticipating his photo safari starting in the fall, Morris was tempted, especially as Schindy "would supply the car and the gasoline"; he and his wife "would provide the travel lore, the tire repairs and the entertainment" (*Cloak* 43). The places Morris mentions visiting are again interesting: the Blue Ridge Mountains, New Orleans, Laredo, Ciudad Victoria, San Luis Potosi, Mexico City, and Cuernavaca; in the last, Schindy became ill, and they finally called off the trip (44–50). Mary Ellen and Schindy, "who found the children dirty and the poverty depressing," had not been happy in Mexico, and Morris says that he "was careful to conceal my thralldom from [his] companions" (49).

His next journey—solo this time—did not take place until 1954, when Morris was armed with his third Guggenheim Fellowship, to take photographs in Mexico. But the problem with Mexico for a photographer with Morris's predilections is that the country dazzled and dazed him with its colorful culture and strange customs. Indeed, Morris's career as an active photographer was virtually over when he took this second trip; Mexico proved simply too exotic for his camera. And besides, by this time, he had already abandoned his idea for "sociological" photo books, and his novels were becoming more conceptual and complex, not lending themselves to the kinds of intimate photo-text experimentation he had brought to the photo-text novel *The Home Place* (1948).

II

Given Wright Morris's personal experiences with life on the road, it is no surprise that so many of his twenty novels deal with road trips of one sort or another. Such travel plays a minor but significant role in *The Home Place*, *The World in the Attic* (1949), *The Works of Love* (1952), *Love among the Cannibals* (1957), *Ceremony in Lone Tree* (1960), and *One Day* (1965). *In Orbit* (1967) is partly focused on "a highschool dropout fleeing the draft" on his motorcycle, about whom "the important detail might escape you. He is in motion. Now you see him, now you don't. If you pin him down in time, he is lost in space. Between where he is from and where he is going he wheels in an unpredictable orbit. To that extent he is free. Any moment it might cost him his life" (Morris, *In Orbit* 9–10)

But road trips play especially substantial roles in three novels: *My Uncle Dudley* and the complementary *Fire Sermon* and *A Life*. These are not typical road-quest novels adhering to the eight-part trip structure suggested by John A. Jakle: "predisposition to travel, trip preparation, departure, outward movement, turnabout, homeward movement, return, and trip recollection" (qtd. in Primeau 6). In fact, all three road trips are aborted enterprises, focused on ends of the road rather than cyclical processes. All three journeys also have large mythic dimensions in which personal transformation is an essential ingredient.

Wright Morris's enthrallment with the automobile was central to *My Uncle Dudley*. The Dudley of the title appears to be a thinly disguised version of Morris's father, and thus perhaps the book is in part an homage to the older man. Presented as something of a rogue hero,

---

Dudley seemingly has the right attitudes toward everything, and the novel vaguely explores several social, cultural, and philosophical issues. But ultimately the novel fails to satisfy artistically and may instead be seen as a compendium of themes that Morris expands on more successfully in later works.

My Uncle Dudley tells the story of an automobile trip planned from Los Angeles back to Chicago—a version of a journey Morris recounts in "The Cars in My Life," with some of the same cast. Uncle Dudley schemes to sell passage for the trip to Chicago, despite the fact that he and "the Kid" have not yet purchased the car to take them there. The cast of characters is perhaps intended to suggest a range of American types: Olie Hansen, Mr. Jeeves, Natchez Blake, Red Ahearn, a red-headed sailor, Demetrios, Pop, and Mr. Liszt, a music teacher. The Kid is the driver and narrator. The automobile he drives is a Marmon, purchased for fifty dollars and later sold for twenty-seven dollars. In "The Cars in My Life," however, the original Marmon becomes immersed in ten feet of water caused by the flooding Mississippi River. Its loss left an impression on the young Morris: "When the Marmon, that sweet runner, went under, so did part of my life" ("Cars" 51).

The trip itself—this section of the novel is called simply "Passage"—is intended to take the travelers to Chicago via New Orleans: "Warm, southern route all the way" (Morris, *My Uncle* 15). Cities along the way include Yuma, Tucson, Bisbee, Douglas, Deming, Lordsburg, Clovis, Amarillo, Oklahoma City, Hope, Texarkana, and El Dorado. The trip ends far short of its goal, in eastern Arkansas, both because the car is hopelessly crippled—"There was a sick, gritty crunch—then that was all" (146)—and because the Mississippi River is flooded.

Despite accounts of blown tires, worn-out valves, and various other mechanical failures, the physical aspects of the trip are hardly memorable. Indeed, the novel gives every sign of confusion regarding its literary purpose, almost as if Morris, having had a similar experience years before, was casting about for some means to tell the tale. Basic themes are difficult to discern beyond a vague Americanism. Several passages give the gist of a philosophy: "Hard to know what a man is—but I know what I like. Two kinds I like. I like the big fella you can't keep down and the little guy you can't keep up" (*My Uncle* 97). And later: "There's no one thing to cover the people at any one time. There's not even any one dream for the people, or any sun or one moon for the people, for any kind of people at all there isn't even one sky. But I'll tell you one thing about the people, this is their land. And the more I see of them the less I want to cover them at all. Hell, there's no need to cover the people—they cover themselves" (103).

Dudley, a flawed heroic figure, had spent four months in jail as a conscientious objector in World War I and had fathered two children with a Navajo woman. In an extended conversation with Jerry O'Toole, at "Valhalla" (near Tucson), Dudley claims to be a "horseless knight," saying, "I got all the armor but I can't get on a horse. And all of that armor shows I really ain't a brave man" (Morris, *My Uncle* 104). His companion in this conversation, O'Toole, has "hair like a sugared doughnut on his head," suggesting a halo, perhaps intended to make him a saintly presence in the scene (107).

The novel ends in Arkansas, where Dudley and the Kid are arrested as vagrants. The incident is modeled on Morris's own arrest in Greenville, South Carolina, during his photo safari—including the same model of bravery, a man named Furman transformed into a character with the same name in *My Uncle Dudley*. There is also a particularly mean-spirited policeman named Cupid. Furman, who believes his purpose in life is to show bravery, has spat in the eyes of all the other policemen, but he has not yet had the temerity to do the same to Cupid. "For spittin in eyes is just what I been called on to do, an what a man really called on for he must. . . . There just Cupid . . . —then I done what I called on to do" (Morris, *My Uncle* 194). It turns out, instead, that upon his release from jail, it is Dudley, not Furman, who spits in Cupid's eye, in an act that will surely lead him to more abuse. Such "bravery" seems the final point of the novel, and it seems quite disappointing to have the novel's ending hang on such a thin conception, while leaving suggestions of the Kid's initiation into young manhood unfulfilled.

Morris was in his early sixties when he composed the much more satisfying pair of books in *Fire Sermon* and *A Life*. Both books have strong elements of myth and ritual, with mundane events carrying timeless significance. They compose Morris's *The Old Man and the Sea*, with much of Ernest Hemingway's mythic simplicity. After nearly thirty years, some of the qualities promised in *My Uncle Dudley* are fulfilled in these two seemingly simple books; some of the universal significance Morris seemed unable to capture in the earlier book here achieves an assured resonance. The books carry sentiment without surrendering to easy sentimentality. Best described as what Ronald Primeau calls "journeys of self-discovery" (69–88), these end-of-the road trips provoke significant change in the eighty-two-year-old protagonist; even though he does not necessarily seek change, character Floyd Warner accepts it with equanimity when it comes.

The cast of major characters in *Fire Sermon* is small, involving through the book's long exposition only the old curmudgeon Floyd Warner and the eleven-year-old Kermit Oelsligle, who live together in a Rubio, California, trailer park. Kermit was orphaned the year before when his family was killed in an automobile accident, and it turned out that Warner, Kermit's great-uncle, was the closest kin able to take the boy in—even though Warner "does not like kids. He thinks they are all a pain in the ass" (Morris, *Fire* 10). The comedy of their situation is often broad, as in this perennial ages-old observation: "At the boy's age (which is almost twelve) the Uncle got up at dawn, harnessed the horses, plowed forty acres of corn and alfalfa, fed and watered the team, then milked five cows and separated the cream before he sat down to supper" (6). Aunt Viola, Warner's sister in Nebraska, who would have taken Kermit in if she were not an invalid, has taken a special interest in Kermit and writes him long, encouraging letters in her own special style; knowing that Warner reads the letters, she always adds loving comments about Warner, calling him "*our old scalawag*" with "*the stubbornest will I ever set my eyes on*" (43; ital. in orig.). But the book changes its focus when a telegram arrives informing Warner that Viola has died. This means that he will have to go to Nebraska to "settle the estate"; the business of the book, then, is ordering of the past. Again, as in *My Uncle Dudley*, the trip itself constitutes the center section of the novel, leaving the final section to transact the concluding business.

If there is any other thing that Warner despises as much as organized religion, it is hippies; this is the 1960s, after all, and Warner is eighty-two. He thinks of them generally as a "pack of mongrels" (Morris, *Fire* 15), "like the strayed and lost remnants of some deranged but irresistible Pied Piper" (18). But now two hippies named Stanley and Joy come into the novel, hitchhikers whom Warner and Kermit pass several times along the highway. Inevitably, Warner picks up the hippies and carries them along to Nebraska. The point of view shifts partially to the boy, who is learning to observe carefully and who was in favor of picking the hippies up. Throughout the "passage," Warner contemplates the boy's future welfare. Despite what he considers the outrageous behaviors of the young, Warner understands that an eighty-two-year-old has little to accommodate the developmental needs of an eleven-year-old. When they ultimately reach Viola's house in Nebraska, Warner turns to Kermit and asks, "You like them, eh?" (145), as if to affirm his own understanding.

In the house and the barn beyond are objects that have been collected for auction—objects like those found framed in Morris's interior photographs in *The Home Place*: tables once holding photographs, household utensils, and objects found inside drawers and cabinets. The detail is excruciating: "There is a ball of tin foil, a pocket watch with a chain, a flashlight, a pocket knife with a broken bone handle, two bed casters, a shaving strop, and a shoebox lid full of black and red checkers. There is more, but it would take all day to sort it out" (*Fire* 134). Obviously, Morris wants to show how symbolic elements, left to Viola "while the others died and left to her those things they valued" (142), have been gathered into one sacred place.

The final chapters are dedicated to the ritual settlement of time. With Viola dead and Warner now the only survivor of the family, what to do with all these objects? The novel's title tells us everything, but what is crucial are the means by which Morris carries this ritual through. At the house, Warner finds the room where Viola spent much time meditating on the past. There, Warner's exhaustion is more apparent than ever before. The boy, finding him slumped in a chair by the window, thinks him dead, but, as Warner suggests, he has only suffered "a queasy spell" (Morris, *Fire* 139). Nevertheless, the "queasy spell" ritually prepares Warner's mind for what follows.

The "fire sermon" ceremony by which time is brought to heel begins with a heedless violation by Stanley and Joy, whom Warner finds naked in Viola's bed. He flails at them with a mop and apparently hits the lamp the two hippies have lit, starting a conflagration that rapidly consumes the room and then the house. In terror, the boy flees into the woods, watching the fire from afar. The fire does its necessary work: Warner watches "the past, lock, stock, and barrel, go up in smoke" (Morris, *Life* 25).

When the boy finally looks around, he finds that he has been abandoned by Uncle Floyd; where he has gone is the subject of Morris's next novel. The Maxwell is gone, although the trailer remains behind. It is clear that Kermit will attach himself to Stanley and Joy; as stated a few chapters earlier, it will be "just the three of them against all the rest" (Morris, *Fire* 111). As for Warner, the fire sermon has further prepared him for significant change in altering his consciousness and reducing his propensity to pride.

In *A Life*, Morris takes Warner's life to its inevitable conclusion, though the narrative is often surprising. It is a simple story, its point of departure being a place not far removed from where readers observed him last in *Fire Sermon*: along the road beside his Maxwell Coupe, "acquired in exchange for a Dodge touring in 1928" (*Life* 2). The road trip in this book takes Warner from Chapman, Nebraska, down Route 183 into Kansas; he eventually reaches the Pecos River region, east of

Roswell, New Mexico, and the homestead on which he raised sheep with his now-long-dead part-Indian bride, Muriel Dosey. Throughout this journey, Warner becomes increasingly more dazed and unsettled, as well as more and more removed from the need to make personal choices.

Morris deliberately prepares Warner's mind for his death. There are three stages through which Warner is mythically "prepared": first, he becomes adventitiously involved in a prayer circle ceremony with several women; second, he asserts his fundamental belief in the sanctity of life by saving a kitten from his perch in the filth of an outhouse privy; and third, he meets a Hopi Indian named George Blackbird in a restaurant, offers him a ride, and falls under his influence and power.

The process is summed up powerfully:

> Into Warner's head, out of nowhere, popped a notion so strange it made him smile. The moment coming up, the one that came toward him like the line on the highway, then receded behind him, was something he had no control over. . . . The Indian, the cat, and the prayer ceremony had come out of nowhere to take him somewhere. He could see it happening. He could see that it was not an accident. He had come this way by his own free choosing, and having chosen as he pleased, he was right where he was. (Morris, *Life* 95)

Although he had always asserted his "stubborn will," in the end his life is taken over by chance. Yet Warner is complicit in the weakening of his volition: in his "agreeably befuddled state of mind" (127), he chooses to accede to the workings of chance, as embodied in George Blackbird.

Blackbird, the Hopi, is a Vietnam veteran and a hardheaded realist. When he finds that Warner is prone to driving off the edge of the road, he takes over the driving. When he sees that the kitten Warner saved is dead, he simply drops it out the window. It is less important that readers think kindly of Blackbird than that they accept the fact that Warner believes in him—especially when Blackbird recognizes and identifies Warner's condition. "You like me, you got no people," Blackbird says (Morris, *Life* 98). Even earlier, upon their first meeting, Blackbird presciently asked: "Old man . . . what you want?" (80).

What Warner wants he hardly knows, but he tacitly accepts all that happens, as if he has chosen it by putting himself in Blackbird's hands. Blackbird seeks Warner out in the dark, holding in his hand something that glints in the moonlight; it is the tuna can cover to the food that Warner purchased for the kitten. Blackbird asks for Warner's hand, and when Warner gives it to him, Blackbird runs the can cover over the old man's wrist. It is an act of murder, but it is clearly more than that for Warner, as well as for Morris: "Everything had happened according to a plan that would prove to be his as much as Blackbird's, so that what he wanted, strange as it might appear, was what he had got" (*Life* 150).

Wright Morris's lifetime of road trips, real and imagined, led him to this remarkable conclusion, in which the road makes possible such memorable experiences of transcendence. Never showing any interest in writing road works in the classic quest tradition, he was more involved in showing the movements and emotions that the road made possible, while celebrating twentieth-century American road culture and his own involvement in it. *Fire Sermon* and *A Life* especially show a writer capable of great change and philosophical acceptance of the inevitable—using the road to get him there.

Works Cited

Morris, Wright. "The Cars in My Life." *Holiday* Dec. 1958: 45–53. Print.

___. *A Cloak of Light: Writing My Life*. New York: Harper, 1985. Print.

___. *Fire Sermon*. Lincoln: U of Nebraska P, 1979. Print.

___. *In Orbit*. Lincoln: U of Nebraska P, 1976. Print.

___. Introduction. *Windy McPherson's Son*. By Sherwood Anderson. Chicago: U of Chicago P, 1965. vii–xix. Print.

___. *A Life*. Lincoln: U of Nebraska P, 1980. Print.

___. "Mexican Journey." *Holiday* Nov. 1959: 50–62+. Print.

___. *My Uncle Dudley*. Lincoln: U of Nebraska P, 1975. Print.

___. *Photographs and Words*. Carmel: Friends of Photography, 1982. Print.

___. *Will's Boy: A Memoir.* New York: Harper, 1981. Print.

Patton, Phil. *Open Road: A Celebration of the American Highway.* New York: Simon, 1986. Print.

Primeau, Ronald. *Romance of the Road: The Literature of the American Highway.* Bowling Green: Bowling Green State U Popular P, 1996. Print.

Cormac McCarthy's Second Literary Trilogy: Dreams of the Fire and Our Fathers _____

Richmond Adams

Various critics have written on Cormac McCarthy's Border trilogy of novels written throughout the 1980s and early 1990s. At the same time, although scholars such as Carol Juge, Dianne C. Luce, and Susan J. Tyburski have explored separate aspects of each work, there has been insufficient exploration of how McCarthy's three more recent works function in the same manner as a cohesive unit. Through *No Country for Old Men* (2005), *The Sunset Limited* (2006), and *The Road* (2006), the image of fire is a repeated symbol. McCarthy's use of "carrying the fire," with its implications concerning some type of Absolute, expresses both a fear and a hope for human civilization in the twenty-first century (*No Country* 309; *Road* 83). As Erik J. Wielenberg suggests, "perhaps to carry the fire is to carry the seeds of civilization" (4) and, even more pointedly, to realize, as the Man tells the Boy in *The Road,* it is "real" since it burns "inside you" (McCarthy, *Road* 278–79). More notably, however, McCarthy's trilogy explores a generation's previous acceptance of postmodernism as an operative world perspective (Gray 39). Even as *The Sunset Limited* does not explicitly reference the metaphor, it is all the same that the Black and White's discussion centers upon the place and reality of the God portrayed within the Judeo-Christian traditions, at least partially, by means of fire.

Such allusions to an Absolute nevertheless suggest something more at work than theological dogmatism expressed in literary form. Rather, McCarthy's three works of the twenty-first century focus upon questions in the aftermath of September 11, 2001 (Gray 39). Through an overarching examination of each work both independently and in the context of the trilogy, I will argue that McCarthy expresses a fear that human civilization might still destroy itself, though it need not do so. In "carrying the fire," McCarthy posits that although postmodernism provides necessary contributions in the areas of race, gender, and class, its logic of externalization undermines the root necessity of an ongoing, stable, and internally manifested moral order. Without such a center, or what postmodernism appears to proclaim only as exemplifying a release from oppressive constructs, McCarthy's second trilogy suggests how it has become increasingly possible for human relationships to deteriorate from a state of resigned uncertainty to nihilistic suicide and eventually cannibalized monstrosity (Lehan xxvi; Glover 2–3). In an essay that dates from the early 1990s but remains directly relevant to McCarthy's more recent works, Edwin T. Arnold argues, "While I recognize and appreciate the postmodern celebration of McCarthy's exuberant violence, his astonishing approximation of chaos, his grand evocation of the mystery of the world, there is also evident in his work a profound belief in the need for moral order, a conviction that is essentially religious" (44). McCarthy uses the metaphor of fire to offer a path by which human civilization can navigate beyond the present darkness—a darkness of its own making.

McCarthy's use of metaphor moves beyond itself by portraying the central and irresolvable problem of postmodernism. By positing itself as a worldview, postmodernism necessarily requires a set of premises supported by forms of argument. Simultaneously, however, postmodernism is an idea that lacks a definition (Hodgson, *Winds* 54). Peter Hodgson, a theologian, also reiterates the incoherence of postmodernism by stating that "since we do not yet have a name for our emerging new paradigm and do not know how to characterize it fully, we simply call it 'post-'" (54). Nathan A Scott, in his speculative article concerning the reactions of theologian Paul Tillich, parallels Hodgson's statement with the assertion that postmodernism does not "have the sort of coherence that lends itself to swift and easy description" (146). Such incoherence, however, assumes a type of coherence and, by doing so, turns postmodernism against itself. This circularity eventually devolves to the brink of metaphysical meaninglessness; incoherence itself is still *something* and, accordingly, can be understood. In an effort to maintain its intellectual viability, postmodernism becomes not an operative definition that is subject to examination and criticism but an interpretive notion of a given critic at a given time and place.

That sort of flexibility, however, undermines postmodernism's ability to articulate its view, as Hodgson puts it, of an age past absolutism that is rooted in pluralism and expressed through "transformative, emancipatory praxis" (*God* 41). Even while arguing that postmodernism's "lack of objective certainty . . . must not of itself be allowed to have an immobilizing effect" (41) on such emancipatory efforts, Hodgson cannot move beyond the conclusions of his own reasoning. To assert a claim of nothingness inevitably moves toward the realization of what is either oppressive or emancipatory. Without some form of stable moral center, Hodgson's "proximate goal," as he says, quoting Karl Jaspers, of a "world order" defined by "a peaceful community of all subject to transmutation in perennial democratic unrest and self-rectification" ceases to appear in a recognizable form (Jaspers; qtd. in *God* 247). Such unrest—if the last century's "deep experience of evil" (30) serves as any guide—will remain "peaceful," "perennial," and "democratic" only in the eyes of those with the power to define or re-define it. Such lack of moral definition in reference to the "deep[ening] experience of evil" is what McCarthy's second literary trilogy attempts to explore.

Published in 2005, *No Country for Old Men* has generated a "large body of reviews" (Cremean 21), many of which have assumed a similarity between what David Cremean calls the "conservatism" of Sheriff Ed Tom Bell and McCarthy himself. "Among the reviewers suggesting this viewpoint," according to Cremean, are Joyce Carol Oates, William Deresiewicz, and Richard Woodward (21). Even while narrowly defining *conservatism* as staying married to one's original spouse and having beneficial relationships with one's parents, Cremean does argue that McCarthy and his sheriff "have at least one major trait in common: they both utter facile pronouncements and make sweeping generalizations" (23). Cremean soon concludes that "despite the great sympathy with which [Sheriff Bell] is portrayed," his judgments throughout the novel are finally "unreliable and suspect" (23).

These same judgments, however, express the perspective that human actions root themselves in some form of discernible relationship between motive, action, and consequence. Even the young boy whose crime of deliberately planned murder opens the novel admitted his guilt and knew the coming result—as Bell puts it, "he knew he was goin to . . . hell" (McCarthy, *No Country* 3). Despite Bell's inability to know "what [to] say to a man that by his own admission has no soul," this causes him to wonder if he is not seeing "some new kind" of criminal; the boy's admission of guilt still, if only tentatively, reaffirms the sheriff's underlying sense of moral order (3). Such affirmation, however, does not ease his growing anxiety over cultural realties that he has little, if any, means of grasping.

Sheriff Bell's musings, however, as expressed through his italicized ruminations, reflect more than simple or "conservative" (Cremean 21) transitions between the novel's narrative sequences. They serve as a way to grapple with the changes across American society that occurred between his return from World War II in Europe and the 1980 in which he speaks. More to the point, Bell's internalized thoughts enable him to realize that he lacks any point of reference for the implications of Chigurh's behavior. Even having witnessed men dying in combat during (probably) the Battle of the Bulge does not adequately prepare Bell for the apparent fathomlessness of antagonist Anton Chigurh (McCarthy, *No Country* 277–80).

At specific instances during the novel, Bell remarks that he is being outgeneraled and overmatched by someone most of his law-enforcement colleagues perceive as just one among many executioners within the already-ruthless drug trade. In admitting his strategic and tactical inadequacy, Bell realizes that Chigurh, as he remarks to a fellow sheriff, is not "a lunatic" (192). Such reasoning, it seems, creates a quandary. Through chasing Chigurh, Sheriff Bell starts to comprehend that any assumptions he may have held about human motivation are inadequate to the task that immediately faces him. Given Bell's lifetime of believing that criminals have some discernible basis for their actions, his increasing befuddlement about Chigurh comes to form the cultural tension at the heart of McCarthy's novel.

Such incompleteness, however, serves a larger purpose within McCarthy's narrative. Chigurh's actions, as Bell quickly discerns, are utterly rational. To accept Chigurh's rationality, of course, calls into question the intellectual and moral basis for the Western civilization within which Bell, among others, has functioned throughout his life. Working as a law-enforcement officer with a sworn duty to serve and protect only solidifies Bell's root belief in the legitimacy of Western institutions. As he gradually comes to understand that Chigurh's actions cannot be dismissed as the unfortunate cruelty of a madman, Sheriff Bell's desperate pursuit increasingly takes a form beyond simply the desire to catch a mass killer. Rather, this desire evolves into a quest, the destination of which is a reestablishment of a functioning moral order.

To do such reestablishing, as McCarthy portrays in *No Country for Old Men*, *The Sunset Limited*, and *The Road*, is to carry the fire. By having his characters carry it (or, in Sheriff Bell's case, see it being carried), McCarthy develops a paradox that he explores throughout his second trilogy. The fire of moral order, it appears, both is planted within and yet remains beyond human experience. *No Country for Old Men* concludes with Sheriff Bell's dream of his father "carryin fire" toward some unknown, but vaguely visible, destination (309). That same fire, however, as the father tells the boy as they walk *The Road*, is within them (*Road* 279). Such a paradox reflects something much more than an academic distinction between enlightened rationalism and fragmented postmodernism. McCarthy's fire instead suggests a desperate groping for moral stability that roots itself beyond human endeavor, idea, or institution. To carry the fire is to understand it as certainly real, but also to see it more basically: as gift and invitation. Sheriff Bell's dream that ends *No Country for Old Men*, in turn, expresses that dynamism.

At its core, however, McCarthy's paradox of an external fire carried within expresses the notion of some Absolute beyond the undefined incoherence that postmodernism comprises. Fire itself, perhaps, is McCarthy's deferential link between his primary readers and their awareness of Western philosophical and religious tradition (Arnold 44). By using an explicit image that alludes to monotheism, McCarthy's three most recent works affirm the necessity of both such an Absolute and, more important, the call for a moral order emanating from that heritage. Moreover, "the fire" carries its own insistence that such an order must be flexible in its stability. Without an acceptance of operative cultural morality, McCarthy fears that civilization will, in short order, descend from murderous indifference to suicidal emptiness to cannibalism. Contrary to postmodernism's claim that freeing human civilization from structures of oppressive power will somehow result in "perennial democratic unrest and self-rectification," McCarthy's trilogy poses the idea that such an unchaining will inexorably lead to a liberation from life in the most unimaginable of ways.

Throughout Bell's search, and despite his evolving insights, the sheriff does not consciously grasp the full implications of the separation he notices between Chigurh and even the murdering boy whose staggering indifference opens the novel (McCarthy, *No Country* 3–4). Bell does, however, process his shifting awareness through the dream about his father (309). Groping for some means by which he might explain his feelings to his wife, Loretta, Sheriff Bell describes a cold nighttime setting with snow on the ground. He observes his long-dead father riding "past me . . . sa[ying] nothin" but still "carryin fire" (309). The older Bell, as the sheriff relates, meant to build a fire in anticipation of his son's arrival. The novel concludes with Sheriff Bell indicating that despite the cold and dark in his dream, the warmth and light of the fire will be waiting for him. For Bell, that sense of something beyond the immediate and material gives him the strength to wake up and face the world that Chigurh is attempting to remake in his own image. Bell might well have said, upon waking up, that the fire's light will always overcome the darkness and that such an image is "okay."

More question than statement, the notion of "okay" rests near the heart of *The Sunset Limited*. McCarthy portrays the conversation between White and Black as an extension of the world that Bell thought he defeated in World War II. Having somehow stepped between White and his desired meeting with the Sunset Limited train, Black spends the play asking for some reason behind White's initiated and soon-to-be-renewed suicide attempts. White, whose work as a university professor embodies Western rationalism as the means to social enlightenment, answers that the things he once believed "dont exist anymore. It's foolish to pretend that they do. Western Civilization finally went up in smoke in the chimneys at Dachau but I was too infatuated to see it. I see it now" (McCarthy, *Sunset* 27). Those infatuations, as White put it, cannot withstand the thrust of their own logic that since nothing is, anything becomes both possible and, in his view, necessary. Since Western civilization and its Enlightenment promises of a self-rectifying world have almost always resulted in even greater calamities, White logically concludes that the best way to live is to let it go, in his case through suicide.

Black's counterargument is not, despite its apparent evangelical language, a doctrinal apology for one version of Christian faith or another. More of a trust that acknowledges the darkness coursing through Western life, Black's faith instead carries the fire of something beyond the cold logic of pitiless rationalism. Black knew quite well that the categories of unmitigated reason were empty long before White reached that same conclusion. It is precisely such awareness, however, that leads Black to claim something beyond the wreckage that has been much of his life (McCarthy, *Sunset* 53, 64). Such an affirmation may incarnate itself in "a horrible place" that is "full of horrible people," but as Black professes, while "the sun dont shine up the same dog's ass ever day," it is somehow still shining (43).

Despite Black's efforts, however, McCarthy finally seems to give the argument to his professorial adversary. White's despair culminates in the idea that since "the things that [he] loved," fragile at best, are now gone, the only rational course left is to meet the Sunset Limited (McCarthy, *Sunset* 25, 60–61). Black's desperate offer that "we can talk about something else," White believes, will only provide another illusion that "things" can be set "right" (141). The fellowship Black offers is one of "pain and nothing more" beyond any form of tolerability except death (136–37). As the play ends, Black begins to follow White's logic, even as he turns to God in a despair of uncertainty. "I dont understand what you sent me down there for. . . . If you wanted me to help him how come you didnt give me the words? You give em to him. What about me?" (142). Even while calling his own trust into question, however, by virtue of simply doing so, Black's despair suggests that McCarthy does not grant White a full victory. In short order, of course, White will be dead and beyond his misery. Black, on the other hand, will return to those in trouble with his story of something rather than nothing (38; 40–41). While McCarthy's play does not employ the phrase, Black's life, work, and hope nonetheless carry the same fire of *No Country for Old Men* and *The Road*. By promising to keep his "word" even while begging for some indication that his efforts with White were "okay," Black manages, at least in part, to reclaim what White had lost (142).

Throughout McCarthy's second trilogy, such a reclamation insists on a form of moral order that emanates from a sense of an Absolute. Arnolds say that "while [he] recognize[s] and appreciate[s] the postmodern celebration of McCarthy's exuberant violence, his astonishing approximation of chaos, his grand evocation of the mystery of the world," he also sees " the possibility of grace and redemption even in the darkest of his tales" (44). Written in the early 1990s, Arnold's contention arguably bears even more resonance in the early twenty-first century than it did twenty years ago. Shortly after Arnold's assertion that postmodernism relishes McCarthy's unwaveringly bleak descriptions of human horror came such expressions of nihilism and violence as the 1995 Oklahoma City bombing and, of course, the events of September 11, 2001. The motivations behind those actions and the near-universal shock at the levels of such meticulously planned violence brought forth something quite other than eruptions of postmodern "exuberance." On the contrary, McCarthy's trilogy posits that at the root of nothingness is a dangerous something that tends toward cruelty and indifference. As *The Road* portrays, these consequences include bands of women being impregnated, not to continue the human species, but for progeny that will serve as food in a world where even the most basic forms of common decency have virtually disappeared (92; 198). In reference to such possibilities, perhaps Sheriff Bell's anxious dream and Black's affirming cry come to serve as bastions of rooted order against the all-too-pervasive tides of intellectual and moral decay.

McCarthy, of course, both carries his fire and gives it the imprimatur of "okay" in *The Road* (56–57). By doing so in a world that has destroyed itself, McCarthy implies that something remains even when the language once used to express it is in the process of dying. In seemingly every conversation between father and son, as they grasp for some form of understood conclusion, one, the other, or each in turn uses "okay" as a means of both ending and yet continuing; the notion of "okay" is also often connected with either warmth or fire. Within the context of their world, which ceased to be "okay" one morning some ten years prior to the events of the novel, such a link comes to serve, at one level, as a metaphorical bridge between adults and children (52).

In building such a bridge, however, McCarthy goes beyond it. Connecting his operative metaphor with the reality of something "inside" that makes it "okay" to be "the good guys," McCarthy expresses the permanent presence of a moral order emanating from a tradition based on some type of Absolute beyond the relativity associated with postmodernism (*Road* 279; 77). In his *After the Fall: American Literature since 9/11* (2011), Richard Gray makes particular note of *The Road* as "a post-9/11 novel . . . to the extent that it takes the measure of that sense of crisis that has seemed to haunt the West, and the United States in particular, ever since the destruction of the World Trade Center" (39–40). Gray's linking of McCarthy's fire with like references in Shakespeare, as well as the high modernism of T. S. Eliot and William Faulkner, grounds *The Road* squarely within Western literary tradition. Such a literary connection, particularly with reference to Eliot's "Fire Sermon" in *The Waste Land* (1922), suggests the need for some type of stable moral premises within which civilization can reasonably function. While Gray limits the "fire" to that carried by father and son, it seems clear that Sheriff Bell, via his own father, and Black's proclaimed faith in a theological father still embody the opportunity that offers human civilization a means of redemption rather than a path to destruction. McCarthy's sense of that moral order and tradition is what Wielenberg calls "the code of the good guys," and it carries the boy past the death of his father toward a germ of trust with his new family at the novel's conclusion. That germ allows the father, the adopted family, and the son between them to remain the "good guys" even as they continue to be engulfed by world's inexorable decay (Wielenberg 5–6).

Their world is, as McCarthy presents, one that would, at the least, call into question the place of any morality whatsoever. Slavery and cannibalism, infants on spits over open fires, and even the boy's mother choosing to abandon her family rather than face being "the walking dead in a horror film" (McCarthy, *Road* 55) all portray a world long since indifferent to its own madness. In a realistic appraisal of their circumstance, the wife's decision to walk to her death consequently appears both logical and, not coincidentally, quite moral. As she puts it, "Sooner or later they will catch us and they will kill us. They will rape me. They'll rape him. They are going to rape us and kill us and eat us and you wont face it" (56). The father also realizes that to either remain or, as he believes possible, travel "south" so that the boy and he might "be warm" will probably lead to a horrendous death (4; 10). But although the father realizes the futility of the journey, he also knows it to be necessary. Such a necessity, at its root, is linked to "carrying the fire" and the moral order to which that phrase alludes. By finally blessing his son with knowledge of the fire inside him, the father gives something not from externalities but rather from a sense of Absolute that is innate, unchangeable, and, even though as fragile as White remembers in *The Sunset Limited*, not extinguishable.

Such eternality still does not lessen McCarthy's assertion that the limitlessness of human depravity, even under the best of circumstances, lurks just beneath the surface of an ostensibly civilized veneer. The works of his second trilogy portray an escalating sense of brutality, violence, and indifference. At the same time, McCarthy does not write fiction that simply rails against the despair of nihilism, cynicism, and suicide. By having Sheriff Bell continue to talk with his daughter years after her death, or Black getting onto his knees in prayer, or concluding *The Road* with the boy expressing even a small trust that the family he meets are also "good guys" who "carry the fire," McCarthy offers something beyond lasting images of devolving amorality. Rather, the trilogy, even as each work within it portrays a civilization spinning headlong toward self-immolation, provides a defiant expression of something that offers an alternative to the destruction represented by the clocks stopping at 1:17. The fire that the man and the boy carry inside themselves, McCarthy seems to say, embodies the light, warmth, and love of "[each] other's world entire" (6). The heart of that world, as McCarthy portrays it, is a functioning moral order based upon some form of human goodness that trusts in something from beyond, but planted still inside, our varied yet commonly human types of experience. What Sheriff Bell's dream, Black's faith, and the courage of father and son embody is that more light and more warmth and, quite possibly, more love wait at the end of their separate, but common, roads. At the last, in a halting attempt to answer Black's question of despair, McCarthy expresses his faith that such light, warmth, and love, rooted in an Absolute and embodied through an internal moral compass, is indeed okay.

Works Cited

Arnold, Edwin T. "Naming, Knowing and Nothingness: McCarthy's Moral Parables." *Perspectives on Cormac McCarthy*. Ed. Edwin T. Arnold and Dianne C. Luce. Jackson: U of Mississippi P, 1993. 43–67. Print.

Cremean, David. "For Whom Bell Tolls: Conservatism and Change in Cormac McCarthy's Sheriff in *No Country for Old Men*." *Cormac McCarthy Journal* 5.1 (2005): 21–29. Print.

Gray, Richard. *After the Fall: American Literature since 9/11*. Chichester: Wiley, 2011. Print.

Glover, Jonathan. *Humanity: A Moral History of the Twentieth Century*. New Haven: Yale UP, 1999. Print.

Hodgson, Peter. *God in History: Shapes of Freedom*. Nashville: Abingdon, 1989. Print.

___. *Winds of the Spirit: A Constructive Christian Theology*. Louisville: Westminster, 1994. Print.

Juge, Carole. "The Road to the Sun They Cannot See: Plato's Allegory of the Cave, Oblivion, and Guidance in Cormac McCarthy's *The Road*." *Cormac McCarthy Journal* 7.1 (2009): 16–30. Print.

Lehan, Richard. *Realism and Naturalism: The Novel in an Age of Transition*. Madison: U of Wisconsin P, 2005. Print.

Luce, Dianne C. "Cormac McCarthy's *The Sunset Limited*: Dialogue of Life and Death; A Review of the Chicago Production." *Cormac McCarthy Journal* 6.1 (2008): 13–22. Print.

McCarthy, Cormac. *No Country for Old Men*. New York: Vintage, 2005. Print.

___. *The Road*. New York: Vintage, 2006. Print.

___. *The Sunset Limited: A Novel in Dramatic Form*. New York: Vintage, 2006. Print.

Scott, Nathan A. "Tillich's Legacy and the New Scene in Literature." *The Thought of Paul Tillich*. Ed. James Luther Adams, Wilhelm Pauck, and Roger Lincoln Shinn. New York: Harper, 1985. 137–55. Print.

Tyburski, Susan J. "'The Lingering Scent of Divinity' in *The Sunset Limited* and *The Road*." *Cormac McCarthy Journal* 6.1 (2008): 121–28. Print.

Wielenberg, Erik. "God, Morality, and Meaning in Cormac McCarthy's *The Road*." *Cormac McCarthy Journal* 8.1 (2010): 1–19. Print.

Girls Gone Wild: American Women's Road Narratives and Literary Tradition_____

Deborah Paes de Barros

I remember quite vividly that evening in 1991 when I went to see Ridley Scott's new film *Thelma and Louise*. I was a graduate student then, doing work on women's literature and the genre of the Western, and barely able to afford the price of admission. The film nearly reduced me to tears; the fact that women could finally, openly, be the heroes of a popular road story was incredibly exciting, but this seemingly revolutionary depiction also ended with the road literally running out beneath the bodies of the protagonists. Women could go on the road, the movie suggested, but only at their own peril. There was no real space for them in that rugged, masculine terrain. I sought solace in popcorn.

As readers, we are culturally conditioned to consider the road as a largely masculine literary endeavor. We think first, perhaps, of Jack Kerouac's narrative *On the Road* (1957) as the nearly canonical textual source for the road's mystique, and the road Kerouac conjures up is indisputably male. More recently, too, there is Cormac McCarthy's lyrical and desolate road story *The Road* (2006), which also focuses on masculine bonds, patriarchy, and fathers and sons. And always behind these tales, constructing the very ground of the American road narrative, is the genre of the Western—that great and bloodied trope claimed for masculinity. We think of the frontiersman out in the dark woods while his wife sits alone in the cabin. We celebrate the cowboy roaming the range. Meanwhile, the woman, who is present in the story only long enough to assure the reader of the hero's heterosexuality (see Eve Sedgwick's excellent study *Epistemology of the Closet*, 1990, for more on this topic), mixes up a mess of biscuits back at the ranch. A kind of urban myth tells us that the West—and therefore the road—is for men.

Of course we know that this notion of the road as a privileged masculine space is largely fictive. In the last decade, a number of scholarly studies have examined and challenged this limited reading of the road. Susan Roberson's *Antebellum American Women Writers and the Road: American Mobilities* (2011), Virginia Scharff's *Twenty Thousand Roads: Women, Movement and the West* (2003), and my own *Fast Cars and Bad Girls: Nomadic Subjects and Women's Road Stories* (2004), for example, all dispute the premise that the road is a masculine territory. Since *Thelma and Louise*, the popular conception of the road has shifted as well, frequently incorporating women into the terrain of the road narrative.

The larger truth of the American road is that women have always traveled it, as a historic actuality and as a discursive adventure. Sometimes these road trips were willfully conducted. At other times, women were forced onto the road against their own desires. Women traveled for reasons of marriage, commerce, art, and even boredom. As Virginia Scharff notes, tales of the American road have nearly always been accompanied by women's narrative excursions. Sacajawea, the famous guide and companion of the Lewis and Clark expedition, traveled across the continent, and her commentary is preserved in the lengthy official accounts. Contemporary writers of women's road narrative—including Mona Simpson, Jayne Anne Phillips, Chelsea Cain, Sandra Cisneros, and Bharati Mukherjee—offer an alternative, feminized road narrative, one that is steeped in a quiet literary tradition. Women's travel texts provide a different lens through which to read the road, often allowing it to function quite differently. For many women authors, travel permits some escape from patriarchy; it encourages bonds between mothers and children—especially mothers and daughters—to emerge; it offers women a new and as-yet-unscripted identity and, in doing so, opens narrative space for change and eccentricity. Moreover, very often in women's narratives the reader learns that destination and defined place are not important; rather, it is in that secret space between departure and arrival—the space between places—that real freedom is possible. The woman on the road, now a nomadic citizen, lives outside prescribed identities, rules, and expectations associated with any place.

In the moment of travel, no person or place claims her. American women's road texts explore this freedom, operating in a discursive space and a genre that provide their own narrative traditions.

The Removes of Mary Rowlandson: On the Road in the Seventeenth Century

Captivity narratives became one of the most popular genres of literature in the early nineteenth century, and of these narratives, none remains as well known as Mary Rowlandson's account of her own experience (Tompkins 110). It may be in part that Rowlandson's tale, *The Sovereignty and Goodness of God, Together with the Faithfulness of his Promises, Displayed; Being a Narrative of the Captivity and Restoration of Mrs. Mary Rowlandson* (1682), still moves us because of her unusual skills as a writer and because so little is known of her life outside of that slim memoir. We do know that Mary Rowlandson was born Mary White in Somersetshire, England, in 1637, and that she came to America from England as a child, sometime before 1650, her first "road" trip then being one of discomfort and deprivation. We also know that she married Joseph Rowlandson, her minister husband—a disciple and employee of Puritan theocrat Increase Mather—in 1656. Joseph Rowlandson was sent, we assume at least at the tacit direction of Mather, to minister on what was then the remote and dangerous frontier, the dark woods of Lancaster, Massachusetts. While Mary Rowlandson's narrative does not cover her youthful travels from England or her thoughts on being relocated to the largely uninhabited West, we can assume that these early road trips were not of her own design.

Rowlandson's narrative records an unwilling progress made through the tribal lands of the Narragansetts, the Nipmucks, and the Wampanoags over the space of eleven weeks. King Philip's War (1675–76; also called Metacom's War or the First Indian War) made the western regions of Pennsylvania, New York, and the New England states precarious for colonialists. It devastated the frontier and imperiled the Puritan "Errand into the Wilderness," leading, as historian Mitchell

Breitwieser notes, to some political tension within the New England theocracy. With nearly half of their settlements attacked, the barely nascent economy floundering, and large numbers of their population dead, many Puritan citizens questioned the prudence of their frontier undertaking. Some argued for new leadership, while others wanted to return to Europe. Increase Mather, seeking to secure his prominent position, contended that these events illustrated God's displeasure with the Puritans' ambivalent attitude regarding their mission and that God would reward them if they held fast to their principles of theocracy and colonization. Headed by the multilingual, educated Narragansett leader Metacomet—Prince Philip—Native Americans came close to toppling the early colonial government. These facts provide the background to Rowlandson's story.

Early on a cold February morning in 1676, Rowlandson's Lancaster farm was attacked. Her husband, Joseph, was absent from the house, but seventeen of Mary Rowlandson's friends and family were killed, including her sister, brother-in-law, and small nephew. The house and surrounding buildings were burned. Rowlandson and her six-year-old daughter Sarah were wounded; they, along with Rowlandson's older daughter Mary, her son Joseph, and some twenty-four others, were taken captive. While Rowlandson was allowed to keep Sarah until the child died a few days later, she was quickly separated from her other children and relatives. Often overwhelmed with grief and fear, Rowlandson—in her eventual account of her captivity—demonstrates remarkable resourcefulness, contradictory attitudes about her captors, and a detectable evolution of character. Moved from campsite to campsite for eleven weeks, Rowlandson lived on the road. She was ultimately ransomed and returned to her family, the necessary twenty pounds raised collectively by the women of Boston when her cash-poor husband was unable to raise the sum on his own. Her remaining children were also soon ransomed, and Rowlandson then moved with her family to Connecticut, where her husband assumed a parish in the relatively safe region of Wethersfield. At the urging of Increase Mather, who arranged for the publication of the text, Rowlandson turned her attention to writing her soon-to-be-famous captivity narrative, which was published in 1682 (Derounian 249).

Joseph Rowlandson died before the book was completed, and for many years, scholars assumed that Mary Rowlandson perished soon after, vanishing from history. More recently discovered documents reveal, however, that Mary Rowlandson survived, marrying a sea captain named Samuel Talcott in 1679. Little more was heard from Rowlandson until her own death in 1711 (she lived robustly on into her seventies), with one tantalizing exception: some historians believe that Rowlandson rescued her adult son, who had been sentenced to the life of an indentured sailor until his mother once again ransomed him.

Unlike the accounts of other frontiersmen, Rowlandson's narrative is marked by her relationship with her children, her increasing ability to deal with a hostile environment, and a bifurcation of attitude as she struggles to balance her own insights with the spiritual and political needs of Increase Mather and the Puritan clergy (Bercovitch 116). The first three chapters, or removes, are largely preoccupied with Rowlandson's dying six-year-old daughter, Sarah. The extremity of Sarah's wound is evident, and for several days before her death, she is unable to drink or eat. Rowlandson remarks that whereas she used to be afraid and "could not bear to be in the room where any dead person was," now she cleaves to the dead body of her child, insisting on proximity. Ultimately, when the tribal band needs to move, Rowlandson is forced to leave Sarah's body behind. Later, as they begin another leg of their travels, Rowlandson is shown the place where Sarah is buried, and "there [she leaves] that child in the wilderness" (Rowlandson 329).

This terrible sense of loss, and of a loss that is not even given a familiar marker, is a familiar theme in the travel literature of frontier and pioneer women. Often urged quickly forward by necessity, they must leave their loved ones behind, in unmarked and unvisited graves. The dead child frequently becomes a symbol of the cost of the journey into the wilderness. As in Rowlandson's tale, there is a dark sadness that often seeps through entire texts. Unlike more masculine frontier texts like that of Daniel Boone, where a more stoic reaction to pain is embraced, women's texts are often marked with acute loss—a loss made even more unbearable because the conditions of their lives do not even allow space for mourning (Breitwieser 33).

Rowlandson's book underscores her concern for her other children as well. Learning that Mary and Joseph are safe, she praises God and endeavors to visit the then-ten-year-old Mary. But when her daughter sees her, the younger Mary falls to the ground weeping, so uncontrollably that the Indians who have custody refuse to let the mother spend time with her daughter. Rowlandson describes the meeting as "heart cutting." The two are separated; their grief is a hazard and inconvenience on the trail. Later, Rowlandson meets with her son, who urges her not to worry about him. While these meetings and Rowlandson's reactions seem natural enough to readers, such concern for children is often discussed in women's road trips. In many female-authored chronicles of the road, children and the emotions surrounding them are primary topics, in contrast to the road trips of many male writers, which tend to be adult centered. For Mary Rowlandson, the road is not the site of adventure and conquest; it is the space of loss and maternal pain.

Of particular interest is Rowlandson's emergence as an entrepreneur. There is little in her background that suggests such an interest. But Rowlandson could knit and sew. She begins to make hats, shirts, and socks that she trades to her captors for more food. Even Prince Philip becomes a kind of customer. When Rowlandson makes him a shirt, he pays her with a shilling that Rowlandson offers to her "master" but is told to keep. She uses the money to buy meat. Still later, Rowlandson is invited to engineer her own ransom. Her captors inquire, what price should be asked for her? After some thought, Rowlandson responds by saying twenty pounds. She wants the sum to give her some value within her new community but also to be at least remotely possible. Even though Rowlandson is a captive, she is nonetheless learning about the exchange of commodities and, in some new way, providing for herself. As a Puritan woman, she lived in households headed by her father and then her husband; now she fends for herself. Despite all of its sadness, the road is in some way for Rowlandson a place of empowerment, albeit in a highly limited sense.

The duality of Rowlandson's attitude toward her fellow captives, as reflected in her narrative, has fascinated readers and critics. Clearly influenced by both Mather and Puritan theology, Rowlandson makes her account a statement about the nature of God and faith, asserting that it is God who is her true rescuer. She attributes the terrible deaths she has seen, most notably her sister's, to a lack of faith and religious conviction. Contemplating her sister's bloody death in front of the Lancaster cabin, Rowlandson remarks that although her sister was surely a steady, God-fearing married woman, twenty years earlier she was less diligent in her spiritual duties. Her death, speculates Rowlandson, was perhaps God's punishment. Rowlandson extends this Puritan dictum to herself. "How many Sabbaths I had lost and misspent," she writes, acknowledging the Lord's goodness in chastising her with captivity and loss (328). This religious tone persists in many of Rowlandson's descriptions of the Indians, whom she describes over and over as "savages" and "hell hounds."

But there is another aspect to Rowlandson's characterizations, a more subtle and rebellious narrative. At a telling moment, Rowlandson goes to visit Prince Philip, who holds a mirror to her face. Here she sees plainly that she is the unwashed savage, rather than her captor (Rowlandson 351). In another remove, Rowlandson's owner's wife loses her own child. Rowlandson refuses to offer comfort, remarking that she too has been in that position. While her reaction may appear to be unfeeling, it also underscores the fact that Rowlandson sees the two of them as similar. If Rowlandson cannot express sympathy, it is not because the Indian woman is different; Rowlandson contends that their situations are now the same. She writes, "I confess, I could not much condole with them. Many sorrowful days I had in this place:

often getting alone" (Rowlandson 346). The Native American wife has changed from being a savage animal, or an agent of the devil, into an equally mournful human, albeit one who is sometimes adversarial. This represents a shift in Rowlandson's thinking and a break with traditional Puritan conceptualization, in which Native Americans had to function as less-than-human savages in a hellish wilderness. It is a shift only possible on the road.

A textual duality is evidenced in Rowlandson's narrative. On the one hand, she continues to express popular Puritan rhetoric: Indians are the representatives of evil, delivery is only possible through the divine, and the wages of weakness or sin will be punished. Her book is authorized, edited, and published by the Puritan theocracy. But in some almost secret way, Rowlandson also codifies an alternative voice: she recognizes humanity in her Native American captors and she sees herself in some new, alternative way. As the text concludes, Rowlandson quietly ignores the directive to accept God's will and that all is well that ends well. As Mitchell Breitwieser notes in *American Puritanism and the Defense of Mourning* (1990), there was little space in Puritan theology or on the frontier itself for the expression of grief. Just as Lot's wife was turned into a pillar of salt for the sin of looking backward, neither the great Puritan mission nor the pioneer movement could allow for much focus on the lost past. Yet Rowlandson persists. In the closing pages of her manuscript, she tells her readers that she has changed. She is restless now, sad, unsatisfied with the "bread" of her existence. Suffering from insomnia, Rowlandson weeps for her loss and for her inability to fit back into the world to which she has been restored.

Rowlandson has, in fact, become a woman of the road, albeit an unwilling one. She sees the world in a radically new way, understands that she is responsible for negotiating her own safety, and weeps for her lost children. Her road narrative stands in stark contrast to the accounts of male theologians and frontiersmen, yet it is a road narrative just the same. Rowlandson establishes themes and tropes that find sustained reflection in the travel texts of American women; these texts are structured by issues of loss, maternity, change, and an alternative vision of the world.

The Nineteenth-Century Road Narrative

As Rowlandson's narrative suggests, women can occupy the road in a different manner than men. A variety of colonial and pioneer texts reaffirm this distinction. While masculine accounts either ignore women entirely or depict the occasional female as a kind of Rebecca Boone figure—an idealized and enthusiastic helpmate back at the farm—women's travel descriptions are different. Like Rowlandson's narrative, these accounts reflect a constant concern for children and a pervasive sense of loss. As Elizabeth Jameson notes in *The Women's West* (1987), the decision to travel was nearly always a male choice. One plains settler, Martha Farnsworth, remarks that she has "cried bitterly all day" (Farnsworth 64). Another, Mrs. Lee Whipple Haslam, condemns the constant violence—often against women—that marks the West (Moynihan, Armitage, and Dichamp 29). And like Rowlandson, too, these western women often ultimately became small-time entrepreneurs, often to provide themselves with an independent source of income and thus an independent life. They made, sold, and washed clothing for a profit. They marketed baked goods. They eventually ran rooming houses and taught school. Instead of being absorbed in the masculine road, they created their own mobile and alternative communities.

Even within the genre of slave narratives, the reader can begin to see the distinction between men and women's travel accounts. Frederick Douglass in his moving *Narrative of the Life of Frederick Douglass, an American Slave* (1845) suggests that his escape and subsequent life can be traced in a direct linear trajectory: he escapes, he travels north, and he becomes a writer and an activist. Douglass finds both voice and fame. In stark contrast stands Harriet Jacobs's *Incidents in the Life of a Slave Girl* (1861). Because she wants to stay close to her children, Jacobs's escape only removes her to a tiny room where, almost unbelievably, she lives for seven years. Even when she eventually goes north, she moves only as far as New York, rather than into the free spaces of Canada. She remains as a maid to the woman who "liberated" her, a Mrs. Bruce, writing in conclusion that "the dream of my life is not yet realized" (Gates 513). She cannot complete her quest, and she fails to see any clear and satisfactory close to her account. Rather than linear, her travels are often circuitous, her purposes unfocused, save for her children. She writes that life is rather like watching patchy clouds and that women's ideas about freedom "are not saying a good deal" (Gates 513). If male progression on the road replicates a kind of quest motif, for women it frequently remains something else. For Jacobs, travel is about her children, about community and emotional connections to others, rather than about the notion that one place is radically better than another.

Going West: Women Rewrite the Frontier

In the late nineteenth century, a number of women writers sought to rewrite traditional frontier literature. Mary Hallock Foote was born in 1847 in upstate New York, in the small, tidy Quaker community of Milton. Trained as an artist at Cooper Union's School of Design for Women (later the Art Institute), she became a member of Boston's close-knit intellectual community, enjoying both literary conversation and artistic commissions from well-known writers like Brett Harte, William Dean Howells, and Henry Wadsworth Longfellow. At twenty-nine, Mary Hallock married Arthur Foote, a young civil engineer, and, with evident misgivings, departed to live in the rugged mining towns of the West. "No girl ever wanted to 'go West' less," Foote later wrote in her memoir *A Victorian Gentlewoman in the Far West: The Reminiscences of Mary Hallock Foote*, published posthumously in 1972 (114).

Partly because of family finances and partly out of a desire to maintain her art, Mary Hallock Foote began to work. She provided illustrations for magazine articles and then developed her skills as a fiction writer. Moving from place to place throughout the West, the Footes eventually settled in Grass Valley, California. While Foote herself described her work as literary realism, suggesting that her stories provided examples of what came to be called local color, her novels and short stories offer real insight into the conditions and psychological realities of women's western experiences.

Foote's best-known works, *The Led-Horse Claim* (1883), *The Chosen Valley* (1892), and "The Harshaw Bride" (1896), share a common theme: they are all tales of young, refined women brought to the West by fathers or fiancés. While open to the notion of romance, the female characters are all disturbed by the crudeness, violence, and commerce-driven destruction of the frontier. In "The Harshaw Bride," Kitty, the tale's protagonist, looks out her boardinghouse window at a landscape despoiled and polluted by the machinery of the mines. "I can't give in," Kitty cries, viewing the phallic imagery of the equipment, the ruptured landscape, and the tainted water (Foote, *Touch of Sun* 256). But Kitty's husband-to-be has paid her passage, she has nowhere else to go, and her fate is tied to the West.

A similar plot unfolds in *The Chosen Valley*. Dolly, the novel's heroine, falls in love with a young mining engineer who tells her that together they will make the desert "sing." Philip, Dolly's lover, has an enormous water-reclamation project in mind that he believes will make the rugged West flower and produce. But Philip's abilities prove to be less than his ambitions; his dam breaks, and the entire valley is flooded. Dolly is saved, but her father is swept away in a muddy wave of water, broken tools, and misspent plans. The environmental sins of this New World Noah find their punishment when the bride calls off the wedding, for she cannot marry her father's killer.

In still another twist on the same plot, Cecilia of *The Led-Horse Claim* is engaged to another young mining engineer, Hilgard, who is a rival of her brother's. Hilgard takes Cecilia down into the bowels of the mine, where she is horrified at the conditions, the darkness, and the heat, and where she believes she can hear her brother working on the other side of the mountain. Eventually, a fight breaks out, and Hilgard shoots Cecilia's brother. In the original version of the story, Cecilia returns to the East and dies. But under pressure from her publisher, Foote changed the text so that the novel concludes with Cecilia's marriage.

In all of these works, and indeed in most of Foote's other numerous stories, certain elements remain constant. The women are reluctant to come west. Their fiancés and spouses are generally engineers or miners. Once there, the women object to the very elements that are typically celebrated in more manly frontier tales; they are shocked by the violence, by behavior that is far from genteel, and by the economic drive to reduce the majestic beauty of the place to commodified rubble. The naturalist Isabella Bird, who lived for years alone in the Rocky Mountains, comments also on this desire to alter the prevalent ethos of the frontiersman. Her biographer Hélène Cheynet notes that while Bird had no desire for regular domestic life, she was nevertheless horrified at the conditions frontiersmen forced upon their wives and the general crudity of their dispositions.

If the West is to become the new Eden, these works seem to say, then the rules of engagement must be altered. Interestingly enough, Foote was a contemporary of Owen Wister, author of the still-famous *The Virginian* (1902). Foote's fame has long been eclipsed by that of Wister. Her work represents a kind of inversion of Wister's West. Wister celebrated the frontier road as a place where "men could be men." At the end of *The Virginian*, Wister's hero has learned the necessity of violence, and he accepts the West on those terms. Mary Hallock Foote's frequently autobiographical literary road is marked by her effort to change the frontier, to make it a space more refined, more gentle, and more protective of its own inherent beauties.

Walking in the Early Twentieth Century

Unlike Mary Hallock Foote, Mary Austin embraced the West. Born Mary Hunter in 1868 in Carlinville, Illinois, Austin went west as a young girl. Her trip was long, but Austin finally arrived in California's

San Joaquin Valley, where she lived in a rural one-room cabin with her mother. Disturbed by her surroundings and by the deaths of her father and younger sister, Austin fell ill. She cured herself, she claims in her autobiography, *Earth Horizon* (1932), by walking. She allows many of her fictional characters to find the same cure; for them, too, the road becomes the space of autonomy, solace, and health. Austin most famously addresses this theme in the story "The Walking Woman."

Written in the first person, "The Walking Woman" is included in Austin's 1909 collection, aptly titled *Lost Borders*, which deals with the ways the road dissolves boundaries between places, people, and fantasy and fact. The narrator of the tales, a traveler in her own right and a persona of Austin's, hears from her fellow tourists in the Owens River Valley about a peculiar woman. The woman's very identity has been erased by her travels; she goes now by the name of "Mrs. Walker," and she embodies the spirit of the road. The stories about Mrs. Walker are vague. Some accounts describe her as beautiful and frail, while others insist that she is old and malformed. Some cowboys say that Mrs. Walker can appear and disappear at will. Mrs. Walker, contends the author, is "the muse of travel," a western Everywoman who moves in a dust cloud like a genie of Middle Eastern legend (Austin, *Lost* 196). Naturally, the narrator is eager to make Mrs. Walker's acquaintance.

The two women do eventually meet, the Walking Woman taking shape near a stagnant pond within a mirage. Her story is poignant and curiously consistent with earlier road tales. The Walking Woman wandered in the hills in her youth until she fell in love with a shepherd, a familiar sight in the eastern Sierras. Enraptured, the Walking Woman shares a pastoral romance, describing a kind of realized (but unlicensed) love that would not be permitted off the road. Spring unfolds around the couple. But eventually winter comes, and with it female complications: the Walking Woman is pregnant. She can no longer "keep to the trails," and her lover needs to find new pasture for his charges. They separate. The Walking Woman gives birth alone to a baby, who quickly dies. She buries her baby alongside the trail, like Mary Rowlandson, and then stumbles in grief along the pathway. Only the rhythms of walking can soothe her and assuage her loss. Like Austin herself, Mrs. Walker is cured by walking, but the experience leaves her marked and unable to settle down happily. The road has made her a permanent nomad, forever altered, unable to enjoy "regular" domesticity. The story concludes with Mrs. Walker disappearing into the desert, leaving only the mark of her two bare feet. The narrator looks down at the footprints and recognizes that they are straight—there is nothing twisted or deformed about them—and that they could be her own. For Mary Austin, the road provides a space of nourishment but also a permanent antisocial marking. Once on the road, it is nearly impossible for Austin's women to resume regular life. They are exiled from any previous contentment. These heroines become literature's "wild girls," at odds with patriarchal culture and its expressions—in the East or on the frontier.

These same themes are visible in the life story of Mary Austin herself. In 1891, she married Stafford Austin and went with him to the Owens River Valley (where there is today a commemorative museum for Austin, on Highway 395, in the town of Independence). Stafford Austin quickly became the school-district superintendent, but he suffered from acute alcoholism—a common problem on the frontier, according to women authors—and was unable to hold his position. Leaving alone her child, who had severe if undocumented health problems, Mary Austin took over the support of the family as a teacher. She eventually had the child institutionalized and moved west to Carmel. Her travels took her throughout the southwest. Horrified at the planned development of California, development that would use the water from the Owens River, Austin became a tireless environmentalist, working (like Mary Hallock Foote's heroines) to preserve the West from the waste of engineers and miners. Her books, including her autobiography *Earth Horizon*, *The Land of Little Rain* (1903), the fantasy *Outland* (1910), and *Everyman's Genius* (1925), all explore these ideas. Interested in politics, art, environmentalism, and feminism, and a constant traveler herself, Austin overtly rejects women's so-called natural domestic roles. She seeks in her work to discover an alternative frontier rooted in a new mythology, challenging the commodified violent West of the typical frontiersman.

Driving the Road to Identity: Late Twentieth-Century Narratives

By the 1960s, the Beach Boys were crooning about a girl who will have "fun, fun, fun" until "her daddy takes the T-Bird away," and women's presence on the road was openly acknowledged. The road unfolded as a temporary place of freedom, at least until the pressures of marriage and family life curtailed the experience. In one of the century's most powerful evocations of road narrative, Joan Didion's novel *Play It As It Lays* (1970) interrogates the brief liberty provided by the highway. Her heroine, Maria—a psychologically frail young woman, a one-time model and B-movie actress suffering in a failing marriage with an autocratic filmmaker and separated from her young, institutionalized daughter—finds autonomy while driving. Maria has no space within her life or culture. Her husband and his director friend own even the rights to Maria's cinematographic image. When she becomes pregnant by a distant lover, she is forced to undergo an illegal abortion. Nearly everything about Maria's life is controlled; even her beauty belongs to her spouse, and her body is not her own. But when Maria drives the freeway, these constrictions vanish. She drives the freeway every day, "as a riverman runs a river, every day more attuned to its currents" (Didion 16). She is on the freeway early every morning, maneuvering her car through the trickiest stretches, eating eggs (with all of their obvious reference to fertility), and finding solace from her sleepless nights.

> Again and again she returned to an intricate stretch just south of the interchange where successful passage from the Hollywood onto the Harbor required a diagonal move across four lanes of traffic. On the afternoon she finally did it without once braking or losing the beat of the radio she exhilarated and that night she slept dreamlessly. (Didion 16)

Driving frees Maria; she is regenerated. As she navigates the bridges over dry riverbeds, stops for a Coke, and plans her own route, Maria finds salvation. She has skills, she has purpose, and—as the eggs suggest—she commands her own body and fecundity. At several critical moments in the novel, Maria takes to the road. After her husband, Carter, forces her to have an abortion and then leaves with his movie-star lover for the desert, where he is ostensibly filming a movie, Maria drives to Las Vegas, once again trying her own luck. And after a quintessential 1960s party in Los Angeles's famed Beverly Glen, where Maria appears barefoot in a silver vinyl dress and is taken home by a befuddled actor who forces his advances on her, Maria steals the actor's Ferrari and once again drives her narrative road. "I don't understand girls like you," Maria's agent tells her when he is forced to rescue her at a police station (Didion 156). Maria's character lies outside the comprehension of the mainstream, masculine world. The road allows her, briefly, to live in a different way.

But, as for many road heroines, the larger world can hold Maria hostage, a by-now familiar theme in women's stories. She has a child. If Maria goes on the road to keep alive her full, fertile sense of self, she is finally brought to heel by threats of losing her child. As the story concludes, Maria herself is held in an institution, speechless, planning for a different sort of world—one that is perhaps impossible—where she can escape with her little girl, Kate. Maria truly represents women in the 1960s. She wears short skirts and is permitted a variety of small freedoms, but her world is controlled by patriarchy. Only when she literally steals the car keys is she free.

The Third Wave: Feminism and the Contemporary Road Story

As the third wave of feminism unfolds in American culture, women's experience of the road has widened. This narrative freedom is evidenced in numerous more recent travel narratives. In Chelsea Cain's cult classic *Dharma Girl* (1996), the road is the place where Chelsea/

Snowbird finds the lost idyllic identity of her youth. Lost in the planned earth tones of an Irvine, California, development, she goes on the road to learn about who she used to be and, in doing so, reforges her own lost identity. In the process in a kind of inversion of the mother-with-child-on-the-road motif, Snowbird reconnects with her mother. The women travel east and backward through time together, recovering the lost innocence of the 1960s. ,

In Marilynne Robinson's lyrical novel *Housekeeping* (1980), the novel's protagonist, Ruthie, ultimately becomes a hobo, living name-lessly on the road, free from any interference. Gently reared by her grandmother to be an accomplished housekeeper, Ruthie is drawn in-stead to transience, to "an end to housekeeping" and an escape from the domestic. Ruthie and her aunt walk away from civilization in the dark, listening to a "new language." The language, suggests Robinson, is free from patriarchy, authority, or any of the old rules of order. Ruth-ie becomes a "drifter," a disciple of the new language, preaching—"like Jesus," Robinson says—a new and unfettered way of being in the world (215). These unfettered nomadic women become the spokespeo-ple for a borderless, unnamed, and undefined space. Patriarchy in all of its expressions ceases to exist, replaced for Ruthie, and for Robinson, with the possibility of new, shifting identities and a language situated outside any cultural code.

Perhaps the most dramatic use of the road as a vehicle toward both identity and freedom is found in Bharati Mukherjee's novel *Jasmine* (1989). Transglobal and hybridic in nature, the text once again cel-ebrates the freedom offered in travel. Its protagonist, Jasmine, is born in India. Her value on the marriage market is initially questioned, and her mother opposes Jasmine's efforts toward modernity. Ultimately Jasmine does marry, but her husband is killed, and she departs for New York. Her travels are grisly; she is raped and forced to work as a kind of involuntary servant. But Jasmine acts out. She kills the rapist, ma-neuvers her way across the country, and ultimately ends up married to a man who was once a part of a couple who employed her as a nanny.

She is a survivor, and she responds to a variety of names. She is the kind of successful nomad whom the theorist Rosi Braidotti would describe as someone "who can sing their way through the wilderness" (17). She has not one name and passport but many. Survival requires flexibility and an understanding that the only real nationality, or place, is the fluid self. Like previous road heroines, Jasmine, too, is tied only to children. Jasmine cares about the child she babysits, the infant she will give birth to, and Du—the hybrid, half-caste Vietnamese refugee whom she adopts. Finally, Jasmine is a kind of shapeshifter; she has no allegiance to a place of departure or a destination. Her space on the road, whatever its name or even her own, is home.

Conclusions

In a way, one can read the history of American women in the history of their travel narratives. If more masculine road literature embraces freedom from the tyranny of women, prizes adventure, and eternally celebrates the virtue of "rugged individualism," women's tales are often very differently calibrated. There is no quest, no fixed point of destination, and no moment of marked arrival. Adventure often translates as hardship and loss, and women's texts frequently value connection, new bonds, and community over individualism. If men must run from what Huck Finn conceived of as the "sivilizing" control of women, female protagonists struggle to escape from the too-typically crude and violent power of patriarchy. Indeed, the reader can perceive a sort of dialogue between the two genres.

For many women writers, the road is different. Theirs is a kind of Underground Railroad, their literature describing both a vehicle and a place where some other kind of life is possible, at least temporarily. These texts tell readers that there is another way, outside of regulation and custom, to be in the world. Certain aspects change, but the commitment to both selfhood and community remains in these women's road stories. One way or another, they tell the female reader that even within culture, there are always alternative points of view. Come outside and play, these books tell us. And bring the children. The experience will change you.

Works Cited

Armitage, Susan, and Elizabeth Jameson. *The Woman's West*. Oklahoma City: U of Oklahoma P, 1987. Print.

Austin, Mary Stafford. *Earth Horizon: An Autobiography*. Boston: Houghton, 1932. Print.

___. *Land of Little Rain*. New York: Viking, 1988. Print.

___. *Lost Borders*. New York: Harper, 1915. Print.

Beach Boys. "Fun, Fun, Fun." *Fun, Fun, Fun / Why Do Fools Fall in Love*. Capitol, 1964. LP.

Bercovitch, Sacvan. *The Puritan Origins of the American Self*. New Haven: Yale UP, 1975. Print.

Braidotti, Rosi. *Nomadic Subjects: Embodiment and Sexual Difference in Contemporary Feminist Theory*. New York: Columbia UP, 1994. Print.

Breitwieser, Mitchell. *American Puritanism and the Defense of Mourning: Religion, Grief, and Ethnology in Mary White Rowlandson's Captivity Narrative*. Madison: U of Wisconsin P, 1990. Print.

Cain, Chelsea. *Dharma Girl: A Road Trip across American Generations*. Seattle: Seal, 1996. Print.

Cheynet, Hélène. "'Travellers Are Privileged to Do the Most Improper Things with Perfect Propriety': Isabella Bird's *A Lady's Life in the Rocky Mountains*." *In-Between Two Worlds: Narratives by Female Explorers and Travellers, 1850–1945*. Eds. Béatrice Bijon and Gérard Gâcon. New York: Lang, 2009. 35–49. Print.

Derounian, Katheryn Zabelle. "The Publication, Promotion, and Distribution of Mary White Rowlandson's Captivity Narrative in the Seventeenth Century." *Early American Literature* 23 (1988): 239–61. Print.

Didion, Joan. *Play It As It Lays*. New York: Farrar, 1990. Print.

Farnsworth, Martha. *The Diary of Martha Farnsworth*. Ed. Marlene Springer and Haskell Springer. Bloomington: U of Indiana P, 1986. Print.

Foote, Mary Hallock. *The Led-Horse Claim*. Ridgewood: Gregg, 1968. Print.

___. *A Touch of Sun and Other Stories*. Boston: Houghton, 1903. Print.

___. *A Victorian Gentlewoman in the Far West: The Reminiscences of Mary Hallock Foote*. San Marino: Huntington Lib., 1972. Print.

Gates, Henry Louis, Jr. *Three Classic Slave Narratives*. New York: Signet, 2002. Print.

Kerouac, Jack. *On the Road*. New York: Penguin, 1976. Print.

McCarthy, Cormac. *The Road*. New York: Vintage, 2007. Print.

Moynihan, Ruth, Susan Armitage, and Christine Fischer Dichamp. *So Much to Be Done: Women Settlers on the Mining and Ranching Frontier*. Lincoln: U of Nebraska P, 1990. Print.

Mukherjee, Bharati. *Jasmine*. New York: Grove, 1999. Print.

Paes de Barros, Deborah. *Fast Cars and Bad Girls: Nomadic Subjects and Women's Road Stories*. New York: Lang, 2004. Print.

Roberson, Susan. *Antebellum American Women Writers and the Road: American Mobilities*. London: Routledge, 2010. Print.

Robinson, Marilynne. *Housekeeping*. New York: Farrar, 1980. Print.

Rowlandson, Mary White. *The Sovereignty and Goodness of God, Together with the Faithfulness of His Promises, Displayed; Being a Narrative of the Captivity and Restoration of Mrs. Mary Rowlandson. So Dreadfull a Judgment: Puritan Responses to King Philip's War, 1676–1677*. Ed. Richard Slotkin and James Folsom. Middletown: Wesleyan UP, 1978. 315-69. Print.

Scharff, Virginia. *Twenty Thousand Roads: Women, Movement and the West*. Berkeley: U of California P, 2002. Print.

Sedgwick, Eve. *Epistemology of the Closet*. Berkeley: U of California P, 1991. Print.

Tompkins, Jane. *Sensational Designs: The Cultural Work of American Fiction*. New York: Oxford UP, 1986. Print.

Wister, Owen. *The Virginian: A Horseman of the Plains*. New York: Grosset, 1911. Print.

The Dark Side of the Road: American Road Narratives in the Popular Dark Fantastic _____

David Bain

Readers of popular fiction in the United States have a long-standing love affair with dark, over-the-top subject matter. The fiction best-seller lists are filled with works in genres such as crime, suspense, thriller, fantasy, and horror. The authors of such works tend to incorporate elements of other literary genres into their narratives, and the American road narrative is no exception. Indeed, road narratives and suspense, fantasy, and horror fiction offer many of the same pleasures, promising escape, discovery, revelation, adventure, and transformation. However, the "rules of the road" change when seen through a dark lens; used largely to examine moral problems and situations, the imaginative structure of popular dark fantastic fiction allows authors to subvert, parody, exaggerate, and literalize the conventions known to readers of more mainstream American road narratives.

No discussion of any aspect of modern dark fantastic or horror literature would be complete without delving into the work of Stephen King. Just as iconic literary critic Harold Bloom famously declared in his book *The Western Canon* (1994) that "Shakespeare is the Canon. He sets the standard and the limits of literature" (qtd. in Gillespie), it can be argued that Stephen King is the canon for contemporary popular dark fiction. As noted editor, publisher, and scholar David G. Hartwell points out in his introduction to King's story "The Reach" in *The Dark Descent* (1987), a critical anthology examining the history and scope of horror literature, "King's eclectic taste and willingness to respond to a variety of styles and approaches points out rich pathways for broadening our conceptions of the nature of horror stories and their virtues" (15). In the quantity, range, and ambition of his work, King simply overshadows all others writing in the field. It would seem there is no convention, mode, form, or subgenre within popular horror fiction that King has not thoroughly explored. So it is no surprise that King is responsible for what has become the quintessential dark fantastic road narrative, *The Stand* (1978), as well as other noteworthy road-oriented narratives such as his Dark Tower series (1982–2012) and *The Talisman* (1984), cowritten with Peter Straub.

With 1990's complete and uncut edition comprising more than 1,150 pages, *The Stand* set the benchmark for what is now recognized as a standard formula for epic horror and dark fantasy novels. In many such works, a large cast of good and evil characters must quest across a drastically altered United States—in *The Stand*, a modern United States that has been mostly wiped out by a superflu. After journeying through this dystopia, the characters must come together on their respective sides, using their unique mundane or mystical talents to do battle for their factions in a final apocalyptic showdown.

Often imitated, *The Stand* itself owes a large debt to a slew of earlier road narratives that explore science-fictional or fantastic settings. The quest motif King employs harkens back to high fantasy epics such as J. R. R. Tolkien's *Lord of the Rings* (1954–55), which Tolkien himself admitted was influenced by quests in numerous ancient European mythologies. King is not, however, the philological and academic literary scholar that Tolkien was; King's influences stem more significantly from popular culture and, in the case of his road-oriented work, quest narratives of a considerably more recent vintage.

King has noted, for instance, that George R. Stewart's ecologically minded 1949 science-fiction road novel *Earth Abides* was a major influence on *The Stand* (King, *Danse* 398). Making extensive use of scientific principles regarding nature's cyclical qualities and social commentary via the main character's encounters and beliefs, *Earth Abides* tells the story of Isherwood Williams, a scientist whose reclusiveness results in his surviving a plague that wipes out most of humanity. The book details his efforts to explore and eventually restore this depopulated United States, which include a number of cross-country reconnaissance journeys.

Examples of best-selling works in which *The Stand*'s influence is evident include, but are by no means limited to, *Swan Song* (1987) by Robert R. McCammon and *The Passage* (2010) by Justin Cronin. In *Swan Song*, the apocalypse has occurred via nuclear war, but while the specific trappings differ—many characters are afflicted with growths around their heads, and the majority of the antagonists are military in nature (though they are still led by supernatural beings)—the overall quest is virtually the same as in *The Stand*, with both good and evil survivors journeying to mystical and mundane meeting points for a final confrontation. In *The Passage*, the first book of a proposed trilogy, the United States has been transformed by a virus that has mutated most of the population into vampiric creatures. Again, surviving characters on both sides must take to the road to find rumored safe havens and infamous strategic locations in anticipation of greater conflict.

In many ways, then, *The Stand* and its descendants in popular fiction are straightforward traditional road narratives, employing themes familiar to readers of more mainstream works: revelatory encounters with strangers, a search for inner or outer harmony, and a journey resulting in eventual transformation of identity. The significant difference is that in dark fantastic epics, the characters must contend with an America that has somehow been radically transformed while wrestling with broad themes of good and evil and seeking to promote one or the other. Discussing *The Stand* in *Danse Macabre*, his 1981 overview of the horror genre, King notes that while his novel and others like it explore the dark side of the human condition and do not necessarily offer any moral solutions, they try "to celebrate brighter aspects of our lives: simple human courage, friendship, and love in a world which so often seems mostly loveless" (403).

The influence of both the moral and the literary structure of *The Stand* shows no sign of waning. In C. Dennis Moore's hefty 2012 novel *Revelations*, the familiar pattern established by *The Stand* takes the form of characters traversing a United States that has become hell on earth after God delivered the righteous to heaven and allowed hell to open up on the planet. The protagonist, Geoffrey, a good man who was cryonically frozen while the apocalypse happened, must quest across this infernal land to discover why he was not taken. While most *Stand*-influenced road narratives focus on a moral quest, *Revelations* is distinctive in tying the journey to a single individual's search for identity and meaning within the larger moral structure rather than to groups striving toward a moral superiority over one another.

The moral aspect of dark fantastic road narratives is not exclusive to books influenced by *The Stand*. Indeed, much popular dark fiction, while not overtly religious, examines moral themes. Hartwell identifies moral allegory as one of three major "streams" in horror fiction, the others being examinations of aberrant human psychology and the nature of reality, and King incorporates moral quests and dilemmas into almost all his work (Hartwell, Introduction 8–11).

King first approached the idea of roads intersecting with those in other realities in an early story, "Mrs. Todd's Shortcut," about a woman who is "mad for a shortcut" (209) and keeps cutting time off a commute across Maine, mostly through deep woods, until she achieves seemingly impossible travel times. The story is told mostly through dialogue in the voice of one of Mrs. Todd's hired hands, who relates how he accompanied her on a trip and encountered strange flora and fauna in the woods, with the affluent Mrs. Todd likely not having enough "woodsy" knowledge to understand the uncanny nature of what she was seeing. The hired hand notes that Mrs. Todd seemed younger, more vibrant, after her travels and speculates that she eventually disappeared into one of her shortcuts, becoming something of a goddess in the strange alternate or parallel world, to which he suggests he may try to follow her. King uses the trappings of the horror and fantasy genres to literalize and exaggerate the transformative power of the road, specifically the rediscovery of youth that older travelers might seek.

Since writing *The Stand* and "Mrs. Todd's Shortcut," King has continued to build on and significantly expand the theme of a nation transformed. In *The Talisman*, for example, King and Straub posit a parallel

United States: the Territories, a medieval country of smaller size but possessing more natural resources. The plot concerns a quest in which twelve-year-old Jack Sawyer, who learns to flip between the worlds, crosses from one coast to the other in order to find the titular mystical object, seeking to save his mother's life and thwart those from his world who would ravage the Territories' resources. King and Straub use the two nations' size differential to have Jack travel more quickly than he might were he confined to his own reality.

While traditional American road narratives sometimes use the specifics of a quest and even existing landmarks as symbols for larger themes, the possibilities for imaginative transformation of the United States by authors of the dark fantastic can easily lend itself to social commentary. King and Straub, for instance, use the very landscape of the Territories for this purpose; the vast majority of the Southwest in their fantasy world is a barren, radioactive waste known as the Blasted Lands, apparently the result of nuclear testing. Jack and his werewolf companion must cross this miserable and dangerous landscape on the bleakest portion of their journey.

While King and Straub use this darkest stretch of the journey to make a larger point in a novel otherwise filled with wonders, Cormac McCarthy's Pulitzer Prize–winning mainstream novel *The Road* (2006) makes use of themes usually reserved for popular genre fiction to make its ecological, humanistic, and literary points—including its counterpoints to what has become the traditional dark fantastic version of the postapocalyptic road narrative. In this novel, McCarthy paints a picture of an agonizingly bleak postapocalyptic world, telling the tale of a man and his son walking endlessly south on the United States' highways, questing for anything resembling civilization. Gone are the grand moral quests, colorful subplots, and mystical characters of King's, Moore's, McCammon's, and Cronin's postapocalyptic worlds. In McCarthy's vision, the United States is transformed into an ash-covered, barren, razed world populated by solitary, broken scavengers or small, desperate paramilitary groups. As critic Ted Gioia summarizes,

McCarthy's "father and son can take nothing for granted—food, shelter, health, physical safety—and the surrounding anarchy suggests that anyone else they encounter will be looking to kill, maim, enslave, or perhaps even cook them up for supper." While plot is everything in *The Stand* and similar works, plot in *The Road* is sparse and episodic at best. Employing the same immediacy of violence and brevity of word and scene he demonstrates in works such as *Blood Meridian* (1985) and *No Country for Old Men* (2005), McCarthy subverts the typical dark fantastic vision of the postapocalyptic United States with a stark presentation of the utter devastation of the human condition one would likely encounter in a world ravaged by nuclear weapons or similar calamity, adding little if any moral commentary or exposition.

Fantastical exploration of transformed versions of the United States and its highways comes to a head, however, in King's Dark Tower series. King has used this sprawling series—itself a road story, a quest through a massive fantasy land that sometimes overlaps the real world—to help unify the majority of his work into a single huge collective story. For example, Father Callahan, a priest who is left to live in disgrace after his faith fails during his fight with the vampire Barlowe in King's vampire novel *Salem's Lot* (1975), enters the Dark Tower series in book 5, *Wolves of the Calla* (2003). The reader finds Callahan somewhat redeemed following several long years lived as a homeless traveler on the highways of the United States—but these are no ordinary highways. In a flashback, Callahan tells other characters that following a near-death experience in New York, he spent five years on the road avoiding the pursuit of various supernatural creatures, taking odd jobs, and living off the kindness of strangers. King's twist is that Callahan frequently wakes up in a version of the world slightly different from the one he went to sleep in; the personal and redemptive transformation Callahan experiences on the road is mirrored by America quite literally transforming around him. For example, detailing one of Callahan's odd jobs, King writes:

Callahan short-orders at the Leabrook Homestyle Diner for three weeks,
and stays two blocks down at the Sunset Motel. Only it's not always the
Homestyle, and it's not always the Sunset. On his fourth day in town, he
wakes up in the Sunrise Motel, and the Leabrook Homestyle Diner is the
Fort Lee Homestyle Diner. The Leabrook Register *which people have been*
leaving behind on the counter becomes the Fort Lee Register-American.
He is not exactly relieved to discover Gerald Ford has reassumed the
Presidency. (300; ital. in orig.)

Again, there is much of the traditional road narrative in Callahan's experience: the odd jobs, the freedom and redemption offered by the road, the reconnection with the land and fellow human beings, the outsider's observation of society. King has simply heightened the more mainstream experience, using ideas suggested by quantum physics to exaggerate the transformative possibilities of the road. This is summarized at the start of the journey, when, after fleeing the dangerous "reality" of New York and noticing the first anomalies in his new (un) reality, Callahan stands at the foot of the New Jersey side of the George Washington Bridge. As the truth of his situation dawns on him, Callahan thinks, "Before me is the weight of America, with all its possibilities." King then narrates:

This thought lifts him, and is followed by one that lifts him even higher:
not just one America, perhaps, but a dozen . . . or a thousand . . . or a mil-
lion. [. . .] *Maybe instead of forty-two continental United States on the*
other side of the Hudson, there are forty-two hundred, or forty-two thou-
sand, all of them stacked in vertical geographies of chance.

And he understands instinctively that this is almost certainly true. He
has stumbled upon a great, possibly endless, confluence of worlds. They
are all America, but they are all different. There are highways which lead
through them, and he can see them." (298–99; ital. in orig.)

Terry Bisson's 1986 novel *Talking Man* presents a noteworthy spin on the dark fantastic theme of America transformed. In this novel, Talking Man, who barely speaks at all, is a godlike wizard who has dreamed the world into being. Having fallen in love with his creation and the United States in particular, he has retired inside it, settling in a trailer outside the Kentucky junkyard he runs. His ex-wife is a soulless wizard goddess named Dgene, who, out of jealousy, decides to destroy Talking Man's creation from the North Pole. Talking Man sets out on a road trip to stop her as the landscape of his dream, competing with Dgene's unmaking, shifts and changes around him: the Mississippi flows north at the bottom of a mile-deep gorge, there are mountains in southern Illinois, characters must slog through the longest traffic jam in history, and there is suddenly no state between Oklahoma and Mexico and no cities in Oklahoma other than Tulsa. In Bisson's book, the American "dream" can vary minute to minute; it shifts and changes, transforms, and could possibly even vanish as one is traveling through it. For the individual characters, the questions of identity that so many road protagonists ask become questions about the nature of reality itself: if reality is not reliable or stable, or even real, then what does that say of identity?

The question of identity is a major theme in another popular darkly fantastic road story, Neil Gaiman's *American Gods* (2001). In both the primary stream of the story and the many seemingly unrelated side chapters that are inserted throughout the narrative, Gaiman's characters search for self-worth, purpose, and the meaning of who they are. The quest for identity is exaggerated in that almost every main character is a god or otherwise mythic character, now fallen into a more mundane existence in a United States that no longer believes in them: Odin the All-Father has become a common grifter, a fire-demon ifrit from Middle Eastern mythology a New York cabbie, and the pre-Christian pagan spirit of Easter a self-deluding San Francisco flower child.

The central concept of the novel, that of immigrants to the United States bringing their gods with them and the gods having trouble adjusting to the hodgepodge of cultures as well as to the ever-changing modern world, is not original to Gaiman—it is, in fact, a familiar convention in urban fantasy and even comic books—but Gaiman was the first to tackle the subject on such a large scale. He incorporates gods from numerous pantheons, pitting them against modern gods such as the obese Technical Boy, who smells of electricity; the chatty, politically correct goddess Media; and the car gods, who seem to gain power from vehicular accidents—"a powerful, serious-faced contingent, with blood on their black gloves and on their chrome teeth: recipients of human sacrifice on a scale undreamed of since the Aztecs" (Gaiman 537).

Although it does not take place after an apocalyptic event, *American Gods* shares *The Stand*'s dark fantastic convention that most travel is for the purpose of gathering forces for a final definitive battle. In this case, Odin, known through most of the novel only as Wednesday, hires a man known only as Shadow (a name that telegraphs the identity theme) to accompany him as he travels the country recruiting old gods for a showdown with the new breed of divine beings.

It has long been a tradition for American road narratives to point out and make use of the mythic scale of the United States. Traditional and mainstream narratives tend to do this by emphasizing descriptions of landscape, distance, and cultures. In postapocalyptic novels such as *The Stand* and fantasies such as *American Gods*, however, the mythic status of the country either becomes exaggerated by the moral scale and importance of the events or, as is especially the case in Gaiman's novel, becomes literalized. While traditional road travelers might quest for a holy place, literature of the fantastic moves beyond the faith of religion—certain locales *are* holy places, specific sites have spiritual or restorative power, and the road is a mythic place. For the deities in *American Gods*, for instance, certain roadside attractions are more powerful than any church, and the humans who build, run, or visit these locations do not fully understand what they are experiencing there.

Another major contrast between traditional and dark fantastic road narratives is the altered sense of home. Even in works by such perennial road souls as Jack Kerouac and Neal Cassady, there is a sense of leaving and return—a sense of return and reintegration into society, of the person they are at "home" having changed due to their experiences on the road. This sense is changed in the dark fantastic; there often is no reintegration, as "home" has been destroyed at the start of the narrative or simply does not exist in the first place. At the end of *The Stand*, two of the survivors, Fran and Stu, apparently find a sense of domesticity in something approximating a preapocalypse suburban home, but they can discuss the future only in uncertain terms. Stu comments that this period of stability is only "a season of rest," and as the characters discuss the outlook for their future, King ends the novel mid-conversation with Stu repeating the words "I don't know" (1149).

Similarly, in *American Gods*, Shadow leaves the United States for Iceland without any concrete "looking back" point:

> He sat down on a grassy bank and looked at the city that surrounded him, and thought, one day he would have to go home. And one day he would have to make a home to go back to. He wondered whether home was a thing that happened to a place after a while, or if it was something that you found in the end, if you simply walked and waited and willed it long enough. (Gaiman 585)

In these darker road narratives, the road does provide redemption, revelation, and transformation, yet the United States is generally seen as unreliable by its very nature. Nothing in it is permanent, and safety and a sense of home are transitory at best; even the new gods in Gaiman's work fear becoming obsolete (537). As Wednesday points out to Shadow, the United States is "the only country in the world . . . that worries about what it is." He explains, "No one ever needs to go searching for the heart of Norway. Or looks for the soul of Mozambique. They know what they are" (116).

While the use of fantasy elements in road narratives such as Gaiman's tends to emphasize and exaggerate the quest for identity, the dark fantastic also has more realistic modes, the thriller and suspense genres, which are employed for largely different purposes but retain the sense of the United States as a dangerous, unstable place. In these narratives, authors tend to explore the same moral ground as King, but the emphasis, at least superficially, is situational; the more peril involved for the characters, the better, at least as far as the typical reader of these popular genres is concerned. In mainstream and traditional road narratives, protagonists—even doomed antiheroes such as Bonnie and Clyde (in the 1967 Warren Beatty film version, at least) or Sissy Spacek and Martin Sheen's young rebels in the film *Badlands* (1973)—revel in the freedom and independence of the road. Even on the lam, they have a wild time. But suspense writers turn this upside down; in their work, the freedom road becomes the highway to hell, as it were. While the road is portrayed as liberating in most road narratives, the suspense genre turns it into a trap.

As Blake Crouch, author of *Run* (2011) and other thrillers making extensive use of road narrative themes, explains, the thriller, suspense, and horror genres

> subvert everything good, happy, and decent in the world. A road trip in most people's minds is a wonderful thing. But people don't read horror and suspense to read about wonderful things. They want to read about people in the most traumatic circumstances possible. In some weird way, that's a pressure release for the stressors, boredom, and humdrum of our lives. It's an adrenaline boost. You don't have those lighter *Bonnie & Clyde*, or even *Badlands* moments in real thrillers (or at least the kind I write like *Run*) because I want to keep my characters under the gun every waking second. (Email interview)

Combining elements of King's and McCarthy's visions of a postapocalyptic United States, *Run* tells the story of a family that must stay in motion in order to avoid annihilation in a world in which the majority of Americans have turned into murderous psychopaths because of an anomalous astronomical event. In this case, the apocalypse is ongoing: those who saw "the lights" recognize those who did not and want to kill them. The Colclough family spends the first half of the novel traveling by car across the often burning or otherwise ruined landscape of the American Southwest, headed north toward Canada, where peace and normalcy are rumored to prevail. The Colcloughs find a temporary utopia in a mountainside cabin but soon must flee by even more desperate means—on foot, by bicycle, as captives.

The fantastic premise of *Run* allows Crouch to explore themes of family and the darker side of human need, human drives, and human limitations. Readers familiar with the clipped style and sudden violence of McCarthy's novels will not be able to read *Run* without noticing similarities. The novel is, on at least one level, a conscious response and homage to *The Road*, but with a thriller novelist's eye and intentions. Crouch explains,

> I think McCarthy is just a fascinating writer, not only from a stylistic perspective but because he writes about life and death on every page of every book (although *Suttree* has its more lighthearted moments). I can't remember where, but I heard once that all books are written, on some level, as a response to other books. *Run* was definitely a response to *The Road*. I'm not in any way saying I think *Run* is anywhere close to the level of brilliance McCarthy achieves in *The Road*, but as much as I loved that book, I wanted more from it. I wanted better plotting to be honest. I wanted more character arc. That's not to say *The Road* should have been any of those things. But for me, in my perfect world, it would have been. So writing *Run* was my answer, I guess. Also, the initial idea for *Run* came as my wife and I had a son and daughter, and so the protection of my family in a changing world was forefront. (Email interview)

Popular fiction is rife with intelligent, ruthless serial killers such as Thomas Harris's Hannibal Lecter or Crouch's Luther Kite, many of whom are capable of "hiding in plain sight" via various disguises.

Often this "disguise" comes in the form of the killer taking to the road, traveling while police and other authorities search locally after discovering one of the killer's victims. Suspense novelist Dean Koontz has used the theme of the killer on the road in a number of his works. In his 1973 novel *Shattered*, a man and his son driving cross-country notice a van that seems to be following them and, at first, make a game of this fact. However, after a physical attack at a motel reveals that the antagonist is a seriously deranged man, the game becomes much more desperate. *Shattered* has some flaws—why, for example, do the protagonists not contact the police, especially after the physical attack?—but it also serves as an early example of Koontz's recurring convention of serial murderers traveling the road, living in relative anonymity while creating mayhem.

Sometimes Koontz uses these traveling killers simply for the purpose of adding the trappings of suspense. This is the case in *Intensity* (1995), one of his most popular novels, in which killer Edgler Foreman Vess is a county sheriff who has converted his mobile home into a rolling jail cell, abattoir, and torture dungeon, making it difficult for other authorities to track him down—and for victims to escape. In other novels, Koontz uses this convention to make larger sociological points; in *One Door away from Heaven* (2001), for instance, the killer, conspiracy theorist and disgraced former professorial "philosopher" Preston Maddoc, travels so that "they" will not be able to locate him while he investigates UFO sightings and espouses a creed based on eugenics (the practice of weeding out those humans with "inferior" genetics), a kidnapped handicapped girl in tow.

Crouch uses similar conventions in his serial-killer trilogy *Thicker than Blood* (2004–2011), in which traveling murderers attempt to convert thriller writer Andrew Z. Thomas, the brother of one of the killers, to their nihilistic philosophies. The books are filled with road trips in which the characters travel long distances in order to murder or prevent murders, gather evidence, or confront each other. Crouch notes that his primary inspiration for his frequent use of the road in his work stems not from other genre-oriented material featuring killers on the road, such as Koontz's novels, but from a more traditional road novel:

> My biggest inspiration for writing about life on the road probably goes back to my reading of [Robert M. Pirsig's] *Zen and the Art of Motorcycle Maintenance* in high school. Pirsig's descriptions of driving a motorcycle through the American west and not knowing where you were going to stop for the night, and using travel as a means to drive the narrative made a huge impression that sticks with me to this day. (Email interview)

Crouch later partnered with J. A. Konrath, author of a long-running series about a Chicago detective named Jacqueline "Jack" Daniels, for some interesting literary experiments. These include a long novel, *Serial Killers Uncut* (2011)—also cowritten, in a bit of literary playfulness, by Konrath's horror-writing pseudonym Jack Kilborn—which combines a number of shorter novellas featuring characters from all three authors' books into a single lengthy, loosely cohesive narrative; and another novel, *Stirred* (2011), which concludes both Crouch's Andrew Z. Thomas cycle and Konrath's Jack Daniels series with the deaths of most of the traveling serial killers.

In traditional road narratives such as those by Kerouac or the film *Easy Rider* (1969), the open road allows protagonists to become outsiders and escape, observe, and at least briefly rise above the "evil" that is society. Koontz's, Crouch's, and Konrath's serial killers, on the other hand, use that isolation and anonymity to hide in plain sight and spread their evil across a society that functions as a victim—and yet they also escape, observe, and rise above society, though in a very twisted way.

Although skewed through the lens of the dark fantastic, these serial-killer narratives nonetheless often use a language similar to that of idyllic, idealistic quests of counterculture youth. Take, for instance, this passage toward the conclusion of *Bad Girl*, a Crouch novella in *Serial Killers Uncut* about twenty-something serial murderer Lucy: "She traveled the country, even up into Canada. She became a wanderer. She never had to take a job. Sometimes, she would run out of money, but there was always someone willing to give a lift to a cute, petite blonde" (Crouch and Konrath 117). This could just as easily be a description of hitchhiking sweetheart Sissy Hankshaw in Tom Robbins's countercul-ture novel *Even Cowgirls Get the Blues* (1976). But the words take on a cruel cast when the reader realizes that Lucy's guitar case contains drugs with which to incapacitate victims; her hunger is not for travel or for the next temporary destination; and, in direct counterpoint to the drug-fueled ecstasies of other counterculture road travelers, the only drug to which Lucy is addicted is the rush of killing other humans:

> She had no friends. No family. Just a guitar case and a hunger that could never be satisfied.
>
> More and more, she was keeping to the quiet, untraveled corners of America. The long, empty interstates of the Dakotas. The desert South-west. She was finding new and exciting things to do in the middle of the night on these long, empty stretches of asphalt, to the poor souls who stopped to offer a ride.
>
> There was both peace and sadness in the knowledge that she would never stop. That she was a hopeless addict. The killing, the blood, was simply all that mattered. She never worried about someone killing her. She had no fear. She only worried about getting caught, getting locked up in a cell away from all these beautiful drugs that were driving around on the American highway system. (107)

Similarly, Konrath's killer Alex Kork could, with the exception of the psychopathic details of the conversation, be almost any teenager la-menting the woes of small-town life in any traditional road narrative as she discusses leaving town with her brother and fellow serial killer, Charles, in a flashback scene from *Serial Killers Uncut*:

> "I'm scared," Alex said.
> "Of what? We're the ones people need to be scared of."

Alex didn't want to tell him the truth. That the thing that scared her most *was* herself . . . what she was capable of. This . . . town was like a cage. Small. Defined. Everyone knew everyone else. Easy to get into trouble, so Alex and Charles had to restrain themselves.

There would be no such restraint Out There.

It was an exciting thought. A sexy one. To be able to unleash their appetites on complete strangers. People who wouldn't be missed. Who wouldn't leave trails for the cops back to their front door. (34)

In writing his novella *Duel* (1971), which director Steven Spielberg adapted into one of his first films in 1971, author Richard Matheson added subtle variations to the tale of the killer on the road and ultimately created a classic road story that transcends the horror and suspense genres. *Duel* tells a tale that is quite straightforward on the surface: a man (his last name is, in fact, Mann) driving through the desert runs afoul of a psychopathic truck driver. At the start of the story, Mann passes the larger but slower vehicle, but as soon as it is able, the truck passes him again, beginning an ever-intensifying cat-and-mouse game in which the truck tailgates Mann dangerously and intentionally blocks the road. The truck eventually damages Mann's vehicle, and the novella ends with a showdown near a cliff. *Duel* is ostensibly nothing more than a tale of a man dealing with the consequences of road rage, but with Matheson's seemingly simple choice never to show the face of the truck driver—nothing more than an arm is ever seen in either the story or the film, which Matheson scripted—*Duel* enters the realm of metaphor. The suspense, and the metaphor, is heightened because the readers never know the psychopath's identity, emotions, or motives; he embodies the idea of the personality-free machines and highways on which society depends revolting against that society. Hartwell comments, "Without a hint of science fiction or an overt whiff of the supernatural, 'Duel' manages to invoke both the science fiction tradition of the menace of the intelligent machine and the monster tradition of the horror genre. It's a psychological monster story, subtly shocking, compelling, fantastic" (Introduction to *Duel* 198).

King has repeatedly cited *Duel* as a major influence on his work, and his oldest son, author Joe Hill, has noted that when he was growing up, he and his father were fans of the film version. Father and son teamed up to cowrite a novella entitled *Throttle*, which was published in *He Is Legend* (2009), an anthology of stories imitating and honoring Matheson. In their spin on *Duel*, an entire gang of outlaw bikers is challenged by a faceless trucker. While King and Hill take the battle to a larger, grander, and bloodier scale, they mostly eschew the psychological and metaphorical subtleties of Matheson's original story, opting instead to present an unadorned high-action thriller. While *Throttle* is a direct, if not thematically ambitious, homage to *Duel*, the influence of Matheson's piece can be seen in subtler form in many other works by King. For example, in his early story "Trucks" (1973), which pushes the "menace of the intelligent machine" to the extreme, the titular vehicles suddenly become sentient en masse, developing a military sort of hive mind with the goal of enslaving humanity. The story details the resistance attempts of one group at a particular truck stop. In this case, the machines not only become the killers, as is implied in *Duel*, but also function as a direct indictment of a society that has become too dependent on them.

While they are not directly road narratives per se, King's novels *Christine* (1983) and *From a Buick 8* (2002) are also worth mentioning, as King makes extensive use of road iconography in them and as both are direct descendents of *Duel*. In *Christine*, the eponymous self-aware, demonic car becomes possessive of its nerdy owner and drives itself on missions to kill in his defense, meanwhile transforming the teen from naïf to lothario to psychopath. In this case, it is the car itself, not the road, that transforms the driver. In *From a Buick 8*, police collect and store a mysterious abandoned car that is never driven anywhere but nonetheless remains a portal into the realm of myth and transformation. The book consists mostly of diverse eerie recollections police share about the car and their theories about its source: the car might, for instance, be alien in origin; it might be organic and alive, despite its strange machinelike parts and general lack of motion; or it might even be a portal between worlds.

As some of the previous examples demonstrate, road narratives in the dark fantastic are frequently a mixture of influence and homage, new spins on preceding works. Author Nick Mamatas, on the other hand, wears his influences on his sleeve—and rightly so—in novels such as *The Damned Highway: Fear and Loathing in Arkham* (2011), cowritten with popular horror writer Brian Keene, and *Move under Ground* (2004). These two novels exist beyond the realm of mere influence, standing as respectful pastiches or parodies. Each novel combines the distinctive voice of a canonical author within the traditional road narrative genre with the purple prose and supernatural trappings of the cosmic-horror tales of H. P. Lovecraft, whose work has only gained popularity since its original publication in the 1920s.

Move under Ground is told in the first person with Jack Kerouac himself as the narrator. The novel begins with Kerouac "hiding out" in the Big Sur region of California following the publication and popular success of *On the Road* (1957). In Mamatas's twist on Kerouac's 1962 novel *Big Sur*, R'lyeh, Lovecraft's sunken city of the Elder Gods, rises from the ocean just off the coast. This sets in motion a road trip quest in which Kerouac must first track down William S. Burroughs and Neal Cassady, the latter of whose letters suggest that he perhaps knows something of the Lovecraftian cults taking over the United States, and then thwart the evil forces attempting to crush the American dream.

Mamatas's prose is flawless as he imitates and combines elements of both authors. The style in *Move under Ground* is primarily Kerouac's beat poetics, but hints of Lovecraft's florid writing, sense of looming menace, and darkness of subject creep into nearly every sentence, as in this passage from the opening of the book, in which Kerouac describes the effects of fame on Cassady:

Those boozy late-night dinners with crazy soulless characters whose jaws clacked like mandibles when they laughed got to him in the end, I'm sure. They were hungry for something. Not just the college boys and beautiful young things, but those haggard-looking veterans of Babylon who started shadowing Neal and me on every street corner and at every dawn-draped last call in roadside bars; they all wanted more than a taste of Neal's divine spark, they wanted to extinguish it in their gullets. (Mamatas 1)

The Damned Highway is a similar stylistic experiment, this time taking on the gonzo journalism of Hunter S. Thompson. The premise is that Keene and Mamatas have unearthed ten new chapters to Thompson's *Fear and Loathing on the Campaign Trail '72* (1973). Thompson himself is never mentioned in the book; instead, the protagonist is making a cross-country bus trip incognito and insists on being called "Uncle Lono," a reference to the title of an obscure Thompson novel, *The Curse of Lono* (1983), as well as to Uncle Duke, a caricature of Thompson from the comic strip *Doonesbury*. The plot of the novel suggests that events of the late 1960s such as the Vietnam War and the Charles Manson killings were all leading up to the rise of R'lyeh. Incumbent president Richard Nixon must win all fifty states in the 1972 election in order to summon the Elder God Cthulhu and bring forth a dark new age, and it is up to Uncle Lono to travel to Arkham, Massachusetts—a fictional town from Lovecraft's works—in order to halt Nixon's plans for world domination.

Whether or not the individual stories take place on the road, the best stories of the dark fantastic literalize what is in the popular subconscious, stating in concrete form what is stated in metaphor in the mainstream. When these stories take place on the American road, they take the reader on a literal journey through figurative places in the country's consciousness. The readers travel through a United States transformed and are thereby themselves transformed; they see their darker selves, the darker aspects of their country, parodied, exaggerated, and subverted. As such, they can, as the protagonists in dark fantastic stories almost invariably do, strive for the light.

Works Cited

Cronin, Justin. *The Passage*. New York: Ballantine, 2010. Print.

Crouch, Blake. Email interview. 11 May 2012.

___. *Run*. CreateSpace, 2011. Print.

Crouch, Blake, and J. A. Konrath. *Serial Killers Uncut*. CreateSpace, 2011. Print.

Gaiman, Neil. *American Gods*. New York: Harper, 2001. Print.

Gillespie, Nick. "Canon Fire." *Reason.com*. Reason Foundation, June 1995. Web. 17 May 2012.

Gioia, Ted. "*The Road* by Cormac McCarthy." *The New Canon*. The New Canon, n.d. Web. 17 May 2012.

Hartwell, David G. Introduction. *The Dark Descent*. Ed. Hartwell. New York: Tor, 1987. 1–11. Print.

___. Introduction to *Duel*. *Visions of Fear*. Ed. Hartwell. New York: Tor, 1992. 198. Print.

___. Introduction to "The Reach." *The Dark Descent*. Ed. Hartwell. New York: Tor, 1987. 15. Print.

Hill, Joe, and Stephen King. *Throttle*. *He Is Legend: An Anthology Celebrating Richard Matheson*. Ed. Christopher Conlon. New York: Gauntlet, 2009. 17–55. Print.

Keene, Brian, and Nick Mamatas. *The Damned Highway: Fear and Loathing in Arkham*. Milwaukie: Dark Horse, 2009. Print.

King, Stephen. *Danse Macabre*. New York: Berkley, 1981. Print.

___. "Mrs. Todd's Shortcut." *Skeleton Crew*. New York: Signet, 1986. 206–31. Print.

___. The Stand: The Complete and Uncut Edition. New York: Doubleday, 1990. Print.

___. "Trucks." *Night Shift*. New York: Signet, 1976. 127–42. Print.

___. *Wolves of the Calla*. New York: Scribner's, 2003. Print. Dark Tower 5.

Koontz, Dean. *Intensity*. New York: Random, 1995. Print.

___. *One Door away from Heaven*. New York: Bantam, 2001. Print.

___. *Shattered*. New York: Berkley, 1973. Print.

Mamatas, Nick. *Move under Ground*. San Francisco: Night Shade, 2004. Print.

Matheson, Richard. *Duel*. 1971. *Visions of Fear*. Ed. David G. Hartwell. New York: Tor, 1992. 198–227. Print.

McCammon, Robert R. *Swan Song*. New York: Pocket, 1987. Print.

McCarthy, Cormac. *The Road*. New York: Vintage, 2006. Print.

Moore, C. Dennis. *Revelations*. Sanford: Necro, 2012. Print.

Stewart, George R. *Earth Abides*. New York: Fawcet, 1949. Print.

Poetics of Place in Roethke's "North American Sequence"

Christian Knoeller

> All roads lead to the self.
>
> Theodore Roethke, "The Mire's My Home"

Growing up in the Upper Midwest, Theodore Roethke gained an appreciation for the region's history and an understanding of how development had transformed the environment there. His vision of environmental history and spiritual relation to the natural world, forged in Michigan, reached its ultimate expression in the poems of the "North American Sequence." An ecocritical perspective helps map Roethke's westward sojourn across the heartland, as well as moments in which the poems incorporate recollected landscapes of the Midwest. The six sections of the sequence suggest the trajectory of a transcontinental "journey" of self-discovery and direct experience of the sublime in relation to nature. In his critical study of Roethke's final book, *The Far Field* (1964), poet Peter Balakian characterizes Roethke's stance in the sequence as Whitmanesque: "in his creation of the self as representative man and visionary explorer, and in his conception of America as a primal territory that is at once a realm of consciousness and geographic space . . . Roethke is a visionary seeker who must also be a cataloging naturalist. . . . Like a Thoreauvian naturalist, Roethke creates the rhythmic beauty of North America's indigenous creatures" (131–3, 148).

In his essay "An American Poet Introduces Himself and His Poems," Roethke renders his geographical inheritance in personal terms: "Everyone knows that America is a continent, but few Europeans realize the various and diverse parts of this land. The Saginaw Valley, where I was born, had been great lumbering country in the 1880s. It is very fertile flat country in Michigan. . . . It was this region that my grandfather came to in 1870 from Prussia, where he had been Bismarck's head forester" (*On the Poet* 7). Roethke situates his interpretation of

190   Critical Insights landscapes in the grand sweep of American history as the Upper Midwest was settled by Europeans who, like his grandfather, were drawn by the abundance of natural resources, such as the seemingly inexhaustible tracts of virgin old-growth timber.

Within two generations, the face of this landscape changed irrevocably as primeval stands fell and verdant wild ecosystems were replaced by second-growth forest or cleared for cropland, exacting a terrible ecological cost: "the loss of ancient woods, the destruction of rivers, the extinction of animals" (Barillas 122). As scholar William Barillas points out, "Roethke was well aware of how drastically his home region had been altered in the half century preceding his birth" (110). Roethke himself describes his family's land holdings as including twenty-five acres "in the town, mostly under glass and intensely cultivated," and alludes to a remnant of primeval forest, "the last stand of virgin timber in the Saginaw Valley" to have survived Michigan's timber boom, as well as "a wild area of cut-over second-growth timber, which [his] father and uncle made into a small game preserve" (*On the Poet* 8). The ecological memory encapsulated here prefigures the crowning achievement of his distinguished career, the "North American Sequence," an exploration of the "various and diverse parts of this land" that has helped define national identity as well as his own poetics of place. Above all, this acclaimed sequence—incorporating a synthesis of disparate places—expresses a transcendental appreciation for wild landscapes as well as an understanding of the historical forces that have reshaped them.

The opening poem of the sequence, "The Longing," reflects both modernist and romantic sensibilities. Blending these two traditions might even be seen as both postmodernist and postromantic (Balakian 136). This dual perspective suggests Roethke's ambition to establish his own legacy in literary history in relation to both British and American verse. Indeed, as critic Walter Kalaidjian argues, the sequence "presents a sustained dialogue with the poet's literary tradition" (159). To do so effectively—to make a lasting contribution—he ventured into long forms; the sequence as a whole, after all, comprises six poems of three to five sections each, in aggregate forming a compact epic (Staples; Malkoff) that Kalaidjian describes as a "consummate celebration of American place" (122). Roethke was at the very height of his creative powers while composing the poems that would be collected in *The Far Field*, the title of which invokes quintessentially American landscapes, perhaps above all the agrarian Midwest.

Roethke reportedly worked feverishly on the project until the final days of his life, leading some to speculate that he had a clear premonition of his imminent death and giving the project a profound personal urgency. Critic Neal Bowers contends that Roethke effectively "communicates to us, through descriptions of his surroundings, that he is meditating upon his own death," juxtaposing the temporal and the eternal to yield a sense of an eternal present (161). Recognition of personal mortality may well account for why he aspired to such heights both artistically and philosophically in these poems.

While the collection was ultimately published posthumously, Roethke succeeded in organizing the manuscript as well as finalizing titles himself. In fact, the poems of the "North American Sequence" itself were ultimately published "exactly as Roethke edited them" (Malkoff 172). Reviewing the collection upon its publication in 1964, acclaimed poet W. D. Snodgrass found the theme of mortality to be so central to *The Far Field* as to suggest implicitly its importance in Roethke's earlier work as well. In his critical study *The Wild Prayer of Longing* (1971), Nathan A. Scott proposes the notion of "sacramental imagination" to account for Roethke's transcendence of the solitary romantic self through his attunement to landscape and deepening reverence for what today might be conceived in terms of biodiversity and ecological integrity, apparently heightened by a growing awareness of his own mortality (qtd. in Dougherty 182–83).

Critics have made much of Roethke's debt to T. S. Eliot, particularly his "Four Quartets" (Balakian; Barillas; Kalaidjian). In fact, "The Longing" closes with several lines often cited in response to Eliot's

line "Old men ought to be explorers," to which Roethke famously re-
torts, "I'll be an Indian" (*Collected Poems* 189). This exchange signals a profound set of contrasts between the two poets: Eliot's view as
an expatriate living in Europe as opposed to Roethke's identification
with the landscapes of North America. As Barillas contends, "Eliot
abstracts place, observing North America at a distance rather than involving himself intimately with the continent's history and landscape"
(133), whereas "at times, [Roethke's] is the eye of the naturalist" (107).
Moreover, a profound difference in perspective is suggested between
Eliot's devotion to the dictates of the Anglican Church and Roethke's
animistic regard for nature from the perspective of "a native namer,
a reclaimer of territory, the perpetual explorer" (Balakian 131), for
whom "sacredness has nothing to do with theology, and everything to
do with biology, evolution, and the primeval life force" (Barillas 117).
Roethke himself confides, "If the dead can come to our aid in a quest
for identity, so can the living—and I mean *all* living things, including the sub-human. This is not so much naïve as a primitive attitude:
animistic, maybe. Why not? Everything that lives is holy: I call upon
these holy forms of life" (*On the Poet* 24; ital. in orig.).

Beyond overt allusions to and deliberate echoes of Eliot—such as
the use of classical elements of air, water, fire, and earth, as well as the
image of the rose—Roethke's sequence actually opens with an evocation of urban industrial blight reminiscent of British romanticism.
These meditations explore metaphysical principles echoed down the
centuries by poets from William Blake to Walt Whitman, as well as
those expressed by American transcendentalists such as Ralph Waldo
Emerson and Henry David Thoreau. In his published letters, Roethke
acknowledges having carefully read and contemplated all four. Indeed, he reports having purchased personal copies of both Emerson
and Thoreau while still an adolescent (*On the Poet* 15–16). His indictment of rampant industrialization harkens back to nineteenth-century poets such as William Wordsworth, with whom he also shared a
passion for direct experience of the sublime in nature. Wordsworth's

"Prelude" exemplifies the double-edged sword of the sublime: awe before nature's majesty and terror at its power. This has led some critics to consider parallels between Roethke and romantic poets such as Blake, as well as twentieth-century midwestern writers such as James Wright, his own student.

If "The Longing" portrays a pervasive modern ennui, as "the spirit fails to move forward," the sequence as a whole constitutes a kind of pilgrimage or quest—literally and symbolically—in search of spiritual renewal (Roethke, *Collected Poems* 187). Yet the poem begins on a despondent note: the spiritual malaise of the postindustrial era, "a more authentic wasteland than Eliot's because it is so rooted in a particular place," and counterbalanced by another romantic impulse, "the imaginative projection of the possibility of union with the world [that] creates the real sense of longing in the poem" (Balakian 138–39). This underlying and at times overwhelming desire gives rise to the spiritual dimensions of the poet's journey beyond the self in search of the sublime. Critic James Dougherty dates this impulse to around 1950, the time of Roethke's first cross-country drive from Saginaw to Seattle, suggesting a newfound "attentiveness . . . to nature, to other humans, and to God . . . recognizing both separateness and identity, assimilation and reverence" (183).

Accordingly, Roethke's exploration of the myriad landscapes of North America, and contemplation of their historical and spiritual significance, is at once a gesture of restoration and redemption. As critic Jay Parini observes, "the metaphorical nature of the journey is given immediate prominence, but the details rapidly make the car trip across the American West the poem's literal setting. . . . A car trip lends a note of realism to what might easily be a wholly metaphorical venture . . . [yet] the poem is not taking place now; the poem is a dream of journeys" (164-65). Dougherty concludes, "Though the journeys are manifestly psychological, they have a spiritual, religious tinge to them as well" (179). Similarly, Kalaidjian contends that Roethke establishes "a kind of intuitive correspondence between the outer highway and the inner spiritual path" (137). While the poems of this sequence ultimately span the continent, the countervailing force of memory leads the poet to return repeatedly to images from his midwestern youth. As essayist Scott Russell Sanders has observed, the landscapes of childhood leave an indelible impression and form a fundamental frame of reference for later appreciation of the natural world in other places (4). In this sense, Michigan forms the bedrock of Roethke's ecological memory.

"The Longing" also provides a first glimpse of landscapes to the west that lie ahead as the sequence progresses: "On the Bullhead, in the Dakotas, where the eagles eat well, / In the country of few lakes, in the tall buffalo grass at the base of the clay buttes" (*Collected Poems* 188–89). Part of what distinguishes the "North American Sequence" from Roethke's earlier work is the particularity in its depictions of place, as opposed to more abstracted or archetypal use of natural imagery. Indeed, the specificity of his ecological lexicon represents a departure for Roethke in *The Far Field*. Similarly, "using a westernized vocabulary of arroyos, buttes, and canyons, the poet conveys an immediate, particular encounter with the land" (Dougherty 189).

Beyond rendering distinctive topography, the poem invokes ecological memory by summoning the legacy of the buffalo. As Dougherty contends, "casting back not in personal memory but in the memory of the continent, he smells the dead buffalo—possibly an Oglala hunt, but perhaps the mass slaughter of the herds that accompanied the suppression of the Sioux and other Plains peoples" (188). Remarkably, Roethke's evocation of history is often so vivid as to seem visceral: "In the summer heat I can smell the dead buffalo, / The stench of their dark fur drying in the sun, / The buffalo chips drying" (*Collected Poems* 189). The saga of the decline and near extinction of the bison exemplifies the ecological havoc caused by westward expansion across the continent throughout the nineteenth century. Some critics identify the signature themes of "environmental destruction and genocidal assault on native peoples" as central to Roethke's legacy (Barillas 138). In *The Midwestern Pastoral* (2006), his study of landscape in the region's literature, Barillas likens Roethke's nascent environmental sensibilities to pioneering ecologist Aldo Leopold's understanding of "the prairie in relation to ecological history," citing "the diminishment of natural diversity regretted by Leopold and Roethke and symbolized by both in the tragic near extinction of the American bison" (132).

Moreover, bison are historically linked to westward migration in that pioneering homesteaders followed age-old buffalo traces, which invariably offered passable routes through the most challenging terrain. Until the late eighteenth century, in fact, thoroughfares for wagons in eastern states such as Kentucky still retraced trails bison had blazed. "In addition to acting as compass lines for colonial migration," Tom McHugh writes in his definitive study *The Time of the Buffalo* (1972), "the trails influenced the patterns of settlement in the heart of the Ohio River valley," accounting for the location of population centers such as Cincinnati and Louisville. "Although the buffalo disappeared soon afterward from most of this area east of the Mississippi," McHugh concludes, "the herds had already stamped the country with some distinctive signs of occupation that would persist for centuries" (49). These are the very sorts of traces—and absences—that led Roethke deeper into the continent and his contemplation of self.

As cultural geographer Richard Manning observes in *Grassland* (1995), his seminal account of North America's prairies, "a single bison does not stand alone, is not an individual. It is, rather, a manifestation of a place, the net result, the capstone of fire, wind, and grass— grass to the horizon—and of the hundreds of plants that live in it. . . . and can only be understood as such" (245–46). Indeed, the bison was an important force in shaping and maintaining the grasslands, including in its interactions with its predators, especially the wolf. As Pulitzer Prize–winning science journalist Jon Franklin observes, "over millions of years, the wolf and its ungulate prey were honed by one another until they constituted a finely tuned ecological machine that flowed across the landscape like a wind, capable of sustaining and perpetuating itself for what might seem like forever" (123). Buffalo remain for us today—every bit as much as for Roethke—the very embodiment of North America's environmental legacy.

Roethke also invokes the figure of the American Indian in a wilderness setting long associated with ecological integrity. In fact, the opening section of the sequence culminates with the names of two tribes, Oglala and Iroquois—an implicit recognition of the diversity of Indian cultures. This reference to Indian nations at the beginning of the sequence signals a link to North America's indigenous past and suggests how our relationship to landscape, place, and environmental history continues to shape national identity. In his essay "On 'Identity,'" Roethke contends that the crux of any quest for identity is the question of "what to do with our ancestors . . . both the literal or blood, and the spiritual ancestors" (*On the Poet* 23). "Roethke meant to address the central failing of the American pastoral after Whitman," Barillas observes, "its elision of Native American experience" (134).

Roethke had a deep-seated sympathy for Native Americans during the era of manifest destiny and westward expansion, which culminated tragically in war and the beginning of the reservation era. Late in his life he reportedly immersed himself in reading histories of the period and even contemplated undertaking another major poetic sequence predicated on a journey to visit the sites of American Indian betrayals and defeats, which he clearly viewed as a moral travesty and a national disgrace. Some critics have gone so far as to suggest that Roethke's figurative identification with the Iroquois in "The Longing" signals tacit approval of the tribe's activism in both the United States and Canada over land and treaty rights while he was writing during the 1950s (Kearful 4–5). Siding with the Iroquois at that point in time could be construed as endorsing tribal sovereignty, native land claims, and Indian resistance movements generally—in short, turning back the tide of colonialism by reversing the lingering effects of manifest destiny.

Roethke's evocation of the indigenous peoples of North America as a fundamental ecological frame of reference, much like that of William Stafford and Scott Russell Sanders, has led some critics to suggest that the "North American Sequence" represents an extension of the land ethic originally posited by Leopold, demonstrating a heightened sense of "ethical and aesthetic perspective on American cultural history and geography" (Barillas 132). Similarly, Balakian asserts that for Roethke "nature and culture are brought into the domain of the poet's identity" (143). Above all, "The Longing" establishes the deeper reason for setting out on the pilgrimage that the sequence as a whole recounts as "an aboriginal trailblazer, making a path through the raw wilderness" (139).

Geographically, the journey begins in the second poem of the sequence, at the confluence of a river with the salt water of the Atlantic Ocean: "Over the low, barnacled, elephant-colored rocks, / Come the first tide-ripples, moving, almost without sound, toward me, / Running along the narrow furrows of the shore, the rows of dead clam shells" (Roethke, *Collected Poems* 190). Several dialectical oppositions central to the sequence are introduced in "Meditation at Oyster River": fresh and salt water, sound and silence, motion and rest. In the final poem of the sequence, "The Rose," each of these is reprised in the elevated diction of mystical lyricism: "As if I swayed out on the wildest wave alive, / And yet was still" (205). This passage exemplifies what Malkoff characterizes as Roethke's penchant for "images of motion in stillness," revealing "essential oneness in apparent diversity" (204). In a landscape of utter flux, he finds a way to portray his own spiritual quest to embrace the natural world in all its grandeur and particularity, and with an immediacy that might be likened to that of Thoreau (Dougherty 194). Intertidal wetlands are exceptionally dynamic ecosystems in which riparian habitats intersect with the seashore. Such transitional zones become a touchstone for Roethke's poetics of place. He celebrates this verdant scene brimming with biodiversity, reciting a litany of life-forms on the coastline, from tiny fish and crabs on the beach to gulls, ravens, deer, snakes, sandpipers, hummingbirds, and kingfishers along the shore.

Roethke is repeatedly drawn to places such as confluences and estuaries—what Kalaidjian terms "a landscape of ecological transition stages" (146)—where merging currents and blurred boundaries provide apt metaphors for his metaphysical yearning and transcendental appreciation for the "spiritual significance of nature" (Barillas 111). Here at the river mouth, he is reminded of a pair of poignant impressions from childhood, both profound beginnings that some critics deem seasonal symbols of rebirth (Bowers; Malkoff): "the first trembling of a Michigan brook in April" and the tumult of breakup as ice shatters and careens downstream on the Tittabawassee, a river flowing through Saginaw (Roethke, *Collected Poems* 191). "The waters of Oyster River and the rivers of Michigan are thus linked," as Dougherty observes, "by spiritual associations of resistance and release" (191). This is an instance of the sequence returning repeatedly to childhood memories of nature in the Upper Midwest—what Dougherty terms "the other terminus of Roethke's spiritual geography" (190).

As Bowers notes, "a loss of the sense of time and the sensation that time is meaningless" often accompany mystical experiences such as the moments depicted in Roethke's meditations (164). Indeed, often the suggestion of communion with nature—whether deer, snake, hummingbird, or morning glory—leads critics to characterize his poetic vision as "inspired by his own native landscape and informed by the transcendentalists" (Barillas 109). Kalaidjian characterizes this stance in transcendental terms: "nature speaks to the poet through its indigenous plants and animals" (139). Instances of identification with nature recur, expressing a sense of mystical union: "And the spirit runs, intermittently, / In and out of the small waves, / Runs with the intrepid shorebirds" (Roethke, *Collected Poems* 192). At such moments it is as if the observed and the observer become one. As the poet himself explains, "the identity of some other being . . . brings a corresponding heightening and awareness of one's own self, *and*, even more mysteriously, in some instances, a feeling of oneness with the universe . . .

induced . . . by intensity in the seeing. To look at a thing so long that you are a part of it and it is a part of you" (*On the Poet* 25; ital. in orig.).

The next poem, "Journey to the Interior," establishes the central symbolism of the sequence: the physical pilgrimage across the continent as a metaphor for metaphysical reflection on the self in relation to nature, a concept presumably dating from Roethke's cross-country drive in 1950, though the poem was not actually composed until a decade and a half later (Barillas 130). According to Malkoff, "both the movement of the car *and* the barren highway are part of the protagonist's psyche" (180; ital. in orig.). Roethke had previously crossed the grasslands, Great Plains, and western mountain ranges only by train; the intensity of his encounter with these landscapes was undoubtedly heightened by actually driving across them.

Bowers posits that the trip itself became "Roethke's metaphor for the contemplative process" (162). Yet, as Balakian observes, "the act of passage and the poet's consciousness are inseparable—the shape of being and the contour of terrain inextricable" (142). Malkoff posits "a correspondence between the poem's outer landscape and the landscape of the protagonist's inner mind; Roethke, in a very important sense, *is* the North American continent, and his explorations of it in time and space continue his search for the self by retrieving the past and analyzing the present" (176; ital. in orig.). This equation is made more complex by its temporal element, the deftness with which Roethke maneuvers between immediate impressions of place and reminiscence, which in turn lends both emotional depth and meaning to the present. Images recalled from his childhood in the Upper Midwest, such as "the highway ribboning out in a straight thrust to the North, / To the sand dunes and fish flies," evoke for Roethke a sense of chilling antiquity and pathos: "The cemetery with two scrubby trees in the middle of the prairie, / The dead snakes and muskrats, the turtles gasping in the rubble" (*Collected Poems* 194).

Such dramatic triangulation of time frames recalls celebrated works by Eliot, of course, but also Whitman's direct address of future generations of readers as if speaking from beyond the grave, as well as Wordsworth's return to Tintern Abbey after an absence of several years, during which he experiences the familiar place in a new way enhanced by the passage of time. Dougherty points to both of these precursors—Wordsworth's "Lines Composed a Few Miles above Tintern Abbey" and Whitman's "Crossing Brooklyn Ferry"—to establish formal parallels with the genre of the "greater Romantic lyric" as advanced by critics such as Meyer Abrams.

Shifting time frames adds the possibility of multiple narrative strands as well as the resonance of accumulated experience. Wordsworth's poem begins by establishing just such a time lapse: "Five years have past; five summers, with the length / Of five long winters! and again I hear / These waters, rolling from their mountain-springs" (lines 1–3). Wordsworth describes having longed during the years since his last visit for the pastoral tranquility of environs surrounding the abbey, finding solace in the ecological memory of a "wild secluded scene" (6) as well as a hint of mystical union: "We see into the life of things . . . a motion and a spirit, that impels / All thinking things, all objects of thought, / And rolls through all things" (49; 100–102).

Though written in 1798, "Tintern Abbey" already arguably suggests what in the following century would become known as transcendental sensibilities: "to recognize / In nature and the language of the sense, / The anchor of my purest thoughts . . . and soul / Of all my moral being" (107–11). This poem exhibits several facets of the romantic perspective that Roethke is heir to in the "North American Sequence." Indeed, the younger Wordsworth might be likened to the younger Roethke, who proclaims in an essay written while a college student, "When I get alone under an open sky where man isn't too evident—then I'm tremendously exalted and a thousand vivid ideas and sweet visions flood my consciousness" (*On the Poet* 4). In the same undergraduate paper, he expresses admiration for the writing of literary naturalists Thoreau, John Muir, and John Burroughs for expressing "a true sense of sublimity of American scenery."

For Roethke, the vivid depiction of motoring precariously off-road reflects "the urge to charge full in the face of mortality" (Bowers 164) while also suggesting the psychological drama, emotional toll, and depth of introspection involved in "the long journey out of the self" (Roethke, *Collected Poems* 193). He describes driving wildly across utterly treacherous terrain in the face of "many detours, washed-out interrupted raw places / Where the shale slides dangerously / And the back wheels hang almost over the edge . . . watching for dangerous down-hill places, where the wheels whined beyond eighty" (193). The daredevil antics of a young man behind the wheel suggest metaphorically both the thrill and the peril of subsequent journeys and the "emotional volatility involved in the visionary experience . . . and the possibilities of annihilation [that] must be part of the poet's striving for transcendental experience" (Balakian 140–41).

Parini similarly characterizes Roethke's "long journey out of the self" as "at once tortuous and delightful . . . in spite of the terrors which seem necessarily to attend the Romantic on his quest for unity of being" (184). Roethke wrestles with aspects of mystical experience akin to Buddhist practices aimed at transcending the solitary self to embrace oneness with all of creation. For Roethke, this contemplative process requires resolving a paradox "at the very heart of mystical experience. . . . This reconciliation of opposites is . . . one of the characteristics of mystical union and an integral part of the sense of unity described by those who have experienced illumination" (Bowers 162–64). Albeit devoid of any dogma or trappings of church doctrine, Roethke's account of this pilgrimage in the "North American Sequence" is consonant with the expression of mystical experience in many religious traditions.

The poem then shifts time and place again, back to the epic journey west, arriving at landscapes of majestic tranquility and intimations of eternity:

> And the sun comes out of a blue cloud over the Tetons,
> While, farther away, the heat-lightning flashes.

I rise and fall in the slow sea of a grassy plain,
....
I rise and fall, and time folds
Into a long moment;
And I hear the lichen speak,
And the ivy advance with its white lizard feet. (Roethke, *Collected Poems* 194)

"Journey" closes with a tone of mystical lyricism, a celebrated quality of the sequence as a whole. Images of the natural world are once again so keenly observed as to yield revelation, ending with an exquisite sense of motion—both physical and metaphysical—coming to rest:

In a tower of wind, a tree idling in air,
Beyond my own echo,
Neither forward nor backward,
Unperplexed, in a place leading nowhere.
....
The spirit of wrath becomes the spirit of blessing,
And the dead begin from their dark to sing in my sleep. (195)

The next poem in the sequence, "The Long Waters," opens with an evocation of classical elements reminiscent of Eliot's "Four Quartets":

Where light is stone.
I return where fire has been,
To the charred edge of the sea
....
Where the fresh and salt waters meet,
....
A country of bays and inlets, and small streams flowing seaward.
    (Roethke, *Collected Poems* 196)

Roethke recognizes that this estuary presents an exceptionally diverse ecological profile, "a rich desolation of wind and water" (197). As Dougherty observes, "the Sequence traces a spiritual process that is founded on his recognition of the substantive presence of the land and sea, the birds and plants" (184). Roethke perceives the verdant wellspring of nature in such an ecosystem, as well as a sense of the ineffable, a "place of change and exchange, a territory . . . where life undergoes perpetual transmutation" (Balakian 137). The behavior of bees, worms, minnows, and butterflies—life-forms historically regarded as simple creatures in the classical great chain of being—remains for the poet deeply mysterious, beyond the reach of human reckoning. Moreover, he recognizes that certain species possess sensory powers of perception that exceed those of humans—and, in all probability, unique forms of cognition.

Roethke's evocation of place repeatedly incorporates not only vivid depictions of flora and fauna but also a keen appreciation of ecological niches and their complex organic webs. Even processes of decay seem palpable as a wave ripples toward "a tree lying flat, its crown half broken. . . . A vulnerable place, / Surrounded by sand, broken shells, the wreckage of water" (*Collected Poems* 197). Recurrent attention to water, and the motion of water, adds cohesion, as does the repetition of several other images throughout the sequence, including birds, flowers, stones, and above all trees, each of which might be conceived of as a kind of symbolic "leitmotiv" (Malkoff 190).

Roethke's ecological memory encompasses old-growth stands in Michigan as well as the recovering second-growth woodlands in the wake of logging. Indeed, these returning forests might be seen as a quintessential emblem of environmental history and trees themselves as the agent of ecological memory in its primary, biological sense. Moreover, given their sheer frequency—trees appear nearly twenty times throughout the sequence—these images repeatedly reveal natural processes reshaping the landscape. "The Long Waters" concludes by describing a kind of communion, contemplating the eternal in a place of flux and change: "I lose and find myself in the long waters; / I am gathered together once more; / I embrace the world" (Roethke, *Collected Poems* 198).

The fifth poem of the sequence, "The Far Field," lends its name to the book as a whole and begins with a deceptively simple yet arresting line: "I dream of journeys repeatedly" (Roethke, *Collected Poems* 199). Beyond reintroducing the trope of a journey, this poem calls attention to the dream world of the unconscious, a wellspring of symbol and mythos beyond the grasp of rational analysis. Dreams and memories were prime sources of inspiration for Roethke's poetry; consider the oft-cited dictum from his notebooks, "I am only what I remember." Parini concludes that "in Roethke's art the memory becomes, finally, a stage whereon the poem of the mind is enacted" (168).

Many of the landscapes depicted in vivid detail are in fact those that he had internalized, transmuted over time: the ecological memory that forms the core imagery in these poems. "At field's end," Roethke writes, "one learned of the eternal" in the face of an "ever-changing flower-dump, / Among the tin cans, tires, rusted pipes, broken machinery" (*Collected Poems* 199). Haunting images from childhood memories, again set in Michigan, are immediately juxtaposed with an archetypal sign of seasonal renewal, the return of migrating song birds—"to forget time and death" in the presence of warblers at the beginning of May— culminating in an incantation: "How they filled the oriole's elm, a twittering restless cloud, all one morning, / And I watched and watched till my eyes blurred from the bird shapes,— / Cape May, Blackburnian, Cerulean" (199). While expressing sentiments traditionally associated with romanticism, Roethke elevates them through sheer lyricism. As Kalaidjian observes, such "lyric narration allows Roethke to abstract meaning from detailed explorations of place" (123). Roethke effectively recovers his earliest ecological memories with remarkable immediacy and particularity, suggesting his deep-seated environmental sensibilities as well as a transcendental appreciation for the significance of nature.

Such intimate encounters with landscape, remembered for a life-time, reflect a visceral relation to nature. Roethke's ecological memory of the Upper Midwest provided grist for metaphysical musing until the very end of his life, as Balakian explains: "Memory becomes mytho-poetic in its ability to bring past and present into a moment of conver-gence, as boyhood experience and present reality are united" (131). Images preserved in memory, such as "the blue shine on freshly frozen snow, / The after-light upon ice-burdened pines" (Roethke, *Collected Poems* 201), are rendered with uncanny clarity that Parini construes in transcendental terms: "clarity of vision . . . heightening of percep-tion generally: a sense of true significance of the physical world [as] inner and outer realms come into Emersonian alignment" (163–64). Dougherty points to Emerson's notion of "the self-redeemed human soul, re-creating the world by seeing it," while recognizing Roethke's self-proclaimed "determination to move beyond the isolation of the Romantic self" (181).

The topography of fields and cliffs then gives way to the aqueous images of yet another confluence: "The river turns on itself, . . . I feel a weightless change, a moving forward / As of water quickening before a narrowing channel" (Roethke, *Collected Poems* 200). In such passag-es, Roethke emerges as a naturalist attuned to the dramatic processes shaping the landscape. A corresponding spiritual dimension arises as the poet interrogates his place in relation to nature, as well as the act of seeing itself, in a manner consistent with Eastern religions such as Taoism.

Roethke's mysticism, though not likely rooted in sacred Asian texts, reveals its depth and profundity in relation to such traditions. Philoso-phies expressed in "North American Sequence" often recall Taoist teachings with their emphasis on water, motion, and paradox—perhaps given their best-known expression by Lao Tzu, as in the following ex-cerpts from the *Tao Te Ching*:

> Man at his best, like water,
> Serves as he goes along:
> Like water he seeks his own level,
> The common level of life,
> Loves living close to the earth,
> Living clear down to his heart. (29)

Water itself, a central symbol in Taoist thought, proves especially conducive to suggesting the ineffable. In the "North American Sequence," Roethke employs water in its many incarnations for similar metaphysical purposes. As Kalaidjian notes, tidal estuaries, lakes, and rivers depicted in the sequence "represent interior landscapes," in contrast to grasslands and mountains, the "concrete locales of the American West and Midwest" (132).

The metaphysical symbolism of water, as Malkoff points out, stems from its being "neither exclusively beginning nor end, but both, since it travels a continuous cycle. . . . This is Roethke's most frequently used symbol of permanence in apparent change" (178). The *Tao Te Ching* states:

> The universe is deathless,
> Is deathless because, having no finite self,
> It stays infinite.
> A sound man by not advancing himself
> Stays the further ahead of himself,
> By not confining himself to himself
> Sustains himself outside himself:
> By never being an end in himself
> He endlessly becomes himself. (28)

Such passages bear an uncanny resemblance to Roethke's expression of his own mystical experience. This is not to suggest that his vision is in any way derivative, given its genesis in introspection, the product of organic processes of poetic perception. Yet he seems to be tapping the same ancient vein of spiritual inspiration. "The Far Field" ultimately arrives at a pinnacle of self-awareness, a recognition inextricably linked to perception of place:

> The lost self changes,
> Turning toward the sea,
> A sea-shape turning around—
> . . . .
> The pure serene memory of one man,—
> A ripple widening from a single stone
> Winding around the waters of the world.

For Roethke, the landscape ultimately provides a fundamental metaphor for perception itself: "My mind moves in more than one place, / In a country half-land, half-water" (*Collected Poems* 201).

The final poem, "The Rose," opens with an assertion central to the sequence as a whole: "There are those to whom place is unimportant, / But this place, where sea and fresh water meet, / Is important" (Roethke, *Collected Poems* 202). The metaphysical importance of such a place is found in the transcendental significance of the natural world: "the place where small streams empty into the ocean, where individual spirits return to be immersed in the depths of the One. It is in this place of flux that the speaker finds his symbol for the eternal" (Bowers 167). Again Roethke contemplates a confluence characterized by remarkable abundance and biodiversity, observing a multitude of birds as if in a single glance—hawks, eagles, seagulls, herons, towhees, kingfishers, scoters, geese, and whooping cranes. Indeed, the sequence as a whole names an impressive total of fifty-eight species and subspecies of birds alone (Kearful). "Was it here," Roethke writes, "I wore a crown of birds for a moment . . . ?" (*Collected Poems* 202).

On the Pacific headlands, having completed his transcontinental journey through memory and imagination, Roethke is struck by the resilience of a delicate flower, the wild rose flanked by driftwood, black sand, and surf. The rose offers a locus of stability amid the flux: "this rose, this rose in the sea-wind, / Stays, / Stays in its true place" (*Collected Poems* 203). Dougherty casts Roethke's depiction of this place in mystical yet decidedly ecological terms: "the rose itself is in a struggle, a state of tension with everything around it—its immediate botanical competitors, its seashore ecology, the sea-wind, the sea pine, the coastal madrona, the interpush of creek current and Pacific wave" (194–95). Taking on a sacramental cast, the sea-rose harkens back to childhood memories of Roethke's father's greenhouses in Michigan, immortalized in his second collection, *The Lost Son and Other Poems*, published in 1948. In the "North American Sequence," such recollections are markedly more expansive, both geographically and philosophically. Even this late in his writing life, recollections from his midwestern youth once again represent for the poet a repository of ecological memory.

In the penultimate section of "The Rose," the focus widens once again to encompass the continent and "returns to the motif of transcontinental journey" (Dougherty 201). As critic Cary Nelson concludes, the final two poems of the "North American Sequence" effectively "fold together all North American landscapes . . . filling 'The Rose' with diverse American places in the culmination of his sequence . . . reach[ing] out to gather all of Roethke's poetry together. We can hear in it echoes of images recurring throughout his career" (10–13). These images reflect the progression of seasons from the returning thrush and blooming lilacs of spring to the "ticking of snow around oil drums in the Dakotas, / The thin whine of telephone wires in the wind of a Michigan winter" (Roethke, *Collected Poems* 204).

Standing on a coastline in the Pacific Northwest, Roethke arrives at another level of self-knowing, made possible by a lifetime of journeys and a keen appreciation of place: "I came upon the true ease of myself / As if another man appeared out of the depths of my being, . . . Beyond becoming and perishing" (*Collected Poems* 205). Yet this sense of self is not separate from the natural world but entwined with it:

> I rejoiced in being what I was:
> In the lilac change, the white reptilian calm,
> In the bird beyond the bough, the single one
> With all the air to greet him as he flies. (205)

There is the sense of exaltation, as if the moment and this very place have been made sacred by the poet's spiritual renewal through union with unadulterated nature. His place in all of creation has been illuminated by a sense of transience and his own mortality, sharpening his perception of the many landscapes he had crossed. In the end, each has become a part of him.

Works Cited

Balakian, Peter. *Theodore Roethke's Far Fields: The Evolution of His Poetry*. Baton Rouge: Louisiana State UP, 1989. Print.

Barillas, William. *The Midwestern Pastoral: Place and Landscape in Literature of the American Heartland*. Athens: Ohio UP, 2006. Print.

Bowers, Neal. *Theodore Roethke: The Journey from I to Otherwise*. Columbia: U of Missouri P, 1982. Print.

Dougherty, James. "Theodore Roethke's 'North American Sequence': Religious Awakening in the West." *Literature and Belief* 21.1–2 (2001): 177–203. Print.

Franklin, Jon. *The Wolf in the Parlor: The Eternal Connection between Humans and Dogs*. New York: Holt, 2009. Print.

Kalaidjian, Walter. *Understanding Theodore Roethke*. Columbia: U of South Carolina P, 1987. Print.

Kearful, Frank. "Regions of the Self: Theodore Roethke's 'North American Sequence.'" *Modern American Poetry*. U of Illinois at Urbana-Champaign, n.d. Web. 20 Mar. 2012.

Knoeller, C. "'I'll Be an Indian': Rereading Roethke's North American Sequence." *Midwestern Miscellany* 36 (2008): 103–18. Print.

Lao Tzu. *The Way of Life According to Lao Tzu*. Trans. Witter Brynner. New York: Capricorn, 1962. Print.

Malkoff, Karl. *Theodore Roethke: An Introduction to the Poetry*. New York: Columbia UP, 1966. Print.

Manning, Richard. *Grassland: The History, Biology, Politics, and Promise of the American Prairie*. New York: Penguin, 1995. Print.

McHugh, Tom. *The Time of the Buffalo*. New York: Knopf, 1972. Print.

Nelson, Cary. "An Essay by Cary Nelson on 'North American Sequence.'" *Modern American Poetry*. U of Illinois at Urbana-Champaign, n.d. Web. 20 Mar. 2012.

Novak, Barbara. *Nature and Culture: American Landscape and Painting, 1825–1875*. New York: Oxford UP, 1980. Print.

Parini, Jay. *Theodore Roethke: An American Romantic*. Amherst: U of Massachusetts P, 1979. Print.

Roethke, Theodore. *Collected Poems*. New York: Doubleday, 1966. Print.

___. *On the Poet and His Craft: Selected Prose of Theodore Roethke*. Ed. Ralph J. Mills Jr. Seattle: U of Washington P, 1968. Print.

___. *Straw for the Fire: From the Notebooks of Theodore Roethke, 1943–1963*. Ed. David Wagoner. New York: Doubleday, 1972. Print.

Sanders, Scott Russell. *Staying Put: Making a Home in a Restless World*. Boston: Beacon, 1993. Print.

Seager, Allan. *The Glass House: The Life of Theodore Roethke*. New York: McGraw, 1968. Print.

Snodgrass, W. D. "The Last Poems of Theodore Roethke." *New York Review of Books* 8 Oct. 1964: 5–6. Print.

Staples, Hugh. "The Rose in the Sea-Wind: A Reading of Theodore Roethke's 'North American Sequence.'" *American Literature* 36.2 (1964): 189–203. Print.

Wordsworth, William. "Lines Composed a Few Miles above Tintern Abbey." *The Poems*. Ed. John Hayden. Vol. 1. London: Penguin, 1990. 357–62. Print.

"The Cost of This Distance": Robert Fanning's *American Prophet* and the Failure to Communicate

Caroline Maun

One would not automatically classify Robert Fanning's *American Prophet* (2009) as a literary work participating in the tradition of American road narratives. There are few highways mentioned, and there is little of the romance of American automobiles, with their emphasis on style, autonomy, and control. If anything, the Prophet is more of a plodding pilgrim than a speeding individualist, as likely to take a bus or a plane as a car. *American Prophet* is a book of narrative poems, and, as Ronald Primeau notes in his book *Romance of the Road: The Literature of the American Highway* (1996), many of the road narratives most familiar—and most thrilling—to readers are written in prose, not poetry. To tell a story about a journey, particularly one facilitated by machines, one needs to convey velocity. In fact, many American road narratives are about distance achieved over time, both physical and psychological, and poetry is generally not well suited to reproducing the phenomenological feeling of speed or the cinematic experience of seeing the world through a windshield. Lyric poetry is best suited for capturing a moment, an image, or a mood. Poetry often slows down our reading of language, placing it within line breaks, stanza forms, and other poetic devices that make us linger over the poet's word choices, and it is generally a contemplative form. In this regard, Fanning's poetry is no different from other contemplative poetry. It is well crafted, the syntax and line endings combining in complex ways to emphasize recurring concepts in his work, and he thereby weaves layers of meaning in individual poems and throughout the volume.

Nevertheless, the structure of *American Prophet* allows Fanning to create an American road narrative in poetry. The recurring character of the Prophet, and his relocation in poem after poem in a different situation and place but with the same, often thwarted goals, creates the experience of his journey. For Fanning, the road mythos emerges between the lines, in the gutters between the poems, in the turning of pages, and, by implication, between the places where the reader observes the Prophet. Additionally, each poem represents the Prophet's fresh, picaresque approach to tackling the issue of the failure of faith in the world; he behaves in each episode with a refreshed resolve that mirrors the emotional experience of an adventure or spiritual journey.

The Prophet's words tend to broaden the meaning of the events he witnesses, even as they are not heard or understood by others. He appears to be from another time, ironically juxtaposed with all the accoutrements and vestiges of early twenty-first-century America. Fanning asks, what could the meaning of a modern prophet in America be? Can modern people, plugged in to all of the available media and constantly exposed to advertising, hear a true prophet's messages through the din of ordinary life? The Prophet's attempts to be heard become more strident as he applies steady yet deliberate thought to how he can be amplified. Whatever the strategy, whenever he is moved to be oracular and deliver weighted messages, his words are drowned out.

The Prophet is a lost traveler. Incorporated into the logos of roadways are the ideas of direction, of efficacy, of being able to find one's way, and of moving forward with purpose, all with a destination in mind. Roads are mapped and marked for travelers. In addition to signage, much energy is spent in making directions electronically accessible in more and more convenient forms. To be lost in this matrix of carefully maintained instruction and information is to be profoundly, spiritually, perhaps determinedly lost. There is not much space for wandering in our culture; in some contexts, to stroll is often to become a vagrant, and to be aimless is to be at best vulnerable, at worst criminalized. Through hesitation, the Prophet often loses the initiative in communication. While he may not be lost in terms of location, he wavers in terms of volition or vocation. Nevertheless, over the course of the book, readers see his dogged resolve to try to do his work and some development in his approach, mission, and character.

American Prophet examines the state of faith in the postmodern world. Fanning begins with two epigraphs, one by poet Matthew Arnold and one by singer-songwriter Morrissey. There is a seeming gulf between these two writers, one a nineteenth-century educator, cultural critic, and poet, the other a lyricist and singer for the 1980s band the Smiths. Yet both identify a decline in faith. For Matthew Arnold, in his poem "Dover Beach," the sea of faith has retreated to reveal the "naked shingles of the world" (line 28), whereas for Morrissey, the "lazy sunbathers" cannot be disturbed by the news that a world war has resulted in the shelling deaths of children. These writers' messages meet on the shore between faith and nonbelief, compassion and indifference. Both writers find that the crisis of faith is centrally concerned with apathy; the Prophet struggles not only with a nineteenth-century mission to warn his people but also with the absence of engagement of his twenty-first-century audience. In the Prophet, readers do not see a proselytizer so much as an advocate. He advocates for people to open themselves up to an awareness of the finitude of life.

To name a book and a character "American Prophet" is to bring to the fore a number of concepts and traditions instantly. Fanning's book is about America. The poems are mostly located in the midwestern United States, but there are also poems set on the shores of oceans, particularly the Pacific. On American roads, particularly in the Midwest, travelers are between the spaces and places of the East, South, North, and West. Midwesterners are in the middle of various extremes, and the Prophet's journeying places him in the center of the country and occasionally at its margins. America is conceptualized by the Prophet as being enormous in scope, made up of one people—his people—to whom he must bring his message. Ironically, the Prophet is called but has no flock; he seems to lack the charisma to attract even a single attentive follower. The Prophet, who is otherwise unnamed, travels in and around his home near Detroit, Michigan, but he also roams across the country. The Midwest is a central platform from which he operates, but he ventures outside the Midwest to try his luck at being seen and heard in other iconic locations. The sequence focuses on the Prophet's role as a wanderer of the American landscape, a prophet who is almost always unable to deliver the urgent and often poetic messages that seem to arrive within and through him. At times lost, at times simply swept away by forces greater than he is, the Prophet—across many poems in a complex sequence—becomes a rich symbol of American dysphoria.

American Prophet is separated into five sections, with a frontispiece poem titled "The Prophet at the Dry Cleaners." The final poem of the volume, and the only one in the fifth section, harkens back to this opening poem and is titled "The Prophet Returns to the Dry Cleaners," signaling the spiritual growth and development that take place as the Prophet goes about his mission. Dry cleaning is a process of laundering clothes that are fragile or formal, made from materials that cannot be washed using cheaper and more accessible water-based laundry methods. In Fanning's opening poem, themes central to the book as a whole emerge from the consideration of this mundane, practical, social activity. The everyday nature of his task is striking, and there is humor in placing a prophet—somebody who is presumably somehow divinely chosen or exalted—in this dull storefront, picking up his alternate black suit. The bells on the shop's door announce his entrance, and readers will come to know that he often must rely on such external, weak, and voiceless means to draw attention to his presence.

In "The Prophet at the Dry Cleaners," the proprietress, an old woman who seems to be an integrated part of the world of "hissing machinery and steam," receives his receipt, described as a "pink slip" (lines 4–5). *Pink slip* is a common term for a document that terminates employment; in this case, though it is simply the means to identify his clothes among the many others, it retains its better-known connotation as well. Will the Prophet, the customer, fire the dry cleaner, or vice versa? Fanning's Prophet has the urge to ask a question weighted with meaning—"*Isn't our flesh a garment heavy enough . . .?*" (6; ital. and ellipsis in orig.)—but the thought is not voiced; the moment is lost.

The Prophet often has words come to him that are roughly appropriate to the situation he finds himself in but that, if spoken, would escalate an everyday situation into a contemplative or eschatological one. For the Prophet, all times, including picking up his laundry, are end times, and all activities, even the ordinary ones, put one's soul at stake.

Fanning draws attention to the conveyor that delivers the clothes in a stilted and haunted progression, loaded down with the garments of many other patrons. The clothing is described in ways that seem forensic—they are bagged and tagged, like bodies at a morgue—and suggest that the people who wear them are mannequins or scarecrows. The clothes for a moment become, through synecdoche, "the faceless men, women and children" in their "wedding gowns" and "Sunday best" (11–12). These garments have been cleaned of all that soils them, of all the evidence of human use and abuse. The Prophet cannot be heard over the roar of the machinery but is soon informed that the fabric of his suit has a hole worn in the breast. His armor has taken damage in a symbolic way that suggests his perpetual heartache over the fate of humanity.

Dressed nearly always in a nondescript black suit, even when it is inappropriately warm or formal, the Prophet assumes this costume as a part of his identity and a symbol of his strange, attenuated power. It allows him both to be separate from others and to blend, against his will, into the landscape. Through the poems, the reader understands that the Prophet is quasi-supernatural in his displacement. Due to a combination of faltering will, circumstances, and what might be cursed bad luck, the Prophet cannot be effective, if to be effective is to wake up his people. The black suit contributes to his invisibility as a cloak of irrelevance. For instance, in "The Prophet's Lament at Spring Break," he stands, fully suited, on a diving board, surrounded by all the familiar trappings of a pool party. He cannot shout over the bass from the radio and he cannot draw attention away from the sun-fueled rituals of mating continuing around him. For a moment he fights the nagging thought that "life *is* short, that maybe they're *right* / to splash and giggle, right to be blind / to the clouds of ash billowing from their burning / cities" (15–17; ital. in orig.). Like Morrissey's "lazy sunbathers," these "glazed citizens bobbing / on inflatable dinosaurs" are "beyond rescue" (22–23). They are, in their somnambulance, reduced to a primitive non-awareness of the larger picture and the grim demise of civilization. They are able to engage only in surfaces—skin, sun, and the satisfaction of animal appetites. The "glaring signs" (19) are completely lost on them in their hedonism, and the Prophet cannot make them see what he sees.

American Prophet succeeds in juxtaposing such surface effects with deeper portents in many poems. In "The Prophet at Elvisfest," he cannot miss the opportunity to be surrounded by the excessive nostalgia and consumerism of the throngs who idolize Elvis Presley. The audience is by definition already looking for something larger than they are, for a greater meaning, and for a charismatic leader—even in effigy. In a lull in the performances, the Prophet ascends the stage and attempts to speak, but the microphone falters. Tapping the microphone, he asks, *"How will we know the voice / of a true King among us?"* (27–28; ital. in orig.), but his voice does not carry. He does not understand that his audience is unprepared for rhetorical questions. In his isolation on the stage, he empathizes with the late Elvis, whose voice and presence also faltered at the end and who also faced a globe of strangers. Usurped by an actor portraying the Elvis of late excess, the Prophet can only silently witness this impersonator enacting the role of healing evangelist to a handicapped woman who is rapt for his attention. The audience members, much older and much changed from when they first encountered Elvis and fell under his spell, also become ironic simulacra of their own youth. They did not attend Elvisfest to become more enlightened; they came to momentarily recapture an escapist idolatry.

American Prophet engages with the Iraq War of the early twenty-first century in "The Prophet at the Matinee." The Prophet is taking in a midday movie, an apocalyptic adventure flick. Through deft word choice and the development of symbols, it is apparent that the moviegoers are modern incarnations of the dwellers in Plato's cave. In *The Republic*, written around 380 BCE, Plato develops an allegory of the cave in which the inhabitants are chained and the only reality they know is the flickering images on a blank wall. This manipulated light and shadow symbolizes for Plato their lack of education and their separation from authentic knowledge, symbolized by the sun. One of their numbers escapes and, able to see the sun for himself, fully realizes the lie they have lived within the cave. He is a philosopher. In Fanning's poem, those in the theater are called "the watchers," and they have come to see a film that recalls in ironic ways the "Mission Accomplished" speech given by President George W. Bush on May 1, 2003. The speech, which took place on the aircraft carrier USS *Abraham Lincoln*, was widely criticized as a premature declaration of victory in the Iraq War and an ill-advised photo opportunity on the part of the White House. In this afternoon film, the "wannabe hero / stands in his zippered flight jacket"; earlier on May 1, 2003, President Bush had been a passenger in a jet that landed on the carrier and had posed for media in a flight suit. He is "pledging with his crew to accomplish / the mission of saving Earth or at least America" (2–5).

Fanning stresses that those in government power with privilege will stay "safe" in fortified bunkers while the continent burns. But even within the context of this horror film, the drain is pulled from the narrative—it turns out to be a false alarm. An unknown and arbitrary force spares the earth from the galactic hailstorm. The Prophet and his people leave the theater, and he notes that "for now / the wide sky [is] clear and the world still here" (35–36). For a while, at least, his people contemplate apocalypse, and the film functions to generate a fleeting appreciation for the intact planet once the show is over. The film achieves for a moment what the Prophet attempts with every contact.

War continues to be the focus in "The Prophet at the Superstore." The Prophet is searching for a night-light, a small gesture toward comfort and security, but the scale of the enormous store dwarfs him and he is lost in the aisles. Hearing sirens and explosions, he goes in search of the problem, knowing "deep in his heart there's a war" (13). Finally, in the electronics department, he sees his people entranced by a wall of television sets broadcasting the iconic night-warfare scenes emblematic of the US engagements with Iraq in the 1990s and 2000s. This warfare is translated on the screen as missile tracers in a green screen produced by night-vision technology—what Fanning describes as a "laser-guided fireworks display" (22). These watchers are also surrounded by sound, enmeshed in the consumer environment; they are watching the real thing instead of a blockbuster matinee, but they function in the same way. Bush appears again to reassure America: "many-faced, his mugs fill this wall of televisions—looming, rouged and ruddy" (35–36). The Prophet attempts to seize the moment to communicate to his people, again described as "the watchers":

> My people, the time
> is upon us! Here we stand face to face
> with the mirrored eye of the fly
> who leads us blindly into the Valley of Death. (38–41)

He is drowned out by the reminder from the public-address system that shoppers should make their final purchases because the store will close in five minutes. The watchers obediently move toward the registers, "pulled by heavy carts" (49). They cannot be mobilized or distracted from their consumerism even while bombs are flying, even when their country has just entered a war.

The Prophet is not completely immune to being swept up in the lures of consumerism or hedonism; he simply cultivates a larger perspective to create distance between himself and his society. In "The Prophet at the Casino," he is in Atlantic City (the road or journey between New Jersey and Michigan implied), where he becomes entranced by the system of risk and reward in gambling. Fanning emphasizes the tawdriness of the buildings, the second-run entertainment, and the mindless repetition of the activities in the casino. It is a self-contained world, another iteration of Plato's cave. Once within, there is no escaping the cameras, which turn the elaborate network of gilded hallways into a surveillance system. The casino is described as a false heaven, but the Prophet associates it with the Death Star of the *Star Wars* science-fiction films. The Death Star was an advanced weapon in the *Star Wars* mythology, capable of doing the unthinkable, easily—it could destroy a planet with the push of a button.

In a lyrical turn in the poem, the Prophet likens the casino to a spider's web, thinking "how sticky intricate / and sweet death tastes here at the slot machine" (24–25). Lured in, he tries it, wins, and a siren proclaims him simultaneously a winner and a criminal. Without pausing, he tries blackjack at a nearby table and loses his winnings, becoming again "a nobody in his thrift / store suit" (35–36). He is able to see that the casino is feeding itself on the customers, who are willing, glassy-eyed victims of this terrible, bewitching circuit. Rather than "play Christ in the temple," he "cuts his losses and turns—flushed straight down / the innards toward the exit" (47–48). He notes the suicide-prevention fences on the rooftop parking lot and resolves to find from now on "what he might save" (55). He recognizes the brutal contract the casino holds with its patrons—it promises fun, or at least adrenaline, while the money lasts, but in the end, once the patrons are broke, they become excrement to be expelled. The Prophet's absolutism can be limiting, but it also provides him with a perspective that illuminates the very real risks behind the alluring façade.

In the second section of *American Prophet*, the narrative poems more straightforwardly engage the road—the road that is forged by movement ahead, no matter what the means of locomotion. In "The Prophet in Flight," the Prophet travels eastward on a red-eye flight toward Detroit, his home base. As is the case in so many poems in this volume, the work engages vision, light, perspective, and mirage. The perspective from the plane affords a different view of the roads below. Rather than the typical earthbound phenomenological understanding of the highways as linear, he is able to see glittering evidence from the lights below of the grid or network that all of the highways, roads, and interstates represent. The freeway lights become "giant pulsing nets spread to defy the gulfs of darkness" (14).

While in "The Prophet at the Superstore" the Prophet shopped for a night-light, revealing his own very human need for security from the dark, in this poem it appears to the Prophet, from high above, that one of the great accomplishments of mankind is this "blockade" of light, a barricade against the dark and all it portends of a return to primitive existence. Light equals civilization in this insight. The Prophet moves forward to address the passengers but is disappointed to find they are deep in sleep, or wearing headphones, watching the in-flight movie. Even at this distance above the earth, the watchers are still tethered to their wires and filling their attention with manufactured images and sounds. He wants to point out to them so they might appreciate— aesthetically, religiously—the minor miracle that is Detroit, below, lit up as they descend, but ironically, he loses sight of the city, and he loses confidence as well. *Those of you on the south side of the plane will now see / Detroit shining and see in its rising light a sign*" (30–31; ital. in orig.). Much of the national popular press about the city of Detroit in the 2000s has been speculative regarding whether it is in permanent and bottomless decline or whether it is rising again in a twenty-first-century renaissance. Fanning engages with the very real issue of Detroit's darkened public light system, which affects many neighborhoods in the city. The Prophet is not able to compete with the pilot's voice as it soothes the passengers and instructs them to prepare for landing.

The next poem in the sequence, "The Prophet in the Blackout," takes place the day after this airline flight within the loose timeline suggested by the poems. In this poem, through various details, Fanning places the reader the Northeast blackout of 2003. The blackout, which affected a wide swath of the Northeast, Midwest, and Canada, broadly interrupted communications and commerce. Occurring in the heat of the summer, it left many people extremely uncomfortable. Although widespread riots did not take place, there were expectations that unrest might follow. In the world of Fanning's poem, the Prophet is researching Cherokee spirituality on the Internet, where the decrees he reads sound a lot like the pronouncements he often makes in tone and rhetoric. The lights and his screen go dark, and just beneath that he senses the panic of his neighbors as they try to bring the power back on.

The Prophet sits in a locked room, indicating again his own desire for security and assessment of the safety of his situation. He hears that the blackout could have originated at the Niagara-Mohawk Power Corporation, further overlaying this poem about light, civilization, darkness, and the vulnerability of contemporary life with a secondary meaning: the Native American civilization that was displaced in settlement and that was free of the dependence on artificial light and power grids. The Prophet realizes that "whether an act of God or man, / this is a blazing sign" (31–32). He leaves his apartment to see how others are doing. He sees quiet looters of a nearby grocery store and comes upon a ragged band of revelers around a campfire, "joking about The End / of the World" (50–51). For the Prophet, the end of the world is not a joke, and he recognizes that even though they are feigning at partying, there is still a very real fear they are trying to dull with liquor. He wants to tell them not to dull their senses—they will need their wits to navigate this situation, particularly if the lights do not come back on. The Prophet is ever in a posture of readiness, able to see the dark possibility of each situation. The next day, after the power has returned and people are lulled back into that comfortable slumber as everything is back to normal, the Prophet returns to the campsite, where a whittled branch thrust into the ground becomes an impromptu sundial, again suggesting that only the thinnest of gauze lies between civilized and primitive existences.

In "The Prophet and the Summer Fair," for the first time in the volume, the Prophet appears to be heard by another person. Searching again for an audience, he makes his way to a community fair, imagining that he can fly like a bird to the gathering to deliver his message.

He observes the egg-and-spoon race under way, where all the world's disappointments seem to be brought down to a child's miniature scale: the children are doomed to crack most of the eggs, and their morale and emotions shatter with each predictable accident. The Prophet tries to tell them, *"Children, it will be like this for you / in the breaking days, carrying the fragile world / of your birth through the distance and wind* (25–27; ital. in orig.), but he is unheard over the sound of the river that lies between him and the gathering and the commotion over the winner. One child who hears him "stands in the field of shattered eggs" and seems to take heed of the warning, guarding the next egg "with his life" (35). The episode is described in lyrical language that suggests that not only has the Prophet had an effect on this child but there is a chance the child will carry this message throughout his life. The message is about perspective and about being receptive to the symbolism of everyday life.

In the mode of a pilgrim, the Prophet travels in "The Prophet at the Barn Looking for the Face of God" to a Midwestern farm, where, through a trick of the light and the chance configuration of wood, hay, and hardware, a face can be discerned by the faithful. The face draws a nightly crowd; at dusk, the farmer flips on lights that will make the image emerge for some who work very hard to see it. The Prophet is drawn to these spectacles of idolatry, with their uncritical and voracious crowds, and the people gathered resemble a mindless herd similar to that at the Elvisfest. There is an improbable link between the collection of surfaces that makes up the barn and a manifestation of the divine, shown by how difficult it is for some viewers to put the pieces together. The crowd, as one, "moves / a little right" and "a little left, / depending on the vantage point of whomever / claims the best view" (17–19). The Prophet tries to instruct those gathered, but a thunderstorm drives most of them inside. Those who see the image are reduced to "writhe and moan now in pools of mud, / baptized by rain, a herd of kneeling swine" (41–42). Fanning emphasizes that their prostration before this random assemblage of surfaces that they take, with great imaginative labor, as a holy sign robs them of their humanity and dignity.

The Prophet confronts the vacuity of early twenty-first-century social rituals, consumerism, and community spaces. His people have forgotten what is important, and his desire to remind them fuels his work and quest. He wishes to deliver his warnings against the excesses, extremes, and emptiness he witnesses; most of all, he wishes to disrupt the mindless fog most people live in most of the time. His voice, however, is often muted by the contingencies of the journey itself. While much American road literature has celebrated the open spaces of the continent, both geographically and ideologically, *American Prophet* tends to emphasize the claustrophobia and gridlock of the road mythos. In "The Prophet in Traffic," he finds himself in a traffic jam and at first thinks it must be a large funeral. Instead, the procession is going toward the stadium, even though it is too late for a football game. Herded along to the gates, the Prophet is swept in with the others and forced to park. He sees a busload of men dressed in black suits, like he is, and he grows more confused. He eventually realizes that it is a ticket-only revival; the crowds are gathering to hear a different sort of preacher, a wealthy one with a large following and a high pulpit.

The loneliness of the Prophet's mission and his resolve to stay the course emerge in many of the poems. Often, he falters not only in communication but in the path, and these glimpses into his wavering are what give the book its surprise and its humanity. The Prophet is the sort of figure people might turn away from, but readers cannot help but admire and respect his determination. He stumbles into pleasure almost against his will, as in "The Prophet Returns Home," where he thinks about the beauty of the people who can barely see him and who cannot hear him, with even his cat seeking shelter under the couch. He falls into his own image-flickering cave, happy to be absorbed in an episode of the science-fiction television series *Star Trek: Deep Space Nine*. The show is one of many programs that extend the American road mythos, with its emphasis on exploration, to the imagined frontier of outer space, and the Prophet is particularly moved by an episode he has seen repeatedly in which a character learns that he himself is a prophet of sorts, "tortured by memory, caught between worlds" (33). Unfettered by human ties of family or friendships, the Prophet is strikingly moved by this story of another reluctant prophet.

The third section of *American Prophet* takes inspiration from the industrial, urban, and suburban landscapes of the Detroit metro area. Fanning explores industrial landscapes, a landfill, and an abandoned railroad terminal. In "The Prophet at the Industrial Complex," his voice falls helplessly on the concrete and metal surfaces of a still-active manufacturing site, one that has obliterated the natural environment with its vast footprint. He shouts, "*I won't be made extinct by your machines!*" but his voice is taken from him by the roar and rush of large spinning fans. He is made diminutive by the lenses of security cameras. In "The Prophet on the Mountain," he seeks higher ground, but instead of the mountain he wishes for, he ascends only a large hill, where he hopes that he might rise high enough to attract an audience. The face of the hill is nondescript, but when he reaches the crest, he recognizes that he is at the top of a vast garbage heap. Gulls are associated with the sea for him, but they have turned scavengers and opportunists in the landfill. The freeway flows nearby through the suburbs, although the city is a "gutted core" (42).

Fanning regards the freeway, the suburbs, and the landfill as one system implicated in the decimation of the city. Similarly, Michigan Central Station figures prominently in "The Prophet at the Train Station." Operational from 1913 to 1988, the station, with its broken windows and graffiti, now stands as an internationally recognized icon for the city's deterioration. Perhaps the most photographed building in Michigan, it has become an unmistakable emblem for early twenty-first-century Detroit. On his way in, the Prophet yells a line from Pink Floyd's song "Comfortably Numb" and imagines that the site holds the energy of all of the passengers who came through it in the past. He imagines immigrants and soldiers as travelers arriving, linking their destinations and their destinies. If that was true for those pilgrims in the past—that the station contributed to their ideas about themselves and how they understood their relation to the country—the implication is that the train station continues to speak to the nation's destiny, albeit in a more macabre fashion. Its abandonment and famous disrepair communicate in shorthand a larger, more severe crisis of neglect. The Prophet is attuned to many of the ironies that such an institution in a state of wreckage represents.

Wanting to escape the city, the Prophet walks along the roadside toward the forest. In "The Prophet Enters the Wilderness," he falls down an embankment; although sore, he is not terribly hurt. Like Henry David Thoreau, he went to the woods to find "solace, some cave or quiet core, a place / to listen to the wind, the crackle of his inner fire" (14–15). He is in retreat for three days, near-fasting. Instead of hearing his inner fire, he is forced to extinguish a fire set by a cigarette thrown from a passing pickup truck. Thinking he is far removed from society, he is startled to learn that he is near a road that he did not previously see. There does not seem to be any escape or retreat from the network of roads and the human ties that they represent. In trying to retreat from the social, the Prophet becomes an accidental hero when he stops the nascent forest fire. In the last poem of the section, "The Prophet's Third Dream," the Prophet stands before a rapt audience waiting for him, and above them he sees a vision of ten million dead birds hung from their necks. His hunger for an audience combines with his vision of apocalyptic death, and even in this imaginary world he is mute.

In the fourth section of *American Prophet*, the Prophet escalates the stakes and seeks greater amplification. In "The Prophet and the Wave of Adoration," he shops for wing-tip shoes, perhaps because he believes he needs an image upgrade, but also simply to try to address his ennui. He attempts to communicate with the clerk, but once again his register is inappropriate and his rhetoric overblown. He asks, *"What will be the cost of this distance / between us in the end,"* referring to the gulf between what he can afford and what a new pair of shoes costs. In

"The Prophet's New Voice," we see the Prophet shopping again, this time for a megaphone. Tired of hearing his natural voice die in the air, he has decided to embrace technology. Later, in "The Prophet at the Terminal Opening," he uses the megaphone to sing to commuters in a fashion similar to the celebrated violinist Joshua Bell, who, on January 17, 2007, was part of an experiment done for an article published in the *Washington Post*: Bell played, incognito, in Washington, DC's L'Enfant Plaza, where security cameras recorded the reactions of more than a thousand pedestrians who passed him. This exercise was conducted as a way to speculate about "the moral mathematics of the moment" (Weingarten), examining whether or not an ordinary commuter, pressed for time on the way to his or her job, might pause even for a moment to listen to exquisite music played live—a performance that many, under other circumstances, would pay hundreds of dollars to witness in a concert hall. The results of the experiment were predictably disappointing. Bell was unable to gather any sustained audience and fared no better than most buskers. The Prophet also finds that his performance is mostly for the birds, as he is largely unheeded by the passing throng.

The poems that follow escalate the Prophet's calling and suggest his increasing desperation. He climbs a billboard at great risk to himself in "The Prophet and the Jaws of Heaven." He ascends a slippery ladder to a large advertisement for toothpaste, where he is dwarfed by the smiling teeth behind him and threatened by sharp icicles above him. He is buffeted by a traffic helicopter that delivers the redundant information to his audience that those below are in a jam. The Prophet's attempt to find an audience fails again, even as he ascends whatever heights he can find.

In an understated display of despair and a poignant demonstration of his isolation, the Prophet becomes a would-be bridegroom in "The Prophet and the Bride of Hope." On a winter day, he spends hours staring at a mannequin bride and imagines himself as a child, at an earlier stage of innocence, understanding, and primal language. He seems delusional, but he also recognizes that there was a time before his obsessive quest when he was able to enjoy a present moment without the constant pressure of what philosopher Jean Baudrillard might call an expectation of a "future catastrophe." In his book *America* (1986), Baudrillard states that he came to the United States because he "sought the finished form of the future catastrophe of the social in geology, in that upturning of depth that can be seen in the striated spaces, the reliefs of salt and stone" (5). Baudrillard is, above all, moved by the ways in which the spaces of America organize to perform an apocalyptic experience of travel and what that landscape does to shape the imaginations and social interactions of Americans. The Prophet's temporary retreat into an illuminated childhood, before language, pronouncements, or the permanently present fear of the end of the world, is a significant turning point in his healing.

Section 4 ends with "The Prophet's Final Dream," which further indicates that the Prophet's desperate quest is nearing its logical end. Inspired by Denise Whitebread Fanning's 2003 art installation titled "What Should We Do?"—a picture of which illustrates the cover of Fanning's first volume of poetry, *The Seed Thieves* (2006)—Fanning's poetry reproduces the image of the papier-mâché figures gathered around dying, fluttering birds. The original installation mutely invited audience members to join the frozen figures in their ethical and spiritual conundrum; the figures of the exhibit and the gathered audience all became witnesses as the mechanical birds flopped in their simulated death throes. In the dream, the Prophet still hopes his frozen audience will listen to him, but the tone of his statements has changed from an exhortation about end times to a tender blessing. Recognizing how fragile they are, he modulates his tone. For the first time, the Prophet forgives his people for their failure to attend sufficiently.

This strongly constructed volume ends with a poem that stands alone in its own section, "The Prophet Returns to the Dry Cleaners." Carrying forward the themes that began the book, the Prophet is still tempted to make a grandiose pronouncement, but he instead speaks appropriately to the social situation. He arrives by bus, noting many individuals he sees on his way. Instead of the old woman at the dry cleaner's, he is served by a young girl, but somehow she is both herself and the older woman at the beginning of the book. She lifts his suit "like a superhero's cape or broken wing," asking how he would like it pressed (27). Rather than escalating this episode by saying something heavy and portentous, he responds simply that he would like the suit pressed "*lightly*" (30; ital. in orig.). By saying so, the Prophet reiterates of one of the major motifs of the book: that of light, visual and spiritual. There is also a self-awareness in the Prophet that he has been too spiritually and verbally heavy and has lost every opportunity to actually talk with other human beings. Early in the book, during spring break, he fought back the notion that his people might be appropriately enjoying the moment in pleasure. Without retreating from any of the true excesses and spiritual deserts he has observed, be they commercial, social, or political, he nevertheless recognizes that human beings are by virtue of their finitude entitled to enjoy their lives. There are some things, like the end of the world, that we cannot worry about all the time. But the book nevertheless maintains that there are many things we can worry about but do not, to the detriment of the quality of our lives and society.

Throughout *American Prophet*, the Prophet's travels become the occasion of the failure of communication, demonstrating the difficult imperative to recapture meaning. Through the Prophet's road travel, air travel, and imagined space travel, the traveling of the imagination, and his personal journey, *American Prophet* extends and complicates the road narrative in American literature. For the Prophet, the cost of the distance between him and his people is everything; his sanity, his mission, and his civilization are at stake. By creating a picaresque figure who develops a deepened empathy for his fellow human beings, Fanning has revealed an unexpected journey to the Prophet's own salvation.

Works Cited

Arnold, Matthew. "Dover Beach." *New Poems.* Boston: Ticknor, 1867. 95–96. Print.

Baudrillard, Jean. *America.* London: Verso, 1988. Print.

Fanning, Robert. *American Prophet: Poems.* Detroit: Marick, 2009. Print.

___. *The Seed Thieves.* Detroit: Marick, 2006. Print.

Morrissey, Stephen Patrick. "The Lazy Sunbathers." *Vauxhall and I.* Sire, 1994. CD.

Pink Floyd. "Comfortably Numb." *The Wall.* Harvest/EMI, 1979. CD.

Plato. *The Republic.* Trans. Allan Bloom. New York: Basic, 1968. Print.

Primeau, Ronald. *Romance of the Road: The Literature of the American Highway.* Bowling Green: Bowling Green State U Popular P, 1996. Print.

Weingarten, Gene. "Pearls before Breakfast: Can One of the Nation's Great Musicians Cut through the Fog of a DC Rush Hour? Let's Find Out." *Washington Post* 8 Apr. 2007: W10. Print.

Journeying Down Freedom Road: The Underground Railroad and the Narrative of Travel _____

Maureen N. Eke

> "I have never approved of the very public manner in which some of our western friends have conducted what they call the **underground railroad**, but which I think, by their own declarations, had been made most emphatically the **upperground railroad**."
>
> (Frederick Douglass, *Narrative of the Life of Frederick Douglass* 440)

Introduction: Framing a Black Road Narrative Convention

In her discussion of the American "road story," Katie Mills returns to her childhood, when she imagined the road on which her mother, a traveling salesperson, journeyed as "a magical place where highly usual people were lucky enough to go" (xi). Mills reads her mother's travels—her entrances and exits from the road or their house—as indicative of freedom, made possible by an automobile. Through her discussion of the movie *Thelma and Louise* (1991), Mills reads road stories as narratives of "transformation" (xii). For Mills, the road represents the site of possibilities—the encounter with magic (or the unexpected, the never-before experienced), the discovery or attainment of freedom, and the experience of change. Although Mills locates her American road narrative as a post–World War II phenomenon, the features of the narrative connect the road literature and its antecedent: the classical quest of adventure-narrative tradition.

Unlike Mills, who traces the American road narrative through the post–World War II beat generation, Ronald Primeau provides an expansive definition that sees the road narrative as a genre that includes the "pilgrimage, quest romance, *Bildungsroman*, and the picaresque" (ix). Primeau's definition recognizes the archetypal nature of road narratives and allows for the consideration of narratives that may not comfortably sit within a contemporary road narrative convention. Thus, according to Primeau, the American road narrative taps into an archetypal story about journeys of self-discovery, reinvention, and freedom. Clearly, such journeys may be spatial, and therefore external (across geographical space), or they may be internal (spiritual and psychological). Primeau's definition and Mills's narrative of transformation provide space for including the Underground Railroad stories in the American road-story canon. This essay attempts to address the following questions: How does the Underground Railroad figure into American road literature? What is the nature of the quest—flight from home—for a protagonist of the Underground Railroad?

African and African American oral and literary traditions are replete with stories of individuals or protagonists who leave their societies in search of something, generally new selves, and who undertake journeys or quests, sometimes involuntarily. In the case of fugitive blacks, the journey was simultaneously voluntary and involuntary. These flights were voluntary because most of the fugitives opted to flee toward freedom rather than remain under the chains of slavery. At the same time, the departures were involuntary, since their status or condition forced the subjects of these stories to leave their families and communities and enter the unknown world. The life of these fugitives was one of loneliness and distrust, as Douglass informs us, because he "saw in white man an enemy, and in almost every colored man cause for distrust" (443).[1] The journey through the Underground Railroad was not glorious, nor was it the romanticized passage that lingers in the American imagination. In his book *Bound for Canaan* (2005), Fergus M. Bordewich recounts a story which George DeBaptiste, a freed slave who was the leader of the Underground Railroad in Madison, Indiana, described his work. DeBaptiste's description of this process to "a Detroit newspaper in 1870, a few years before he died" (Bordewich 3), provides readers with a glimpse of the dangerous work of the Underground Railroad.

In the traditional quest narrative, a protagonist leaves home in search of adventure, promising to return, but the protagonists of the Underground Railroad stories did not leave places they could comfortably call home. The separation from community or home was not because the subjects desired the romance of the road rather than the security of a stable home. Rather, such homes, if the slave plantations could be described as such, were sites of dehumanization and traumatization. Slaves fled under the threat of death, or at least physical and psychological anguish. Moreover, flight from such a place was permanent; there was no promise of a return, except perhaps to rescue family members left behind. It was only upon leaving such a place that a slave could claim autonomy or even a sense of self through the attainment of freedom. This emergence of an autonomous self is evident in the slave narrative that sometimes encloses the story of the Underground Railroad. For instance, escaped slaves such as William Wells Brown, Ellen and William Craft, Frederick Douglass, and Harriet Jacobs claimed an authorizing self only after their escape from slavery, through the slave narratives that detail their experiences.

Within the African American literary tradition, the slave narrative as a story about flight provides a framework for examining the Underground Railroad as a narrative of the road. The slave narrative, which represents the psychological, spiritual, and spatial journey of many captive blacks from slavery to freedom, serves as a trope for exploring the Underground Railroad experience as an example of the American road narrative because the stories of slavery sometimes contain discussions of the experiences of the fugitive before attaining freedom, and the Underground Railroad was a conduit through which many attained that freedom.

In many ways, the Underground Railroad occupies an interstitial location between life under slavery and the vision or promise of freedom. Because the slave narrative provides strong examples of some of the experiences of fugitives as they seek freedom, this paper will occasionally refer to some slave narratives to underscore features of the road journey as they relate to the Underground Railroad. Indeed, the stories of the Underground Railroad, like those of the slave narratives, include daring feats, disguises, and strategies that protagonists deployed. Examples often include the story of Henry "Box" Brown, who had himself boxed and shipped to Philadelphia. Another is Ellen Craft, who disguised herself as a white man while her husband posed as her servant so that both could escape to freedom.

The stories of the Underground Railroad also include the voices of those who assisted the fugitives in their escape and served as guides, conductors, and station masters. These stories of flight make it possible for the protagonists (here real people) to narrate their experiences of self-realization through a quest for freedom, the various challenges they encountered, and the examination of the self. An examination of the Underground Railroad as a road narrative can combine primary source materials—such as the records, letters, and autobiographies of slaves and activists, including William Still, Levi Coffin, and Laura Haviland—and historical, cultural, mythological, and archetypal criticism. Joseph Campbell's archetypal study of the hero's journey is also useful.

The American Midwest played an important role in the journey of slaves from captivity to freedom. Ohio and Michigan were central in this road journey. Fugitives fleeing northward often headed to Ohio as the entry point into regions where they would be free. Michigan served as home to many free blacks, also becoming a prominent site of Underground Railroad activity and a refuge for blacks fleeing to Canada. Consequently, several Michigan cities, including Adrian, Ann Arbor, Detroit, Kalamazoo, and Marshall, would figure as important sites of antislavery activities, and several Michigan residents would become figures of the Underground Railroad.[2] Notable among these Michigan citizens are Laura S. Haviland and George DeBaptiste. Indiana, Wisconsin, and Illinois also contributed to the Underground Railroad story. The midwestern states became important because they joined the nation as free (that is, nonslaveholding) states. Consequently, fugitive blacks used them as safe havens from slavery. These states would eventually become sites for the contestation of freedom for blacks, especially after the passage of the Fugitive Slave Acts of 1793 and 1850, which did not protect the rights of fugitive blacks nationally. Thus, even when fugitives fled to free states, they could still be recaptured and returned to the southern slaveholding states. The fate of Seth Concklin in Indiana is an example.

Indeed, as Bordewich notes, "nowhere in the Northern 'free states' was freedom for African Americans fully guaranteed or protected." He adds, "In 1840, more than ninety percent of Northern free blacks lived in states that either partially or completely disenfranchised them" (245). For instance, Ohio punished the harboring of fugitive blacks and required that free blacks carry certificates of manumission. In Illinois, Ohio, Indiana, and Iowa, blacks could not testify in cases involving whites (245). If free blacks were not truly free, then fugitive blacks fared much worse. Consequently, in the face of continued threat to their freedom, enslaved blacks and those who supported their quest for autonomy had to use alternative methods to permanently secure freedom. The Underground Railroad served that purpose.

Although many communities claim some historical role in the story of the Underground Railroad, it was not a formally organized system of railroads or routes but "an informal constantly changing network of routes over which fugitive slaves were passed along, often at night, from Border and Southern states to Canada or to a safe city in the North" (Hendrick and Hendrick 3). George and Willene Hendrick acknowledge that "runaway slaves were helped in an organized way before 1830, but there was no widely recognized name for this activity" (3).[3] For Albert Bushnell Hart, the Underground Railroad "was simply a form of combined defiance of national laws, on the ground that those laws were unjust and oppressive" (Siebert viii). Hart's definition, therefore, sees the Underground Railroad as a rights movement and an attempt to challenge both the legitimacy of slavery and the system of owning human beings as property. Hart also notes that, as a form of defiance, the Underground Railroad "had the excitement of piracy, the secrecy of burglary, and the daring on insurrection" (ix). Indeed, as Frederick Douglass stated, a fugitive slave was a thief who had stolen himself (as property) from his master. Certainly the number of slave uprising in many Southern communities even before the American Revolution is clear indication that enslaved Africans were fighting to liberate themselves upon their arrival in the new world.[4] The Underground Railroad was only one aspect of that struggle, and it had to be concealed.

As a result, the history of the Underground Railroad is shrouded in mystery, and the date of its actual inception is unclear. Bordewich states that "fascination with the Underground Railroad manifests itself most vividly in a persistent hunt for tunnels through which fugitive slaves were allegedly spirited to freedom" (xv). Other forms of fascination relate to the presence of trapdoors, attics, hidden closets, nooks, rooms, or barns in old homes that may have provided hideouts for fugitives. Furthermore, Bordewich suggests that "because the Underground Railroad was secretive, and because much of its story has been forgotten, or deliberately suppressed, its memory has sheered away into myth and legend like no other piece of our history" (4). But, he emphasizes, "the essential nature of the Underground Railroad lay in the character and motivation of the people who made it work, not in bricks and mortar" (xv). Indeed, the Underground Railroad represents an early form of a multiethnic collaborative resistance against injustice in the United States. As such, Bordewich is correct in describing it as America's "first civil rights movement," for the movement brought together fugitive and freed blacks as well as whites whose singular objective was to end slavery.

This collaboration would bear fruit in the number of fugitive blacks who attained freedom with the help of people involved in the Underground Railroad. According to George and Willene Hendrick, "it has been estimated that from 1830 to 1860, 9,000 escapees passed through Philadelphia; Levi Coffin is said to have helped about 3,000. Rev.

Rankin assisted about 2,000, but some of these passed through the Coffin station" (6). Others were rescued by Harriet Tubman and "hundreds of little-known people, black and white," who "did not publicize their work" (6). Clearly, the actual number of fugitive blacks who made it to Canada by the time of the Civil War is uncertain. The Hendricks suggest "between 20,000 and 75,000" (6). This lack of certainty again underscores the secretive nature of the Underground Railroad and its activities, especially because those involved were violating both federal and state laws.

Space Clearing: The Record's Conundrum

Writing about the Underground Railroad raises the challenge of distinguishing between fact, fiction, and a romanticized narrative of the Underground Railroad that many Americans hold. This tension between the historical reality of the experience and its mythology has undermined research in the area. Truly, what does one accept as fact, given the abundance of myths, stories, and claims of Underground Railroad activities and slave hideaways in so many communities in the United States? Ironically, this history, which now seems to have become tourist fodder for many towns, at some point in US history was a forbidden subject. One might ask, if so many communities were as involved as they now claim or suggest in the Underground Railroad, why did it take so long to end slavery in the United States? The transatlantic slave trade ended in 1808. The United States signed the agreement but continued its plantation slavery until 1863, after the Emancipation Proclamation Act. Even then, it would take the Civil War to finally put an end to the institution of slavery in the United States.

A significant problem in researching the Underground Railroad lies in documentation. Although William Still published an impressive volume of records and transcribed stories of many who passed through the Philadelphia station, it is still difficult to find actual accounts written by those who undertook the journey. Most accounts are rendered retrospectively, years after the flight and attainment of freedom. For instance, William and Ellen Craft, who escaped from slavery via the railroad, did not write their story until many years after their departure to England. Harriet Tubman narrated some portions of her story to Sarah H. Bradford, years after her freedom and only a few years before her death.[5]

Although the slave narratives provide some evidence about the nature of the Underground Railroad journeys, the stories are often cautious about such revelations. An example is Frederick Douglass's refusal to reveal the identity of those who helped him or even share his route of escape. His criticism of those who made such information public underscores the dangerous nature of the work; Douglass feared that such overexposure could threaten the escape of more enslaved blacks from the South. But many fugitive blacks did not keep written records of their journeys, escape routes, and helpers or make public their plans to escape. The urgency and desire to attain freedom, as well as the life-threatening nature of an escape, evoked enough fear that fugitives often did not tell anyone of their plans. When they did, it was often to trusted family members who were left behind. For example, although Tubman escaped with her two brothers, they eventually left her and returned to slavery. Bradford indicates that for the fugitives, "the way was strange, the north was far away, and all unknown, the masters would pursue and recapture them, and their fate would be worse than ever before; and so, they broke away from [Tubman]" (28). Indeed, to contemplate escape, speak about it, or engage in it meant death if caught. Escaping from slavery or supporting any activity that freed slaves violated the laws of the land as enshrined in the Fugitive Slave Acts.

Besides, most slaves could not read or write, and if they did, they only wrote about their experiences after they attained freedom. Certainly, writing while still in flight was a privilege fugitive blacks could not afford. Indeed, William Still acknowledges the lack of record keeping by underscoring the secrecy the Underground Railroad and its activities demanded. According to Still, "the slave and his particular friends could only meet in private to transact the business of the Underground Rail Road. All others were outsiders. The right hand was not to know what the left hand was doing" (xvi). Still adds that even the fugitives did "not know the names of their helpers, and *vice versa* they did not desire to know theirs," because the "risk of aiding fugitives was never lost sight of, and the safety of all concerned called for still tongues" (xvi; ital. in orig.). Consequently, the activities of the Underground Railroad were preserved in the participants' memories.

The group did not maintain records until William Still's accidental meeting with his long-lost brother, Peter Still, whom he had not seen for forty years. William Still writes that after "the wonderful discovery and joyful reunion" with his brother, he realized that "all over this wide and extended country thousands of mothers and children, separated by Slavery, were in a similar way living without the slightest knowledge of each other's whereabouts, praying and weeping without ceasing, as did this [Still's] mother and son [Peter]" (xvi). Still began to keep records of the work of the Philadelphia Vigilance Committee to help fugitives connect with their lost families. He hid his records to preserve the security of fugitives and their helpers. These records serve as testimony to the immediate experiences, hopes, struggles, and memories of fugitives who passed through the Philadelphia Underground Railroad station. His records also highlight the complexity of the Underground Railroad, as well as the diversity of those who were involved in antislavery activities.

Although William Still created the most comprehensive documentation of the Underground Railroad, a few other people recorded similar work. Wilbur Siebert provides a catalog of the names of various people who kept a diverse range of records of either their activities or their observations of the activities involving the Underground Railroad in their communities. These people also were constantly aware of the danger of preserving "written evidence of complicity" (Siebert 7) in helping fugitives escape.

Flight: Crossing the Threshold

Africans resisted slavery from the time of their arrival in Jamestown, in the Virginia colony, in 1619. Captive Africans "began to escape, and slave owners began to call for official action to solve the problems" (Hendrick 5). Clearly, both the enslaved and their enslavers understood the significance of freedom; for the captive Africans, life in an unknown environment, away from their captors, or even death was preferable to slavery. Therefore, as a road narrative, the story of the Underground Railroad begins with a departure—the crossing of a threshold—that takes the protagonist away from the life he or she knows. Although there is a catalyst for such flight, the journey does not truly begin until the subject crosses this first threshold.

In his book *The Hero with a Thousand Faces* (1949), Joseph Campbell delineates the journey of the hero—the monomyth—beginning with the call to action and the hero's acceptance or refusal of the call, followed by his departure from the community. If a desire for adventure propels the heroes of road narratives and quests, then the desire for freedom and dignity sets the protagonists of the Underground Railroad to flee. Slaves were objectified and defined as chattel; they were sources of cheap labor and items for economic exchange. Some slaves were able to purchase their freedom, and if they were lucky enough, they paid tremendous sums to purchase the freedom of family members. Freedom for blacks was further threatened by the Fugitive Slave Acts and local laws in several southern states that prohibited the manumission of enslaved blacks.[6] Consequently, the only means of attaining freedom were rebellion, death, or flight.

Campbell's description of the adventure of the hero is formulaic, "represented in the rites of passage: separation—initiation—return" (3). Between the separation and the return in the hero's journey lie the struggles, tests, and transformation. While the mythic hero returns to share his wisdom or boon with the community, the central figures of the Underground Railroad stories could not do so and did not often plan to return to the place from which they fled. If an escaped slave did return, the goal was generally to rescue others who were still in captivity and lead them to freedom. One example is Harriet Tubman, who traveled into the South on several occasions before the Civil War to lead slaves to freedom. William Still writes of how his manumitted brother Peter had secretly returned to Alabama to visit his wife and children, hoping to purchase their freedom; upon arriving there, however, he failed to do so, fearing that his attempt might "[awaken] the ire of slaveholders against him" (4).

In Campbell's monomyth, the hero's quest begins with a call to adventure, which the hero either accepts or tries to flee from but, in the end, accepts reluctantly. While Campbell's hero might be drawn into a quest by an accidental encounter, for the protagonist of the Underground Railroad, this call is "the awakening of the self" (Campbell 51), a realization that something is amiss, followed by the desire to correct it. The fugitives whose accounts William Still recorded emphasized the wrong they felt as slaves, which propelled them to flee in order to secure their own freedom.

For instance, John Thompson in a "Letter from John Thompson, a Fugitive Slave, to His Mother," which he sent to William Still, underscores his attainment of freedom—the ownership of himself as a driving reason for his escape. He tells his mother, "I am now a free man Living By the sweet of my own Brow not serving a nother man & giving him all I Earn But what I make is mine and iff one Plase do not sute me I am at Liberty to Leave and go some where elce & can ashore you I think highly of Freedom and would not exchange it for nothing that is offered me for it" (33). Thompson claims agency by asserting the right to act on his own volition. Not only can he now keep his earnings, he also can choose where to work and exercise the right to leave. The importance of this self-assertion is accentuated by the second half of the letter, which lists the number of times he was sold—at least three— before escaping finally to freedom. In addition to dehumanizing him, each sale further severed him from his family. Thompson's fate was not unusual, for the slave narratives in general inform us that the life of a slave was punctuated by the looming presence of such sales and the denial of the individual's rights as a human being.

William and Ellen Craft reinforce this position. William Craft states that "the mere idea that [he and Ellen] were held as chattels, and deprived of all legal rights," including the right to any children they produced, caused them to flee (3). He adds that even white or nearly white children were sold into slavery; he also catalogs the ways in which slavery traumatized blacks either through economic exploitation, physical and sexual abuse (7), or fragmentation of families (9). Further, Craft notes that his wife, Ellen, recognized her gender marginalization, that "the law under which [they] lived did not recognize her as a woman, but a mere chattel, to be bought and sold, or otherwise dealt with as her owner might see fit" (21). The astuteness of Ellen Craft's awakened consciousness has to be acknowledged, for as early as 1848, she was acutely aware of her subordination and particularly the ways in which slavery activated both sexism and racism as weapons against her. Ellen Craft was an early black feminist like several other black women, both free and captive, including Frances E. W. Harper, Sojourner Truth, Harriet Tubman, Harriet Jacobs, Pauline Hopkins, and Maria Stewart. In her 1861 autobiography, Harriet Jacobs echoes Ellen Craft's reading of her position as a woman and a slave; in defiance of her master and rejection of his amorous overtures, Jacobs would hide herself in an attic for seven years before escaping to the north.

Like the Crafts and other fugitives, John Malvin fled to the north for a better life. In *The Autobiography of John Malvin* (1879), he portrays a life of abjection under slavery. Like Frederick Douglass, Malvin underscores the starvation of enslaved blacks. Malvin's clothing was so wretched and his food so scarce, "consist[ing] of one peck of corn meal a week," that he was forced to "resort to other means to obtain food" (6). He adds that his quest for freedom was ignited by a desire for "the luxury which [he] observed among the neighboring slave-owners, and the style of living of [his] master" (6). Malvin's story highlights the inequities that fueled the flight of the fugitives in general. Moreover, it reaffirms Douglass's claim that his first attempt to flee was "an attempt, on my part, to secure my liberty" and to live "*upon free land*" (432; ital. in orig.). These protagonists' assertion of agency challenges the stereotypical assumption held by slave owners that black captives were happy in their captivity and, as such, would not initiate their own escape. Harriet Tubman also fled because she wanted to own herself. According to Sarah H. Bradford, at "about twenty or twenty-five years old," Harriet Tubman heard one night that she and "two of her brothers were very soon . . . to be sent far South with a gang, bought up for plantation work" (26), and decided to escape. She consulted with her brothers, and they agreed to escape with her that night to the north, where freedom awaited them (27).

Unlike Douglass, Brown, Jacobs, or Tubman, Malvin describes his journey to the north in search of freedom as an adventure, in which he succeeded in convincing the local clerk to provide him with travel papers. In presenting his escape as an adventure, and in stealing himself from slavery, Malvin affirms Albert Bushnell Hart's contention that the Underground Railroad had the excitement of "piracy." Regardless of the nature of the escape, the protagonists of the Underground Railroad emphasize the primacy of the desire to be free and to own themselves.

Thieves, Tricksters, Rogues, and Rebels

In appropriating the quest narrative as a paradigm for exploring the Underground Railroad, one notes that, as in the quest—especially in its manifestation as a picaresque narrative, where the protagonist must depend upon her or his wits for survival—the subject of the Underground Railroad story must also be a trickster and a rogue. A common factor among the stories of the Underground Railroad is the protagonists' assertion that their acts constituted a form of theft, because they were stealing themselves away from those who claimed to own them. Consequently, the quest for freedom was not an easy task for fugitives. They deployed various strategies to elude those who held them in captivity and thus secure their passage to freedom. An example is Henry

"Box" Brown, who had a large box built in which he was shipped by overland express from Richmond, Virginia, to a friend in Philadelphia. He spent twenty-six hours in transit. Likewise, twenty-five-year-old William "Box" Peel Jones "had himself boxed up by a near relative and forwarded by the Erricson line of steamers" to Philadelphia (Still 24). So also did Lear Green, who escaped from her master, "James Noble" of Baltimore, in a chest (149-52).

Other modes of escape include gender switching and cross-dressing. An often-cited example is the previously mentioned case of Ellen and William Craft, who dressed as a white male planter and his servant and escaped by train to Philadelphia.[7] Ellen was so successful in her disguise that even white citizens traveling on the train with them did not recognize her as black. In other cases, fugitive blacks sometimes hid for extended periods before escaping. In her autobiography, *Incidents in the Life of a Slave Girl* (1861), Harriet Jacobs tells her readers that to escape Dr. Flint's clutches, she spent seven years hiding in a garret "only nine feet long and seven wide," the highest part of which was "three feet" (297). Clarissa Davis also hid for two and half months before escaping to Philadelphia dressed in men's attire (Still 32–34).

Conductors, Drivers, Guides, Stockholders

The story of the Underground Railroad is not complete without a consideration of those who made it possible for fugitives to reach freedom. A careful investigation of work on the Underground Railroad suggests that while blacks often fled on their own, many were also assisted by benevolent supporters, abolitionist whites, and free blacks. These activists—both men and women, blacks and whites—were often referred to as stockholders, drivers, and conductors. They volunteered to serve despite knowing the dangerous nature of Underground Railroad work. Seth Concklin, who died while trying to rescue the family of Peter Still, is a good example. In his autobiography, Levi Coffin describes in detail his activities in the Underground Railroad, beginning as a child, when he took "supplies of bacon and corn bread" in his corn sack to fugitives hiding near his home and sat with them in their hiding places while they ate (36). Later, as an adult, he would agree to help freed blacks in their efforts to conceal fugitives or forward them to Canada. One of the fugitives he and his wife sheltered was Eliza Harris, who was made famous by Harriet Beecher Stowe's *Uncle Tom's Cabin* (1852). In addition, Coffin worked with Reverend Rankin of Ripley, Ohio, who also sheltered Eliza Harris before sending her to the Coffins. In Michigan, Laura S. Haviland, who also collaborated with Coffin and George DeBaptiste, helped to transport or forward fugitives to Detroit and then to Canada. She also accompanied Coffin and his wife on their visit to Canada to meet free blacks in the summer of 1854. In a section of her autobiography, *A Woman's Life-Work* (1887), Haviland describes how she and her husband, Charles Haviland Jr., leased twenty acres of land to Elsie and Willis, a fugitive couple (56). Haviland would become deeply involved in driving fugitives across towns to catch the train to freedom (60).

Conclusion

Much of the story of the Underground Railroad still remains untold. There is no doubt that it belongs to the road narrative convention as a quest story. Its protagonists may not be figures of epic poems, legends, or myths, but like those figures of the classical quests, the protagonists of the Underground Railroad undertook journeys in search of a different type of prize: freedom, a boon that is self-healing and collectively recuperative. Like the heroes of ancient quests, those of the Underground Railroad had to cross a threshold to initiate their journey, encounter obstacles, and slay a metaphorical dragon or demon—slavery—before receiving their boon. Conductors, drivers, and stockholders at various stations served as guides throughout the journey. Like the legends and myths, the Underground Railroad story, although real history, continues to intrigue audiences with its mystery and romance. This essay is a humble attempt to help unravel this mystery.

Notes

1. The accounts of fugitives and their helpers confirm this claim. See Still.
2. The Second Baptist Church of Detroit, Michigan, established by thirteen free blacks in 1836, became one of the stops, if not the last, on the Michigan Underground Railroad that led fugitives to Canada. It is said that Sojourner Truth, John Brown, and Frederick Douglass visited the church. In 1847, a group of whites and blacks living in Marshall, Michigan, resisted the attempt by Kentucky slave catchers to return to slavery the Crosswhites, a family of fugitive blacks who had escaped to Marshall.
3. See Siebert, chapter 11, for a discussion of possible Underground Railroad activities before 1800.
4. Several slave revolts occurred before the Revolutionary War. The most notable was the Stono Rebellion (1739) in South Carolina, which resulted in the deaths of over twenty white citizens and led to South Carolina's ban on teaching slaves to write. Several notable slave revolts took place after the Revolutionary War: Gabriel Prosser and Jack Bowler (1800), Charles Deslondes (1811), Denmark Vesey (1822), Nat Turner (1831), and Amistad (1839).
5. See Sarah H. Bradford's preface to her 1897 edition of *Harriet: The Moses of Her People*, which the author wrote in an effort to raise funds to save Tubman's home.
6. William and Ellen Craft quote a number of codes or laws established in several Southern states designed to ensure that blacks remain enslaved in perpetuity (10–11).
7. See Craft and Craft for a detailed description of Ellen's clothes, the disguises, and how the couple created such effective disguise.

Works Cited

Bordewich, Fergus M. *Bound for Canaan: The Epic Story of the Underground Railroad, America's First Civil Rights Movement*. New York: Harper, 2005. Print.

Bradford, Sarah H. *Harriet, the Moses of Her People*. New York: Lockwood, 1897. Print.

Campbell, Joseph. *The Hero with a Thousand Faces*. New York: MJF, 1949. Print.

Coffin, Levi. "Selections from Levi Coffin's *Reminiscences*." Hendrick and Hendrick 29–98.

Craft, William, and Ellen Craft. *Running a Thousand Miles for Freedom*. Athens: U of Georgia P, 1999. Print.

Douglass, Frederick. *Narrative of the Life of Frederick Douglass, an American Slave, Written by Himself*. Gates and McKay 385–450.

Gates, Henry Louis, Jr., and Nellie Y. McKay, eds. *The Norton Anthology of African American Literature*. New York: Norton, 2004. Print.

Haviland, Laura S. *A Woman's Life-Work: Labors and Experiences of Laura S. Haviland.* Chicago: Waite, 1887. Print.

Hendrick, George, and Willene Hendrick, eds. *Fleeing for Freedom: Stories of the Underground Railroad as Told by Levi Coffin and William Still.* Chicago: Dee, 2004. Print.

Jacobs, Harriet. *Incidents in the Life of a Slave Girl.* Gates and McKay 279–315.

Malvin, John. *Autobiography of John Malvin.* Cleveland: Leader, 1879. Print.

Mills, Katie. *The Road Story and the Rebel: Moving through Film, Fiction, and Television.* Carbondale: Southern Illinois UP, 2006. Print.

Primeau, Ronald. *Romance of the Road: The Literature of the American Highway.* Bowling Green: Bowling Green State U Popular P, 1996. Print.

Siebert, Wilbur. *The Underground Railroad from Slavery to Freedom.* Mineola: Dover, 2006. Print.

Still, William. *The Underground Railroad: Authentic Narratives and First Hand Accounts.* Ed. Ian Frederick Finseth. Mineola: Dover, 2007. Print.

Thompson, John. "Letter from John Thompson, a Fugitive, to His Mother." *The Underground Railroad.* By William Still. Rev. ed. Vol. 1. Middlesex: Echo, 2006. 33. Print.

"Surprised to Find Itself in a Tree in the Chicago Suburbs": Images of Home and Travel in the Nonfiction of Mary Morris _____

Mary Beth Pringle

Travel literature features places visited, but it may also treat homes left behind. Such a double focus is evident in Mary Morris's travel memoirs, which detail journeys to Mexico, Russia, California, and river towns along the Mississippi. They also explore Greater Chicago, Morris's hometown. "I come from the Midwest, from the bluffs along the shores of Lake Michigan," Morris explains in *Nothing to Declare: Memoirs of a Woman Traveling Alone* (1988), situating her childhood self somewhere on Chicago's north shore (23). Because she calls Chicago home, readers might expect all four of her memoirs—*Nothing to Declare* as well as *Wall to Wall: From Beijing to Berlin by Rail* (1991), *Angels and Aliens: A Journey West* (1999), and *River Queen: A Memoir* (2007)—to offer up images of an urban Chicago heartland. But they do not. Consistent with portrayals of home by other contemporary female writers, Morris describes a Chicago that is more barren and painful than "very beautiful" (*Nothing* 23), a locus of exile as bleak and distressing as the lonely vistas she often seems to encounter on the road.

In fact, home, today's women writers often claim, is not the "sweet" place of nineteenth-century cross-stitched samplers. Introducing *A Place Called Home: Twenty Writing Women Remember* (1996), Mickey Pearlman sums up lessons about home she learned from the writers whose essays she has anthologized. Pearlman herself was raised in the South, where, she says, the assumption that everyone itches to get back to "the land of cotton" runs strong. She held to this assumption for a long time, even though it was not true for her (2). Despite feeling sure that "Norman Rockwell images would not emerge in prose from this group of talented and edgy essayists" writing for *A Place Called Home*, Pearlman was still stunned when she began "to receive—by fax and snail mail—so many essays about childhood homes as places *to get away from*" (3; ital. in orig.).

Over and over again, contributors to her volume, including Mary Morris, tell stories about home shaded by references to racism, anti-Semitism, unloving or damaged parents, loneliness, and loss. Pearlman quotes Henry James, who believed writers "start from the port of grief," and adds, "As a group they pay attention to pain—theirs and everyone else's—which is, indeed, their job" (4). Her observations are confirmed by others writing about women's travel literature. In their introduction to *Travel Writing and the Female Imaginary* (2001), Vita Fortunati, Rita Monticelli, and Maurizio Ascari refer to Julia Kristeva's comment that "writing is impossible without some kind of exile" and that women's travel literature is "the expression of a quest for . . . self which has been repressed in the symbolic and social order" (6).

Mary Morris's essay in the Pearlman collection is like the others in its painful depiction of home. "Illinois follows me around like some bad deed I've done," Morris writes, "like some stalker I can't shake." She reports agreeing with Johann von Goethe that "all writers are homesick, that all writers are really searching for [a] home" they can bear to live in ("Looking" 29). Nevertheless, she herself is repeatedly blocked from accessing such a place, especially the literal home of her childhood. Although her adult dreams frequently return her to Chicago, where it is snowing "billowy thick flakes, and I feel myself shrinking, growing smaller," she never really arrives. Of course, it always looks as if she will. "I am in a snowsuit, my hands in mittens. Tracks appear, human tracks, and I follow them to my white house on Hazel Avenue and I go home. Up to the front door but I always wake up before I'm inside" (30).

There are reasons why Mary Morris cannot enter the house of her heart. Her parents, she complains in "Looking for Home" and also in her travel memoirs, sell the place without consulting her, before she is ready to let it, and her childhood, go. The deal is struck suddenly, and a college-age Morris finds herself living with her family in a downtown

Chicago apartment. "The new apartment wasn't finished, and door-knobs kept falling off, locking us in empty rooms," she writes. "My brother and a friend were arrested at the Democratic National Convention in Chicago for handing out bread, and the police broke their fingers" (*Angels* 78). Worst of all, her mother even gives the family's dog to a supermarket cashier, because it barks in the city.

How to deal with a home that, in practical ways, has vanished? Ambivalently. On one hand, Morris recalls a childhood vision of her father proudly standing in the cellar, patting the beams of the house he is having built. On the other, she remembers cutting her forearm with a razor blade that day at the construction site, watching the blood seep down her wrist and onto the unsealed wood floor. "A part of me remains" carpeted over in that place, Morris observes, leaving readers to puzzle out the implications of that ambiguous, even creepy, image ("Looking" 35).

Still, given the myriad ways in which Chicago has been depicted in fiction, nonfiction, and poetry, Morris's portrait in *Nothing to Declare* of a city devoid of tall buildings and wedged against a looming lake seems surprising. Nowhere to be seen is a modernized version of Carl Sandburg's "stormy, husky, brawling, / City of the Big Shoulders" (lines 4–5). Gone are the hog butchers, toolmakers, railroad workers, painted women, lured farm boys, and the faces "of wanton hunger" (8). Gone is the "city with lifted head singing so proud to be alive and coarse and strong and cunning" (10). Morris replaces these dynamic metaphors with four people—two parents and two children, one of whom is the author herself— stranded in a desolate natural environment: a troubled suburban family, sandy bluffs, sparse grasses, and, once, a perched bird.

Morris's first memory of Chicago in *Nothing to Declare* links the city to her mother, but also to pain:

We are living on Roscoe Street which means I am less than two, and my mother says I cannot remember this, but I am sure I do. We are going somewhere. I am dressed in blue and my mother wears beige. She is yelling at me, telling me terrible things, and I am not crying. I am stubborn, standing still. When I tell this to my mother, she says I am a liar. She says I have made it up. Pure invention. I never raised my voice to you, she says. (42)

Like her mother, Morris's father is also negatively connected to images of Chicago in *Nothing to Declare*. Mary Morris travels, and her father is the seated leg of a mathematical compass, stuck in Chicago and trying to control where she, the other leg, goes. To that end, he blankets American Express offices around the world with letters to his daughter, just in case she visits that particular country. She receives one such letter in Honduras on her way to Nicaragua, warning her to avoid being careless like her friend Linda, who has flipped her car three times. He is sure, he says, not without irony, that she will not go to Nicaragua because it is too dangerous. Morris is in Nicaragua on the next page.

Morris's mother is also strangely involved in her daughter's journeys, indirectly, perhaps unintentionally, pushing her to leave home. "It was my mother who made a traveler out of me," Morris says, "not so much because of the places where she went as because of her yearning to go." Morris feels responsible to travel for her mother, the woman who "had many reasons—and sometimes, I think, excuses—for not going anywhere" herself (*Nothing* 21). An image of her mother is particularly poignant. One Chicago Halloween, she concocts an elaborate costume for herself—a dress made of blue taffeta and white fishnet gauze, onto which she had pinned and sewn travel sites: the Taj Mahal, the pyramids. Paris, Tokyo, Istanbul, and Tashkent. Morris notes, "Instead of seeing the world, my mother became it," leaving the daughter with a sense of obligation to vicariously fulfill her mother's dreams (21).

In fact, in *Nothing to Declare*, Morris describes herself as a traveler very much like the "perched bird" she sees as a child on her way home from school. Lost in and bewildered by the landscape, the bird is "larger than myself," balanced in a tree not far from Morris's house (23). It appears "weary and a bit confused"—"surprised," in fact, "to find itself in a tree in the Chicago suburbs." In awe of the gigantic creature, Morris settles in to watch as it "stretche[s]" and "flutter[s]" its mighty wings (23). Much later, her mother, frantic that her daughter has not arrived home from school on schedule, finds the girl face-to-face with a bald eagle. Even then, Morris wondered "what led it to suburbia, so far away from where its nest *should* be" (24; emphasis added).

Like the bald eagle, Morris sees herself as out of place and Chicago as antithetical to her real identity, a false and temporary home. Represented by a curious synecdoche, Chicago is a barren suburb on the shores of Lake Michigan, a place where "you might stumble on an arrowhead," a place where there are "a few trees, bent and tied to the ground a century before by Indians" (Morris, *Nothing* 23). This Chicago, in short, resides in a distant, unreachable, and alien past.

In fact, feeling "out of place" in Chicago may be what inspires Morris to become a traveler. As a child, she goes on "adventures that [involve] walks along ravines or on the old Indian trails" and turns alienation into imagination, cataloging "plants, creatures, bits of stone" (*Nothing* 77):

> In my childhood fantasies I saw myself as an adventurer, a pioneer, a woman hero. I was an Indian maiden, named White Eagle or Running Deer, who rode a pinto bareback and hunted buffalo, with bow and arrow, at a full gallop. . . . I was faith keeper, peacemaker, diviner, matchmaker, interpreter of magical signs. I envisioned myself in wagon trains and tepees, in jungles and exotic desert lands, discovering an unknown species of reptile, blazing trails across virgin terrain. (76)

These imaginary adventures strengthen Morris and ready her for the real trips she will make as an adult. Sometimes, she reports, she takes her clothes off in front of a mirror in order to admire the body, her own, that accomplishes all these feats. Alone, she is pleased by her "taut limbs," her body's "incipient roundness." She says, "I tried to imagine it in another *place* at another time" (77; emphasis added).

The places Morris visits in *Nothing to Declare*, especially San Miguel de Allende in central Mexico, resemble Morris's imagined Chicago: alien, unreal. Morris calls San Miguel part of "old Mexico, a lawless land. It is a landscape that could be ruled by bandits or serve as a backdrop for the classic westerns, where all you expect the Mexicans to say is '*hombre*,' '*amigo*,' and '*si, senor*'" (*Nothing* 3). She has traveled there from New York, where she has been living, to spend down a travel grant and to write, having heard from friends that "Americans who want to get away often go there. It is a place of exile" (4). Like the Chicago of Morris's imagination, it is more rural than urban. Comprising pale desert colors and "scattered yellow flowers," San Miguel seems like a cardboard backdrop for the lonely rituals Morris engages in during her stay. "The solitude is dramatic," she writes, and her descriptions make that solitude real (3). Having already connected Chicago and San Miguel by means of sadly windswept vistas, she says, "I have been, and am, a woman who has often found herself, through circumstance and fate, alone" (23).

Just as her first memory of Chicago reveals a frightened Morris, her stay in San Miguel is also characterized by fear. "I can say," she writes, "that I have never been more afraid in my life than I was in San Miguel" (*Nothing* 25). But the fear is not solely of what will happen to her while journeying in a strange land. Instead, she acknowledges, "Mostly I was afraid because of what I carried in my heart" (26).

The borders between Chicago and San Miguel, as well as those separating her hometown from the Central American countries she visits on the same trip, blur. In a jungle, she spots butterflies she studied as a child while a member of Chicago's South American butterfly club. The butterflies' colorful wings evoke memories of a butterfly book her parents gave her and trips to the Field Museum. "They were all right there," she says, "the ones I had spent years studying and then forgetting. And now they were all here, for me to remember" (*Nothing* 84).

In a dream at the end of *Nothing to Declare*, Morris becomes the "traveler eagle" who hypnotized her as a child in Chicago. After a long flight to her grandmother's Ukrainian village, after mating midair with a mysterious male bird, Mary Morris flies "to a place where I know I do not belong. I fly to the Midwest." There, she makes it "to a tree in a small woods near a lake, and there I rest." Although the "rest"—presumably on the shore of Lake Michigan—might appear to be satisfying, it is not. When, as the eagle, Morris opens her eyes, she spots a "small girl standing by the side of the road, watching me. . . . She wants to come with me." That small girl is Mary Morris, too, the part of herself that still feels exiled. Even though Morris, as the eagle, says, "I open my wings, because she is asking, and I take her in," that image represents only temporary calm, not reconciliation (246).

The image of Chicago Morris depicts in *Wall to Wall: From Beijing to Berlin by Rail* seems at first more positive than the one in *Nothing to Declare*. In *Wall to Wall,* two homes embody Chicago: Morris's Russian Jewish grandmother's downtown apartment and her parents' place north of the city. Morris describes her grandmother's small living space in exotic terms as "the first foreign country I ever traveled to" (6). It is filled with the luscious Old World odors of baking breads, of "savory fruit stews," of "whispers in thick, impenetrable tongues," and of the fairy tales her grandmother tells her of "Baba Yaga, the cannibal witch, or Jack Frost whose embrace was death, or the girl turned into a firebird, her feathers spreading beauty across the land as she died in the talons of the evil prince." The grandmother relates true stories from her childhood in the same "voice, conspiratorial, almost," about her escape to America and the oppression and fear in Russia that made her leaving necessary (6).

Morris idolizes this grandmother, who represents the positive elements of Chicago and who is also one of her travel inspirations. She is "a teller of tales, a dreamer with translucent blue eyes that made me think not of the marbles the boys played with in her alleyway, but of globes and oceans and distant lands." From this grandmother, Morris hears heroic stories about her family, in particular a Russian great-grandmother who protected her children from the Cossacks by burying them alive in little graves "in the ground with reeds sticking out of their mouths" (*Wall* 5). These stories make the child Mary Morris's mouth "taste . . . of soil" (6). More than anything, the adult Morris wants to visit Russia so she can find "the place where the little graves were" (9).

By way of her Russian grandmother, Morris could claim Chicago as her true home. The grandmother does not just live in the city; she belongs there, her father having made his way west from Ellis Island to Chicago and settled in long ago. In those days, Chicago "was a small but emerging city on a seemingly endless prairie," where "the winters were difficult and my great-grandfather tended to pray rather than work" (Morris, *Wall* 40). Whatever Morris's great-grandfather's relationship to Chicago, her grandmother's is firm and satisfying. Even as an old lady in her nineties, nearly blind and "crippled with arthritis," she would dress up in white gloves and a veil "and take the bus to Marshall Field's whenever there was a sale on pistachios." There is something magical about this grandmother—Morris says she was rumored to have "psychic powers" (73)—and about the Chicago that is her home. But in *Wall to Wall*, Morris's family's house on Hazel Avenue also continues to represent Chicago, and it is still portrayed as a site of difficult memories. This time, readers learn that "the house is gone, long ago sold to a man who has married a woman half his age," and that it now has a flag in the front yard and white wrought-iron furniture (21). Even though years have passed, Morris cannot forget about this home. Visiting Chicago as an adult, she stays with a one-time neighbor and "sp[ies] upon [her] former life" (21). Whole doing so, she jealously imagines another little girl sleeping in the room "where my father tucked me in. Where I read my first books, whispered my first secrets to girlfriends on the phone" (21–22).

But what she misses about that house is the happiness she seems *not* to have experienced while living in it. Both of Morris's parents lead disappointed lives and, according to their daughter, visit unhappiness on their children. Her mother, who might have preferred a London career in fashion design, becomes instead a Chicago homemaker. Her father, a perfectionist, suffers his children, who are not. For him, there is only one way to do a job. Morris's and her brother's efforts to learn that one system disappoint him: "The napkin was never in our lap on time. The bread never broken before it was buttered" (*Wall* 151). Morris hides in books, her world a "made up one" (152). Eventually, of course, such efforts at containment fail. After an "explosion," Morris determines to "set out on journeys, wandering the world. I would find that part of me I'd had to hide" (153).

In *Wall to Wall,* Morris's efforts to find a home more emotionally satisfying than Chicago fail. First, there is her faltering relationship with a partner of several years. The two travel to Shanghai to his conference, after which, Morris assumes, they will continue together, traveling westward by train to Berlin. When her partner refuses to accompany her, Morris goes on alone. A curious lethargy complicates the trek, and Morris learns she is pregnant. Alone, awash in hormones, she barely manages to finish what she has begun.

Morris starts her journey—this time through China, then Russia—optimistically. She wants more than anything "the stamp on my passport that would enable me to enter the land of my Jewish ancestors by rail" (*Wall* 3). She believes Russia to be an ideal part of her past; it is not. That fact does not keep her from imagining, however, that her grandparents and those who preceded them lived spiritually rich lives there, compared to her own life in Chicago. They "grew up in the land where their spirits dwelled. They grew up with their own *place* myths" (87; emphasis added). In contrast, Morris describes her existence as "dull," herself as "a *desdichada*, a Jew, a lost one, searching for my clan" (87). That Morris wants to return to Russia so she can see the graves where her grandmother and siblings were temporarily buried alive, a ghastly image, does not bode well for her search for a home.

But there are other reasons why the trip across Russia in an attempt to find a home more satisfying than Chicago seems doomed. Morris's mother has warned her that her Russian Jewish history hardly affords her safety as a woman. Her female relatives slaved their lives away in Russia and in Chicago. "Women, my mother said . . . , lived terrible lives. They were abused, but who would listen. They suffered, my mother said, but whom could they tell" (Morris, *Wall* 50).

That the 1986 nuclear disaster at Chernobyl occurs right before her trip is significant. Chernobyl serves as a poisonous metaphor for the Russia Morris visits. In fact, she must decide whether to continue her journey near the site of the catastrophe or avoid the area in order protect her unborn child and herself. Morris eventually opts to skip the Ukraine, where the fallout is worst, even though it is the place she most wants to see. She notes this accommodation to the fetus indirectly, almost grudgingly admitting that "four years later . . . the death rate of children in Minsk from leukemia [would] leap from one a year to one a week" (*Wall* 231).

In *Angels and Aliens: A Journey West*, her third memoir, Morris continues the thread of nostalgia, regret, and loss. This time, though, she is angrier, her image of Chicago still more deeply tainted by painful memories of her parents and home. In *Angels and Aliens*, Morris details a teaching term she spent in southern California, a place she reveals over two hundred pages to be consummately and unsurprisingly superficial and alienating. She flies there from New York with the daughter born after the Russia trip, still suffering the bad behavior of the child's father, who was supposed to accompany her but again does not. As the plane lands in California, she tells readers, once again, that she wants "to retire to a place where everything is different from what has been. Where I can forget what needs to be forgotten and begin again" (Morris, *Angels* 4).

As in her earlier memoirs, Morris paints an ambivalent, but ultimately negative, picture of Chicago and home, offering as a disclaimer that "creative people, even if they had a happy childhood, tend to remember an unhappy one" (*Angels* 16). Although Morris recalls parties, a mother who blew her good-night kisses from her bedroom doorway, a father who read her bedtime stories, her feet crunching through fall leaves, and adventures in the woods around her house, these positive memories are tainted by darker things: her tears at a party where a magician pulls a rabbit out of a hat, her mother prying her fingers off when Morris clings to her on the first day of kindergarten, her father perennially behind a newspaper or correcting her for misusing her spoon.

Morris's father, in fact, emerges as an especially negative representation of home. Nothing his daughter does seems to please him. She does not stack dishes in the dishwasher properly, does not set the table right, does not make salad or clean her room properly. Even her mother seems to be under the father's angry spell. Once, when the dog chews on the living room sofa, shredding it, Morris's mother, terrified, tries to sew the upholstery back together "before the 5:10 arrive[s]" (*Angels* 33).

A particularly telling anecdote about Morris's relationship with her father occurs when she is about three or four years old and trying to copy her name in a legal tablet as he has taught her. After struggling to make the shapes of letters and fearing to disturb her father, who is working on papers himself, she slips the tablet filled with her name into his line of vision. "I am standing on tiptoe," Morris writes, "peering at the tabletop. I see his fingers come down. 'The R is backward,' my father says. I look at his finger, study the R. Even now I can see his finger, pointing at the page" (*Angels* 94). She has failed, utterly, and at such an early age.

Although Morris shows that her father is the root of much of her childhood pain, in *Angels and Aliens*, she more than once rationalizes his bad behavior: He had scarlet fever as a boy. He lost part of his hearing. He yells because he cannot hear himself. He has always had to support someone in the family. She also, however, acknowledges his negative effect on her adult life. At one point, Morris speculates whether her father's bad behavior made her vulnerable to being mistreated by her daughter's biological father, who, she notes, "spoke so quietly that I had to lean close to listen"; her father, by contrast, frequently yelled, so the quieter man made Morris think, "This must be good. I must be safe" (*Angels* 118).

If Morris looks to her mother for corroboration of her memories about home, she does not get it. Her mother "remembers things differently" than she does, distancing Morris from her own version of history. The mother, perhaps needing to, "remembers quiet Sundays, family picnics"; Morris says, "I remembered that nothing was ever right. That everything I did was wrong—the way I folded napkins, carried dishes. Someone was always yelling at me. . . . Rage boiled inside of me. My father shouting about lights being left on. My brother's hand being dipped in a scalding tub so he'd stop setting fires. These come to me in snatches" (*Angels* 208). Morris's mother even corrects her memories of seemingly inconsequential matters. "She says that the maid who got pregnant was Anka, not Herta, and that it was Herta who took my music box away. She says someone was always home when I got back from school. So why do I remember an empty house, unmade beds?" (208).

In *Angels and Aliens*, Morris continues to mourn for and fear aspects of the house on Hazel Avenue. She fondly recalls its "white walls and wood trim, its sturdy white brick and picket fence. Its green shutters and big lawn," but she also reports a chilling detail, one of the carpenters who worked on the house bringing over "the head of a deer he had killed" (29). That head, later stuffed and hanging above the fireplace, presides eerily over the family's basement playroom throughout her childhood.

Other Chicago images are ambivalent: the bluff at the end of Hazel Avenue, for example. Although Morris spends happy times as a child playing near it, and although it is "where [she] told [her]self [her] first stories," at fourteen she threatens to kill herself there, to fling herself off it if she ever becomes pregnant (*Angels* 74). Better that, she observes, than revealing to her father any of her sexual secrets.

In her fourth travel book, *River Queen: A Memoir*, Morris revivifies her embittered father and, through him, her blighted childhood home.

Although her father died at age 103, Morris will not let him go; he is the impetus for a dispiriting journey she makes down the Mississippi River between Wisconsin and Tennessee. During the trip, Morris obsesses about her father and the home life he ruined. She is so busy blending stories about her father's connections to the river with those concerning her unhappy Chicago childhood, in fact, that readers learn little about the actual places visited on the voyage.

Like Morris's earlier travel memoirs, this one is downbeat from the start. It begins on board a creaky houseboat, *The River Queen*, in the midst of an electric storm. Morris is alone on the boat; it is night; she is fearful; although the boat is docked at a marina, the bed Morris is on pitches from side to side in rain and wind. All the wisdom she has garnered from a handbook on water travel says to get off the river in "a dielectric breakdown," but she reports having "nowhere [else] to go" (*River* 1). She means that observation to be taken literally and figuratively. She is locked into this voyage, into this rickety boat with its absent pilots, just as she is locked into haunting memories of her home on Hazel Avenue in Chicago.

Reasonable readers may wonder why the thoroughly urban Morris commits to such a rustic trip afloat. Answers to this question relate back to Morris's father. Through her father, Morris writes, the river "became part of my landscape, my natural terrain. My father's stories of living in Hannibal [Missouri] and his friend's farm on the river took hold of my imagination. It became a piece of what I called *home*" (*River* 3–4; emphasis added). A second answer is more straightforward: "The first time I was ever on a river was with my father. We had rented a boat on the Fox and my father steered. I was surprised that he knew how to pilot, but it seemed he had lived a different life before I was born, one that I would rarely be privy to" (15). Morris is powerfully drawn to what she cannot know, especially where her father is concerned. A river journey is an opportunity to reflect on those mysteries. But the trip will not be easy. As she reports, "The drugs I've been taking these past few months for sleep and anxiety have worn off. Since my father's death last May, I've awakened in the night, short of breath" (2).

As Morris's earlier memoirs establish and this one emphasizes, all of Morris's life has been spent under her father's spell. As a child, she is acutely aware that her father is a mixed bag of emotions. He had, she writes, a reputation for being "charming, handsome, debonair," but she quickly adds, "Underneath, as my brother and I knew, my father was a very angry man. Seething in ways few could imagine. Street angel, *home* devil, the Yiddish expression goes" (*River* 16; emphasis added). Beginning with a sketchy snapshot of her father, Morris paints a portrait of a mercurial individual whose emotions unpredictably waxed and waned. Although she assures readers that his "anger was never physical," she mentions many abusive speeches. "Words can kill," she adds (17). As *River Queen* begins, Morris is still trying to make sense of her dead father's troubled behavior. "To this day," she says, "his outbursts are incomprehensible to me. He never apologized. He never acted as if anything was wrong. He'd blow up and call us names, then make us popcorn or take us to play golf, as if nothing had happened" (17).

As in her previous travel memoirs, Morris connects her father to literal home space—the Midwest, Chicago—in *River Queen*. She reminds readers that "my father built the house where I grew up on the banks of Lake Michigan" (56). She repeats that her blood stains the house's wooden floors, the result of an accident she had there with a razor blade when she was three or four. Despite the eeriness of the detail, Morris follows it with a telling juxtaposition: "I loved that house. . . .My father loved that house as well" (56). He was, she says, fated to occupy that space. As a young man, he visited a fortune-teller somewhere in Pennsylvania who told him that he would receive a letter containing an offer he would accept. He would go to Chicago, marry a woman, "have two children and live near a lake" (49).

Not all of Morris's Chicago memories are blighted in *River Queen*. At one point, reflecting on her youth in Chicago, Morris recalls fondly:

When I think of childhood, I think of horse chestnuts, girls walking together to school, the trains. Camel hair coats and saddle shoes. The sound
of my father leaving for work and coming home. The Chicago Northwestern he took twice a day. F. Scott Fitzgerald would agree. At the end of *The
Great Gatsby* he wrote, "That's my Middle West. Not the wheat or the
prairies or the lost Swede towns, but the thrilling returning trains of my
youth." (59)

But for every detail that is pleasant, there are many more that are not.
On the river and thinking about her father, Morris mentions his "outbursts," noting they "were confined to our four walls." The occasional
"waiters who didn't make his vodka tonic just right or busboys who
didn't clear fast enough got a hint of his rages," but it was mostly his
family that he tormented: "He called us names. He told us we were stu-
pid or selfish or spoiled brats. Once when I was visiting from college,
I came home for dinner half an hour late. The meal was already eaten,
the table cleared, and my father began to yell at me. He yelled until my
brother stood between us and told him to stop" (114).

Morris pays a familiar price for enduring so much anger and violence at home: she becomes violent herself, throwing a much-loved pet
rabbit around by the ears, killing a guppy, tying up a neighbor's dog
and beating it with a stick. As an adult, she recognizes the signs: "Now
I know, of course, that such action is a sign of sociopathic behavior
in children. Was I a sociopath?" She avoids answering the question.
"If I could control the world around me—the world of rabbits, fish,
and dogs—the way my father wanted to control us, keep us in line, if
I could get them to do it, then maybe everything would be all right. I
wanted these creatures to obey me as I tried to obey him" (*River* 228).

But this trip suggests another response to victimization, another fallout from obsession. It is that Morris struggles, often unsuccessfully, to
really *see* the sights she is traveling to write about. Of course, there are
moments in *River Queen* when Morris seems to successfully lay aside
her grief. Once, for example, she begins, "We're traveling at about

eight miles per hour and three of those come from the river's natural flow. Your average marathoner can do better than that. At this speed I can see the underside of a bird's wing." Just as readers think they are about to really see the river, Morris offers up the following vision, presumably something she glimpses along its shoreline: "The eyes of a disenchanted woman, hanging laundry up to dry. Children taunting a mongrel at the river's edge. The bait wiggling on a fisherman's pole. The grimace of an old man, his life behind him now. It's more poem than story, but the long narrative kind" (43). Suddenly, Morris seems to be back in Chicago. There is the mother "disenchanted," struggling to make the home pleasant and habitable. There are the children—Mary and brother John—being cruel to an animal. There are suffering worms dangling off the fisherman's line. And there is the father with his perennial "grimace," staring off at a dissatisfying life that is "behind him now." No matter how far Morris travels to write about a landscape, no matter how diligently she tries to make sense of what she sees, her views outward often seem blocked by distressing remembered scenes of home. For Morris, every "long narrative" begins and ends with Chicago's pain.

Morris never actually lives in Chicago after age eighteen, when she heads to college and a life on the East Coast, claiming she will never come back except for short visits. On rare trips to the area, she rushes not to the Loop but to the lake, driving "thirty miles out of the city" to do so (*Angels* 74). But even these stays are bittersweet. She stands "with my back pressed to the tree bent back in the wind along the bluff, at the place where so many years ago I'd planned my own death" (74). Through the years, she says, she has thought of buying a home elsewhere, but she has never been able to do so. "I had already had a home in Illinois," she says. As for some new house somewhere away from Chicago, she observes, "I didn't want to live with someone else's memories" (*Wall* 139). "I am caught in this web between a desire for permanence and a deep sense of loss," she writes. "It is as if my dark

Russian soul, plunked down in the Midwest, has been exiled, banished, relegated to another place" (138).

Morris posits that what is true of her experience of Chicago is also true of other midwestern writers. Southern writers stay in the South, she says, to write about it. But "Midwestern writers—Twain, Cather, Dreiser, Wilder, Hemingway, Fitzgerald, Nathanial West—wrote about the Midwest from either coast. . . . The Midwest, with its flat, unrippled surface and its child's dream of innocence and balance, is a good place to *remember*" (*Wall* 138; emphasis added).

There is an indie album called *Illinoise*, music and lyrics by Sufjan Stevens, containing a collection of songs about Stevens's and Morris's home state, including one song titled "Chicago." In it, Stevens's words echo Mary Morris's thoughts about Chicago and the Midwest: "I drove to New York / In a van with my friend. . . . If I was crying / In the van with my friend / It was for freedom / From myself and from the land."

Works Cited

Fortunati, Vita, Rita Monticelli, and Maurizio Ascari, eds. *Travel Writing and the Female Imaginary*. Bologna: Pàtron, 2001. Print.

Morris, Mary. *Angels and Aliens: A Journey West*. New York: Picador, 1999. Print.

___. "Looking for Home." Pearlman 25–39.

___. *Nothing to Declare: Memoirs of a Woman Traveling Alone*. Boston: Houghton, 1988. Print.

___. *The River Queen: A Memoir*. New York: Picador, 2007. Print.

___. *Wall to Wall: From Beijing to Berlin by Rail*. New York: Penguin, 1991. Print.

Pearlman, Mickey, ed. *A Place Called Home: Twenty Writing Women Remember*. New York: St. Martin's, 1997. Print.

Sandburg, Carl. "Chicago." *Selected Poems*. San Diego: Harcourt, 1996. 4. Print.

Stevens, Sufjan. "Chicago." *Illinoise*. Asthmatic Kitty, 2005. CD.

Shoreline Sansaras

Arvid F. Sponberg

Any shoreline road is a state of mind. Along their edges, lakes and rivers lure us into imaginings, fantasias, sansaras. Water touching land launches us beyond quotidian matrices of here and now, duty and desire, responsibility and resistance. The abscissa and ordinate of the humdrum fall away and we rise; we gyre and gimble.

My wife and I walk the beaches in the Indiana Dunes, so we often drive US-12 between Ogden Dunes and Michigan City, Indiana. Oak groves and bogs on both sides of the highway hint at the difficulties that dune morphology of northwest Indiana has presented to people in every era. Before modern road building, the region was impassable. Since then, the region has been invisible.

In the minds of many Americans, the whole Midwest sags under the put-down *flyover*, and northwest Indiana earns the complementary dismissal of *drive-through*. Most people cannot find a good reason to stop in northwest Indiana. Every day, Interstates 80, 90, and 94 funnel hundreds of thousands of people and tons of freight through the shoreline corridor. The superhighways replaced US Highways 6, 12, 20, and 30. They carried growing loads from the 1920s through the 1960s. US-30 runs over the Lincoln Highway, the first transcontinental autoroute, pioneered by Indianapolis headlight entrepreneur Carl Graham Fisher and his wealthy friends, including Tom Edison, Teddy Roosevelt, and Woodrow Wilson. Henry Ford passed on the opportunity. He thought highways should be built by the government, not private citizens. When my wife and I visit our friends Jan and Wolf, we pass a sign with a capital *L* a quarter mile north of their house. The sign marks a corner where a section of the original Lincoln Highway meets a county road.

No good reason to stop in northwest Indiana. The joke is at least five hundred years old. Underneath US-12 lies the Sac Trail, used by Native Americans humping their household goods from winter hunting grounds. For centuries, the Pottawatomie, Sac, Mascouten, and Miami

Frank V. Dudley (1868–1957); *Sandland's Even Song*, 1920; oil on board, 38 x 50 inches; Sloan Fund Purchase; Brauer Museum of Art, 2001.44; Valparaiso University.

used the Dunes only for summer foraging. One source ends a paragraph about the Mascouten this way: "Although the evidence is not entirely satisfactory, it is probable that this tribe entered Wisconsin from southern Michigan, passing around the southern end of L. Michigan" ("Mascouten"). *Passing around* is the important phrase here, followed by *not entirely* and *probable*. Like Willie Loman, northwest Indiana always feels "kind of temporary" about itself (Miller 51).

Nothing is certain along my lakeshore. Dunes move. Lake levels rise and fall. Light and shadows, clouds and humidity cast doubts on claims to permanence. Marram grass creeps over the dunes, followed by jack pine, then oak and maple. Knowledge of the Dunes' succession of plants and animals entered human affairs in 1904 through the work of Charles Cowles, a University of Chicago botanist. Unique ecological microsystems exist here and drove a half-century-long campaign to establish the Dunes as a national park.

Frank V. Dudley (1868–1957); *The Wind's in the North*, 1944; oil on canvas, 27 x 30 inches; gift of Percy H. Sloan; Brauer Museum of Art, 53.01.019; Valparaiso University.

The best artist of the Dunes is Frank Virgil Dudley (1868–1957). Two of his paintings, *The Wind's in the North* (1944) and *Sandland's Even Song* (1920), stand out in particular. In *The Wind's in the North*, the Dunes flash into a contest between glare and shadow. The darker patch of blue to the right of the pine, striated with wave shadows, steers our eyes out of the picture into wild, windy spaces. The imagined lake beyond the right edge buttresses the mass of the pine, making us feel the wind's force. The pine, a cascade of darkness, drags our eyes back to the painting's center, a shimmering vortex. The broad shadow climbing from beneath the pine up the dune's slope attaches the marram grass, and us, to the earth. But the shadow also complicates our progress. This painting is not about moving forward. That is out of the question. Stymied by the slope, the wind, and the vortex, we can stand only by struggling to keep our balance. And if the wind dies, we will tumble.

Sandland's Even Song gives us the same terrain from a completely different perspective. We are much farther from the water now, and we can barely discern the bluish mass of Lake Michigan forming a vague horizon. Between us and the lake, our eyes descend into canyons of trees in which we could very easily lose ourselves. Balancing the faded russets of the forest, a large, pale pink cleared dune top opens at our feet. Littered with windfallen branches and scattered grassy patches, it affords us limited space to move. If we stay to the left of the two tall, tattered pines, we could carefully make our way down the slope. But as we do, we notice a top branch of the further pine. Its shaft drives straight through the upper center of the picture and lands our eye at last on the moon—or is it the sun?—glowing through the hazy twilight that softens every edge in the composition. This picture, which is about possibilities, invites us to dreams and visions.

Some writers live in the Dunes but do not write about the Dunes. Harry Mark Petrakis lives in the Dunes but writes about his Greek heritage. Carl Sandburg wrote most of his biography of Lincoln while walking the Dunes beaches up the road near Harbert, Michigan. People who write about northwest Indiana do it while living elsewhere. Jean Shepherd, the most famous writer of "da region," wrote and talked plenty about Hohman, Indiana—a fictionalized Hammond—but from eight hundred miles away in New York City.

Up the River from the Dunes

Drive US-12 east into Michigan, then follow I-94 for sixty miles. Arrive in Kalamazoo, the home of Bonnie Jo Campbell, a writer bringing attention to southwest Michigan, a sort of "drive-through" neighbor of northwest Indiana. Campbell has been respected by other writers of fiction for nearly twenty years. Her story collection *American Salvage* (2009) was a finalist for the National Book Award, and her novel *Once upon a River* (2011) received the broadest critical acclaim.

The novel tells of Margo Crane, sixteen years old in 1980, when the novel is set, and the outcast granddaughter of the Murray clan, whose metal-fabricating factory pollutes the fictional Stark River and the lives of nearly everyone living along its shores. Campbell imagines that Stark River flows into the real Kalamazoo River, which flows into Lake Michigan at the real town of Saugatuck. In this way, Campbell draws boundaries for new fictional territory, which she also explores in her novel *Q Road* (2002).

Though Margo stands apart from her Murray relations and from teenage girls in earlier eras of American fiction, she strongly resembles two currently popular fictional heroines: Lisbeth Salander of *The Girl with the Dragon Tattoo* (2008; *Män som hatar kvinnor*, 2005) and Katniss Everdeen of *The Hunger Games* (2008). All three hunt—Salander with her computer, Everdeen with bow and arrow, and Crane with a customized Marlin rifle that she steals from Cal Murray, her uncle and rapist. Margo's theft of the Marlin lets Campbell put Margo in intimate relationship with the power that will keep her from starving to death and give her standing in the Stark River community.

> Margo's heart pounded as she extracted the Marlin, the gun Cal had let her use on special occasions, because it was like Annie Oakley's, he said. Margo ran her hands over the squirrel carved into the walnut stock, the chrome lever. Cal had kept the gun oiled and polished. An electrical charge passed through her as she touched the gold-colored trigger. . . . She lifted the rifle to her shoulder and pointed it out the window. She pressed her cheek against the stock and looked over the iron sights at a bit of orange plastic ribbon stapled to a fence post. If she was going to leave this place and all its familiar landmarks, she would have to take this gun. She . . . gripped the Marlin in her left hand. She felt the ghosts of Murrays watching her. (Campbell 68)

Salander and Everdeen have cosmic goals. Salander penetrates national security networks to topple evil corporations and treasonous spy networks; Everdeen revolts against dystopian oppression operating through policies of enforced starvation masked as entertainment.

Like Salander and Everdeen, Margo Crane fights for survival, but unlike them, she fights only for herself. Campbell restricts her world to the shores of the Stark River. Margo lives in various places on the river, but we never see her more than a few hundred feet inland, except for her visit to a Planned Parenthood clinic in Kalamazoo. Indeed, Campbell takes pains to show that Margo sees herself as inseparable from the river. The following passage is characteristic; its motifs recur throughout the novel:

> Margo rowed upstream, *warmed herself against the current*. . . . After about two hours of hard pulling in the dark, she found a shallow stream, maneuvered herself a few yards up into it, out of view of river traffic, and *tied her boat to the roots of a tree*. She curled up in her sleeping bag on the back seat of her boat *as she used to curl on the couch* to wait for Crane to come home, and fell asleep. *Rocked by the motion of the river*, she slept hard and for a long time, until the sun was high the following day. . . . By the afternoon of that second full day of rowing, she was tired and hungry beyond any exhaustion or hunger she had known. With each pull of her oars, *she felt herself liquefying*. A few times she paused and *put her hands into the water to soothe them*. When snow began to fall around her, *she wondered if she might dissolve* before she got where she was going, like the big flakes that fell on the water. (71–73; emphasis added)

The life of the world beyond the river barely impinges on Margo's thoughts, feelings, or purposes. For six months, she edges close to what passes for normal living in late twentieth-century America by living with Michael, who tries to draw her into town life, church, school:

> She had gone once [to Michael's church], had listened to the minister. The man meant well, she could tell, but he was as dull as a schoolteacher. She had enjoyed the guitar music, but she didn't like the way people wanted to shake her hand and talk afterward. She didn't dislike people, she told Michael, but at church there were too many all at once. He said it was

okay that she didn't go, but he was disappointed she didn't want to be part of his community. He was also disappointed that she didn't show any interest in school. He thought Margo needed to set personal goals, that it was not enough to live a beautiful life on the river, fishing, shooting, and collecting berries, nuts, and mushrooms. (153)

This restriction affects the reader in ways that Jane Smiley emphasized in her *New York Times* review:

Because Margo is so strong and idiosyncratic, because she possesses such great natural innocence, the reader would like her to transcend her circumstances, but the constant refrain of her life, as young as she is, is not transcendence but consequences. She is doomed to pay the price for her ignorance, pay the price for her enthusiasm, pay the price for her affections and pay the price for the sins of those who came before. The damaged world she lives in remains an ecosystem in which animals and humans, field and stream, purity and pollution, love and hate are tightly interconnected. It would be too bad if, because of Campbell's realistic style and ferocious attention to her setting, "Once Upon a River" were discounted as merely a fine example of American regionalism. It is, rather, an excellent American parable about the consequences of our favorite ideal, freedom. (Smiley 2)

While driving through Campbell country to a meeting of the Society for the Study of Midwestern Literature, I think once more about Campbell's vision and Smiley's words. Whether and when regional literature becomes national are questions that inform, directly or indirectly, every discussion of midwestern literature in ways unknown for decades in discussions of the literature of New England and the South. Of course Henry David Thoreau, Ralph Waldo Emerson, and Nathaniel Hawthorne are American writers now, but they were provincial writers from the viewpoint of nineteenth-century London. Of course William Faulkner and Carson McCullers and Eudora Welty are

American writers now; they were regional writers, but readers all over the world no longer think of them that way. Who thinks of Mark Twain as a Missouri writer, or F. Scott Fitzgerald as a Minnesota writer, or Ernest Hemingway as an Illinois or Michigan writer, or Toni Morrison as an Ohio writer? No one, of course—they are American. So when Smiley has to remind readers that Campbell is more than a regional writer, she is guiding them along a trail—a kind of mental shoreline once trod by earlier generations of readers—from one mode of literary knowing to another.

What qualities must a literary work possess to complete the journey from regional to American? Smiley's review suggests that an important attribute is the theme of damages risked and endured during the pursuit of freedom. Freedom and consequences—we live on the shoreline between them.

Up the Western Shoreline of Lake Michigan

Once again I am driving US-12 through the Dunes of northwest Indiana, but now I am heading west—into Chicago. On my right I pass ArcelorMittal Steel, the world's second-largest steelmaker and current owner of four square miles of dunes. Next I pass Midwest Steel, occupying about two and a half square miles of lakeshore; then, crossing the Gary, Indiana, city line, I travel for nearly eight miles along the southern edge of the US Steel Works. Between Midwest and US Steel lie the town of Ogden Dunes and the West Beach portion of the Indiana Dunes National Lakeshore. These unlikely neighbors always remind me of a conflictual family—forced to live together by peculiar historical circumstances and a common desire for access to the shore but able to agree on very little else, certainly not on the best uses of the land and water they need.

People who bemoan the presence of the ugly industrial landscape and its deleterious effects on the quality of the water and the air forget that a little more than a century ago, nobody wanted the Dunes. When Judge Elbert Henry Gary proposed to build a state-of-the-art steel manufactory on the sand hills east of Chicago, he earned praise for at last finding a practical economic use for what all regarded as essentially a worthless desert. Moreover, his plans to build a model town for his workers, including the latest improvements not only in housing but in education and other social services, were hailed as convincing evidence that industrial and human progress walked hand in hand. It is one of history's obscure ironies that in 1898, eight years before Judge Gary broke ground for his grand design, Professor Henry C. Cowles of the University of Chicago published his doctoral dissertation explaining the scientific significance of the Dunes's unique succession of plant genera and coining the word *ecology*.

I just wrote that no one wanted the Dunes in 1900, but that is not quite correct. The sand, an obstacle to anyone trying to move across it or grow anything in it where it was, proved transformative when carried to other places. Worthless when piled by nature in heaps along the southern shore of Lake Michigan, it became nearly priceless when distributed by humans in the right amounts a few miles up the shore to the northwest. People walk, run, and roll in pleasure on the Chicago shoreline. No city in the United States has for its main street a thoroughfare quite like Lake Shore Drive. Few know or seem to care that the ground supporting Daniel Burnham's superbly planned constellation of parks and museums and the roads connecting them includes of millions of tons of Indiana sand ("Implementation"; "Lake Shore Drive"; Rodriguez).

The eagerness and energy with which Chicagoans manipulated their shoreline, displacing water with sand, may partly explain Chicagoans' intense relationship with real estate. When you have to make it up yourselves instead of just exploiting what nature provides, you tend to pay closer attention. Of course, residents of any city obsess about real estate; Chicagoans are not special in that way. But Chicagoans' relationship with where, how, and with whom they live has a unique history that continues to define every facet of the city's character. Even the city's literary and theatrical histories bear the imprint of its real-estate obsessions. We can find a complex exploration of this relationship in two plays: Lorraine Hansberry's *A Raisin in the Sun* (1959) and Bruce Norris's *Clybourne Park* (2010).

Hansberry's play has a unique place in US theater history; it is the first play by a black woman to run on Broadway, as well as the first Broadway play directed by a black director, Lloyd Richards. It is also the first play to succeed in getting large numbers of mainstream white audiences to accept a realistic view of the lives of working-class African Americans. Whereas Broadway and Hollywood, throughout the first half of the twentieth century, caricatured blacks to emphasize the differences between them and whites, Hansberry showed audiences that the aspirations of the Younger family are identical to everyone else's: Get a better education, find a better job, own a business, work hard, sacrifice, move up, and the best evidence of your success will be a nicer home in a nicer neighborhood.

Hansberry knew this life because she lived it. Her father, Carl Hansberry, owned the Lake Street Bank in Chicago and in the 1940s led a series of successful court cases that overturned and outlawed restrictive covenants in real-estate transactions. As the Youngers do at the end of the play, the Hansberrys crossed Chicago's residential color line and faced the consequences of their bid for freedom. Hansberry described one of them in an autobiographical passage that appeared in 1959 in the *New Yorker*:

> My mother is a remarkable woman, with great courage. She sat in that house for eight months with us—while Daddy spent most of his time in Washington fighting his case—in what was, to put it mildly, a very hostile neighborhood. I was on the porch one day with my sister, swinging my legs, when a mob gathered. We went inside, and while we were in our living room, a brick came crashing through the window with such force it embedded itself in the opposite wall. I was the one the brick almost hit. (qtd. in Choate 8)

In *Raisin*, the Youngers move to a fictional Chicago neighborhood called Clybourne Park. (There is a Clybourne Avenue in Chicago.) Bruce Norris makes this neighborhood the setting for his play. The first act, set in 1959, presents Russ and Bev (no last names for Norris's characters) in the midst of packing their belongings. They are moving to a new house in a new suburb and they have sold their house to a black family named the Youngers. Their preparations are interrupted by a visit (secretly arranged by Bev) from their pastor, Jim, who comically tries and fails to get Russ to explain the reasons for his now-quite-lengthy withdrawal from the social and business life of the community. While the pastor is there, another visitor calls: Russ and Bev's neighbor Karl Lindner, whom alert students of Hansberry's play will recognize as a character in *Raisin*. Lindner has just come from his failed attempt to persuade the Youngers not to move into the neighborhood. Now Karl vigorously tries to persuade Russ and Bev to renege on their agreement to sell to the Youngers. Complications mount when Karl's hearing-impaired and pregnant wife joins the discussion. The knot of white homeowners scuffling verbally about preserving the color line in late 1950s Chicago is observed with increasing dismay by Bev and Russ's black maid, Francine, and her husband, Albert. Pressures on Russ mount. Finally he explodes in a denunciation of all the pleaders and the entire neighborhood. In his fury, he reveals the motive for their move: they can no longer stand to live in the house because it is the scene of their son's suicide. They no longer want to live in Clybourne Park because the neighbors have been ostracizing their son, a Korean War veteran convicted of committing atrocities against innocent Koreans. In this act, Norris accomplishes a feat rare among American playwrights, successfully linking psychological, social, and political themes.

In the second act, new characters take the stage. The year is now 2009. During the intervening fifty years, Clybourne Park has become an entirely black neighborhood. However, a young white couple,

Lindsey and Steve, have made an offer on the now-run-down Younger house. They want to demolish it and build a three-story condominium. Complications arise when the Clybourne Park Historic Preservation Association, represented by Kevin and Lena (another tip of Norris's hat to *Raisin*'s main character), objects to what it sees as the beginnings of white gentrification, a continuation of racial division under another name. The parties to the dispute have each brought their attorneys. What follows is a polished, effective satire of racial politics in Chicago in the context of Americans' obsessions with real estate and the conflicts they generate between the pursuit of economic freedom and the consequences of that pursuit for the achievement of social justice.

These two plays are far from the only literary works that raise up characters living on the Chicago shoreline for our edification and entertainment. The list of novels, stories, plays, poems, and memoirs is long and distinguished. Carl Smith's *Chicago and the American Literary Imagination, 1880–1920* (1984) is a good place for the uninitiated to begin. Some post–World War II writers can be followed in the first section of Carlo Rotella's *October Cities: The Redevelopment of Urban Literature* (1998). Also helpful is Rotella's article "Literary Images of Chicago." Carla Cappetti's *Writing Chicago: Modernism, Ethnography, and the Novel* (1993) overlaps with Smith's and Rotella's books. Writers not discussed by these three scholars must be pursued one by one, because no comprehensive study of Chicago literature yet exists.

Are You into Wisconsin Yet?

US-12 carries me into Chicago but leaves the shoreline at East Ninety-Fifth Street and South Ewing Avenue. (It heads west—a direction that does not interest me—for 2,166 miles to Aberdeen, Washington, and the Pacific Ocean.) I am familiar with this corner because ever since the Skyway raised its fare to $3.00 sometime in the 1990s, I have preferred the surface streets on the southeast side of Chicago. They offer much more to see, hear, and smell, and the subtly changing character of the city is much more apparent, especially as the seasons revolve. So instead, I continue north on US-41—South Shore Drive, Lake Shore Drive, Sheridan Road—often to my sister's house in Evanston, and at least once a year into Wisconsin and on to my old hometown of Marquette in Michigan's Upper Peninsula. I feel as if my life has US-41 as one of the strands of its DNA.

You may imagine, then, that the publication of Chad Harbach's novel *The Art of Fielding* (2011) caught my interest. Harbach combines a baseball story, two love stories, and a meditation on the freedom and consequences of the pursuit of athletic glory, remedies for loneliness, and literary scholarship.

The setting is a small liberal-arts college right on the shore of Lake Michigan. Harbach is not specific, but a reasonable conjecture from references to actual highways and locations would be that it is in Kewaunee County, south of Door County, not far from the point where I-43 angles northwest from Manitowoc and heads toward Green Bay. The college's name—Westish—derives from a word used by Herman Melville when, in the novel, he traveled from New York City to see the Great Lakes and gave a lecture on Shakespeare. In the lecture, Harbach has Melville say, "Humbled, I am, by the severe beauty of this Westish land, and these Great Lakes, America's secret sinew of inward-collecting seas" (74). A different passage in the lecture has the most profound effect on one of the novel's main characters, Guert Affenlight, president of Westish College:

> It was not before my twenty-fifth year, by which time I had returned to my native New York from a four years' voyage aboard whalers and frigates, having seen much of the world, at least the watery parts, and certain verdant corners deemed uncivil by our Chattywags and Mumbledywumps, that I took up my pen in earnest, and began to live; since then, scarcely a week has gone by when I do not feel myself unfolding within myself. (Harbach 61)

Affenlight reads these lines when he is an undergraduate football star at Westish and working as an aide in the library. He discovers the manuscript of the Melville lecture. Harbach writes:

> Upon his first reading, Affenlight failed to untangle the syntax before the semicolon, but that final clause embedded itself swiftly in his soul. He too wanted to unfold within himself, and to feel himself so doing; it thrilled him, this oracular promise of a wiser, wilder life. He'd never traveled beyond the Upper Midwest, nor written anything a teacher hadn't required, but this single magical sentence made him want to roam the world and write books about what he found. (61)

Affenlight is not the only character on the shores of Lake Michigan enraptured by magical sentences. Henry Skrimshander, a seventeen-year-old Westish baseball player from Lankton, South Dakota, also carries a manuscript in his hand and heart: Aparicio Rodriguez's *The Art of Fielding*, a manual about playing the position of shortstop. It is a smorgasbord of sansaras.

> 26. The shortstop is a source of stillness at the center of the defense. He projects this stillness and his teammates respond

> 59. To field a ground ball must be considered a generous act and an act of comprehension. One moves not against the ball but with it. Bad fielders stab at the ball like an enemy. This is antagonism. The true fielder lets the path of the ball become his own path, thereby comprehending the ball and dissipating the self, which is the source of all suffering and poor defense. . . .

> 3. There are three stages: Thoughtless being. Thought. Return to thoughtless being.

33. Do not confuse the first and third stages. Thoughtless being is attained by everyone, the return to thoughtless being by a very few. (16)

Harbach's novel fuses the fictional, the metafictional, and the real. Like Campbell, Hansberry, and Norris, Harbach pursues the freedom that literature confers and achieves a work of art that brings attention to actual and metaphorical shorelines of our lives. For his characters, pursuing visions of freedom on these shorelines has less happy consequences. Henry, on the very brink of a perfect season, suddenly loses his ability to throw a baseball accurately and, as a consequence, seriously injures his teammate Owen Dunne. Guert, at age sixty, falls in love with Owen and, as a consequence, loses his job and then his life. But the novel itself, and Harbach's skill in writing it, brings great satisfaction to many readers.

The Art of Fielding, *Clybourne Park*, and *Once upon a River*, taken together, confer new and serious cultural interest on shorelines and adjacent lands of Lake Michigan. Each work has traveled the path from regional to national significance—and, in the case of Norris's play, to international significance as well, having won four top awards for best new play, the Pulitzer and Tony in the United States and the Olivier and Evening Standard in the United Kingdom. Travelers will always enjoy the attractions of the various landscapes and towns offered by the highways along the shores of Lake Michigan. To them they may now add a deeper appreciation for the superb literary art that these shorelines inspire.

Works Cited

Campbell, Bonnie Jo. *Once Upon a River*. New York: Norton, 2011. Print.
Cappetti, Carla. *Writing Chicago: Modernism, Ethnography, and the Novel*. New York: Columbia UP, 1998. Print.
Choate, E. Teresa. *Hansberry in an Hour*. Hanover: Smith, 2010. Print. Playwrights in an Hour.

Cowles, Henry Chandler. *Ecological Relations of the Vegetation on the Sand Dunes of Lake Michigan*. Chicago: U of Chicago P, 1899. Print.

Govinda, Anagarika. *Creative Meditation and Multi-Dimensional Consciousness*. Wheaton: Theosophical, 1976. Print. Quest Bk.

Hansberry, Lorraine. *A Raisin in the Sun*. Rev. 30th anniv. ed. New York: French, 1988. Print.

Harbach, Chad. *The Art of Fielding*. New York: Little, 2011. Print.

"Implementation." *Encyclopedia of Chicago*. Chicago Historical Society, n.d. Web. 18 June 2012.

"Lake Shore Drive." *Encyclopedia of Chicago*. Chicago Historical Society, n.d. Web. 18 June 2012.

"Mascouten Indian Tribe History." *Access Genealogy*. Access Genealogy.com, n.d. Web. 30 May 2012.

Miller, Arthur. *Death of a Salesman*. New York: Viking, 1949. Print.

Norris, Bruce. *Clybourne Park*. London: Hern, 2010. Print.

Rodriguez, Karen M. "Shoreline Erosion." *Encyclopedia of Chicago*. Chicago Historical Society, n.d. Web. 18 June 2012.

Rotella, Carlo. "Literary Images of Chicago." *Encyclopedia of Chicago*. Chicago Historical Society, n.d. Web. 18 June 2012.

___. *October Cities: The Redevelopment of Urban Literature*. Berkeley: U of California P, 1998. E-book.

Smiley, Jane. "Bonnie Jo Campbell's Rural Michigan Gothic." *New York Times Sunday Book Review*. New York Times, 22 July 2011. Web. 13 June 2012.

Smith, Carl S. *Chicago and the American Literary Imagination, 1880–1920*. Chicago: U of Chicago P, 1984. Print.

Key to the Highway: The Road in the Blues _____

Phil Patton

I

"Key to the Highway" is an old blues song that has been recorded by Charlie Segar, Big Bill Broonzy, Little Walter, and other musicians. It turns on a joke: the highway is not locked; no one needs a key; it is free. But the song and others about the road offer a key to the spiritual map of the blues, that assemblage of poetry and imagery that is so central to the American experience.

The highway is a major metaphor in the blues, and "Key to the Highway" is just one of many blues songs about the road and the highway. The titles of road-themed blues songs go back to the earliest blues, like Tommy Johnson's "Big Road Blues" (first recorded in 1928), and include "Highway 61," recorded in variations by many artists, including James Son Ford Thomas, and "Highway 49," sung by Big Joe Williams. Robert Johnson made "Crossroads Blues" famous and sang of the road in "Sweet Home Chicago."

The spiritual landscape of the road is laid out in blues lyrics. The core myth of the road was tied to myths of freedom and escape, in both a social and a spiritual sense. The freedom of the road, however, is also a source of loneliness, restlessness, and rootlessness. The road exacts a price.

The myth of the road is an old trope in American culture. "The road" usually refers to the road west, the route of the pioneer and the wagon train, along the classic lines of American myths of the frontier and manifest destiny. The road also crops up in music and literature. The way west, the route to economic escape or prosperity, is tied to another numbered highway. Route 66 figures not only in the pop song of the same name, recorded by artists of all styles, but also in John Steinbeck's *Grapes of Wrath* (1939) and Jack Kerouac's *On the Road* (1957) and even in the Disney-Pixar animated film *Cars* (2006). (The highways were given their numbers by state and federal agreement in the mid-1920s.)

Culturally, Route 66 finds its counterpoint in Highway 61 north, which runs from Congo Square, the old slave market in New Orleans, all the way to Hibbing, Minnesota, home of Bob Dylan, creator of the landmark 1965 album *Highway 61 Revisited*. Whereas Route 66 heads west, Highway 61 runs north. For poor people in the American South, especially African Americans, the freedom of the road was only the freedom to go—to flee north. This was an experience central to American song and story.

So the cultural geography of rail and road, from south to north, touches on key racial, economic, and artistic issues in America. The migration of African Americans from the South, the land of cotton, to the North, the land of factory and city, was the greatest in America's history—even larger, in sheer numbers, than the movement west. Between the beginning of World War I and 1970, some six million people made the move north. This migration is charted in two notable books, *The Promised Land: The Great Black Migration and How It Changed America* (1991) by Nicholas Lemann and *The Warmth of Other Suns: The Epic Story of America's Great Migration* (2010) by Isabel Wilkerson.

Many of these African American migrants left the Mississippi Delta first by railroad and then by Highway 61, on a bus or in a car. The Delta, from which so many blues singers arose, is an area of rich soil, ideal for raising cotton, along the Mississippi River. It takes its name from its pyramid shape, which resembles the Greek letter *delta* (Δ). The Delta was a social and economic pyramid as well. Atop the pyramid sits the city of Memphis, Tennessee, home of those who owned the land and dealt in the cotton. The base of the pyramid was the great mass of poor sharecroppers.

The pyramid plays a large role in the nomenclature of businesses in the area. Indeed, Egyptian imagery is abundant. Memphis echoes its forerunner city in Egypt. The climate invites comparisons with the

Highway 61 runs north from New Orleans to the US-Canadian border in Minnesota.

Nile Delta, the sharecropping population with the children of Israel and their enslavement by Pharaoh.

Sharecropping was a halfway state between slavery and free labor, in which families lived on plantation land and worked the fields, ostensibly in exchange for a portion of the value of the crop when it was sold. But because the plantation owner did the accounting, there was rarely any value to be shared; instead, the sharecropper was in perpetual debt. Even within Memphis, the tip of the socioeconomic pyramid is sharply defined; the center of life in the city, the Peabody Hotel, is famously said to mark the edge of the area. As the local saying goes, "The Mississippi Delta begins in the lobby of the Peabody Hotel."

Fleeing the sharecropper system, young men would hobo and make a living playing in the streets. Many blues singers were literally at home on the road, moving from club to club or walking from place to place as itinerant street performers. Bessie Smith, the "Empress of the Blues," traveled up and down the road and died in a car accident on Highway 61. Magic Slim sang "The Highway Is My Home."

II

Some singers were quite precise in describing the literal track of a road. For example, Big Joe Williams, who was based in St. Louis, begins a version of "Highway 49" by listing an itinerary of the towns it passes. In a litany reminiscent of a railroad conductor or bus station announcer, he sings, "Highway 49, leaving out of Memphis down to Clarksdale, Mississippi . . . until Hattiesburg, until Gulfport, Mississippi and that's the end of it."

But the songs about Highway 61, the most symbolic of roads, place it in various geographical locations, many of them different from where it actually ran. Such dislocations are key: the imaginary geography of the road as it shows up in the songs proves that it is not attached to a real landscape as much as to a spiritual one. For example, a 1933 version of "Highway 61" by Will Batts and the Jack Kelly Memphis Jug Band—one of the earliest recorded examples of the song—says, "It runs from Atlanta Georgia to the Gulf of Mexico" (Kelly). But Mississippi Fred McDowell sings:

> Lord, that 61 Highway is the longest road I know.
> Lord, that 61 Highway may be the longest road I know
> She run from New York City, down to the Gulf of Mexico.
> (McDowell)

Further on, he testifies that Highway 61 "runs from New York City right by my baby's door," indicating an emotional connection in the absence of a physical one; Highway 61 runs nowhere near New York, except perhaps in the heart.

III

The road is a place of charged spirituality, nowhere more so than at the crossroads, a place of destiny in Greek mythology and African folklore. The crossing of roads echoes the crossing of rails "where the Southern [Railway] cross the Dog"—the Yellow Dog or Yazoo Delta Railway. This line of the iconic first blues song was captured by W. C. Handy in a railroad station in 1903.

In "Cross Road Blues," Robert Johnson sings about going to the crossroads, where legend has him selling his soul to the devil for the skill to play guitar. The medium in which this legend lived was not the song itself but the interviews and interpretations of the blues industry, the record companies and music publications. The crossroads even became specific: the intersection of Highway 61 and Highway 49, near Clarksdale. (This is an unlikely twist; the intersection is actually far from an isolated crossroads, and for much of their courses, these two numbered roads are nearly parallel.)

Having taught Johnson to play, according to the legend, the devil eventually returned to collect his soul, presumably using as his agent the man who killed Johnson in a dispute over a woman. In "Me and the Devil Blues," another Johnson song, a dark vision emerges when he sings about his ghost taking to the road north on a bus. "You can bury my body down by the highway side so my old evil spirit can catch a Greyhound bus and ride" (Johnson).

Johnson has now grown so mythical, thanks to Greil Marcus, Robert Palmer, and other critics, that we must place Johnson in our cultural pantheon beside Edgar Allan Poe and Herman Melville. He fits within the tradition Harry Levin traced in *The Power of Blackness* (1958).

IV

The life of the blues singers of several generations was one of wandering on the road, riding rails, and touring. The autobiography of David "Honeyboy" Edwards, *The World Don't Owe Me Nothing* (1997), is a revealing account of the life and methods of a blues singer and his experiences on the road. Edwards, who died in 2011 at the age of ninety-six, was a remarkable figure; his career began when he was a teenager, following and performing with Robert Johnson in Mississippi, and continued into his nineties.

In his book, assembled from recollections, Edwards describes life for an apprentice bluesman. Edwards was barely fourteen when, around 1930, he began to play on the streets and ride the rails. At times he played on plantations as an attraction for local bootleggers; these dances were lit by informal lanterns in trees, Coca-Cola bottles filled with kerosene and stuffed with wicks, creating contemporary versions of the African bottle trees of the southern landscape. Sometimes he played to help gather crowds for patent medicine shows that traveled between small towns. Eventually, like many blues singers, he was recorded by traveling folklorist Alan Lomax.

But for many decades, music was more about performing live than it was about recording songs for posterity. This meant that the music was more mutable and folkloric. Songs and lines were borrowed and swapped with little sense of ownership. Edwards describes putting together a song from existing pieces: "I went and recorded it . . . . I never heard of nobody else recording it. Everybody used to take everybody else's numbers and do something with them. That's where the songs come from. You sit down, get one verse out of one number, one verse out of another . . . . Or take two or three verses and play a different tune with it" (172–73).

Recurrent lines and phrases and modified melodies meant that songs mutated wildly in the early blues. These bits of song are called floating verses. Singers would often incorporate the numbers of local roads or the names of local towns in their lyrics, like a politician using local names in his stump speech. This in part accounts for the use of road names in songs. Varying names and numbers also made rhyming easier.

Only when the phonograph became common did things change.[1] The first phonographs were wind-up clockwork devices for a countryside that was not yet electrified. Once a song was on vinyl, audiences listened to it over and over again, and they demanded that the live performance match the record.

V

Highway 61, of course, also ran from north to south, symbolically, as the pathway of northern discovery of southern music. (In contrast, we think of Route 66 as running only from east to west—never the reverse.) This return trip was a complex journey of appreciation mingled with exploitation, elevation with condescension.

The great parable of the process came in 1938, when the New York record producer John Hammond, having come across recorded music of Robert Johnson, tried to find him. But neither Hammond nor his scouts in Mississippi could find Johnson, who had already died—probably poisoned by a jealous rival. So for his famous Spiritual to Swing concert that December in Carnegie Hall, Hammond wheeled out a phonograph and played records by the creator of "Phonograph Blues."

Early bluesmen traveled by foot, rail, and bus. Only later did the key to the highway turn into an ignition key. Few bluesmen would have been able to afford a car, although Charley Patton, a star of the Delta, was said to have acquired a Chevrolet before his death in 1934. Certainly Robert Johnson would have been hard pressed to dream of owning a Terraplane, the fast, streamlined Hudson referred to in his song "Terraplane Blues." (Ironically, John Hammond did own a Terraplane.)

But the evolution from blues to rock and roll followed the highway. "Rocket 88," the song with the best claim to be the first rock and roll song, is credited to Jackie Brenston and His Delta Cats. It was actually written by Ike Turner. And it literally took its sound from Highway 61.

In March 1951, a group of young musicians and their gear headed up 61 from the Delta to make a recording in Memphis. Their leader was Ike Turner. On the drive along Highway 61 in an overloaded Buick, the amp slipped from the roof and bounced off the pavement. The group recovered their equipment and proceeded to Sun Studio on Union Avenue. But as Turner later described it, the blow permanently altered the sound of the speaker. When Sam Phillips, the legendary producer, stuffed the broken amp with paper, the result was a woofing sound that people liked and that helped make the record a hit. Ike Turner's trip up 61 marks a symbolic link between blues and rock and roll.

VI

The musical traffic on Highway 61 ran both ways in the 1960s. In his autobiography *Chronicles: Volume One* (2004), Bob Dylan wrote about Highway 61 and how he thought of it when he was growing up in Hibbing, Minnesota, near Duluth:

> Highway 61, the main thoroughfare of the country blues, begins about where I came from . . . . I always felt like I'd started on it, always had been on it and could go anywhere from it, even down into the deep Delta country. It was the same road, full of the same contradictions, the same one-horse towns, the same spiritual ancestors. . . . It was my place in the universe, always felt like it was in my blood. (240–41)

The road north figures as a literary trope as well, tracing a similar cultural geography along the road Faulkner sent his characters on in his last novel, *The Reivers* (1962)—the physical and symbolic road from Mississippi to Memphis. His racially mixed pair steal an old Winton car and head up the muddy road to adventure in a picaresque tale, later filmed with Steve McQueen.

The flat landscape of the Delta through which Highways 49 and 61 run is well treated in photography that matches the music.

Contemporary photographers Birney Imes and William Eggleston treat it; Walker Evans and other Farm Security Administration photographers shot Highway 61; and the writer Eudora Welty, who also worked as a government photographer during the Depression, dealt with the road in both image and story.

It is evident from photos that only in the 1940s did paved roads and electricity come to many parts of the Delta. Honeyboy Edwards recalled hitchhiking along Highway 61 when it was still gravel; a Walker Evans photo of a hitchhiker near Vicksburg suggests how the lonely the road looked. The arrival of the tractor, displacing the mule, and the mechanized cotton picker, displacing the human picker, changed the landscape dramatically and set off a second wave of migration up Highway 61 to the North.

The road as symbol was also modernized. When giants of rock and roll like Eric Clapton and the Rolling Stones recorded versions of such blues classics as "Crossroads," "Highway 61," and "Key to the Highway," the blues highway might be said to have rejoined the main route of popular music. Aretha Franklin turned it into "The Freeway of Love," Bruce Springsteen suburbanized it, and the Talking Heads existentialized it as the "Road to Nowhere." With Dylan's later homages to Charley Patton in "High Water (for Charley Patton)," from his 2001 album *Love and Theft*, Highway 61 was revisited again and again. The road was firmly established as one of core tropes not only of the blues but of all popular American music.

As many blues remind us, "The road goes on forever."

Notes

1. Thanks to Sears Roebuck or Montgomery Ward, phonographs were remarkably affordable. Such goods could be sent by Rural Free Delivery, a government program that, among other things, improved the quality of rural roads so the post office could reach isolated farms.

Works Cited

Dylan, Bob. *Chronicles: Volume One*. New York: Simon, 2004. Print.

Edwards, David Honeyboy, Janis Martinson, and Michael Robert Frank. *The World Don't Owe Me Nothing: The Life and Times of Delta Bluesman Honeyboy Edwards*. Chicago: Chicago Rev., 1997. Print.

Johnson, Robert. *Robert Johnson: The Complete Recordings*. Columbia, 1990. CD.

Kelly, Jack, and His South Memphis Jug Band. "Highway No. 61 Blues." *The Sounds of Memphis (1933–1939)*. Story of Blues, 1987. CD.

Levine, Lawrence W. *Black Culture and Black Consciousness: Afro-American Folk Thought from Slavery to Freedom*. Oxford: Oxford UP, 1977. Print.

Marcus, Greil. *Mystery Train: Images of America in Rock 'n' Roll Music*. New York: Dutton, 1975. Print.

McDowell, Fred. "61 Highway Blues." *61 Highway Mississippi*. Comp. Alan Lomax. Rounder, 1997. CD. Southern Journey 3.

Palmer, Robert. *Deep Blues: A Musical and Cultural History of the Mississippi Delta*. New York: Viking, 1981. Print.

Williams, Big Joe. "Highway 49." *Blues on Highway 49*. Delmark, 1962. LP.

Yafa, Stephen H. *Cotton: The Biography of a Revolutionary Fiber*. New York: Viking, 2005. Print.

Travel Guidebooks, Cultural Narratives, and the American Road Quest _____

Steven K. Bailey

From *A Walk across America* (1979) by Peter Jenkins to Bill Bryson's *The Lost Continent: Travels in Small-Town America* (1989), the American road quest features prominently in travel writing and other subgenres of literary nonfiction. No two road quests ever unfold in quite the same way, of course, as the journeys undertaken by Jenkins and Bryson clearly illustrate. As an idealistic young man, Jenkins set out to discover America by walking across the continent. Bryson, on the other hand, sought to rediscover the United States as a jaded middle-aged expatriate who had spent the previous two decades overseas. Nonetheless, their narratives share some common characteristics of the American road quest: an open road, chance encounters, perhaps a faithful human or canine companion, and, if not a destination, then at least a motive for open-ended travel. Though road-quest narratives typically feature such elements, they almost always neglect to mention another necessity: travel guidebooks and road atlases.

Road-quest narrators rarely acknowledge the use of atlases and guidebooks, but I suspect that these texts often facilitate their adventures. In fact, I will argue that American road quests, like travels abroad, are frequently shaped and directed by the guidebooks and road atlases that travelers carry with them. The sheer ubiquity of these guides and atlases, as well as their ability to function as how-to manuals for understanding unfamiliar terrain, makes them two particularly powerful genres. Guidebooks, for example, not only tell readers what to see but also tell them what to think about what they see. This power to influence how readers interpret the places they travel to is further enhanced by the objective tone of travel guides, which claim to present unbiased factual information rather than subjective interpretations. As a result, guidebooks tell readers what to think without the readers even noticing, much less questioning, what they are being told.

With this in mind, I consider in this essay how midwestern guide-books and road atlases are designed primarily for objectivity and usability. In other words, these texts package factual how-to information in formats that are easy for the reader to use. Building on the critical approaches taken by scholars examining international travel guide-books and other forms of instructional texts, I argue that while this focus on objectivity and usability may appear to suggest that guides and atlases are ideologically neutral, such a focus actually works to uphold dominant cultural narratives and position these narratives as normative and uncontested. This essay concludes that rather than confirming dominant narratives, travel guidebooks and atlases should challenge these narratives, render the ideologies—the values, beliefs, and assumptions—that underpin them visible, and open up space for counternarratives. In doing so, guidebooks and atlases can provide travelers with more nuanced understandings of the cities, counties, and cultures they encounter on the midwestern road quest.

Objectivity and Extreme Usability

Scholars have devoted considerable attention to nonfiction travel narratives, which range from Marco Polo's late thirteenth-century *Travels* to Elizabeth Gilbert's 2007 bestseller *Eat, Pray, Love: One Woman's Search for Everything across Italy, India, and Indonesia*. However, contemporary travel guidebooks and related genres such as the road atlas have largely escaped critical scrutiny, despite their substantial role in determining how travelers come to know the places they visit. In his critical study of travel guides to Vietnam, for example, the historian Scott Laderman argues that scholarly treatments of travel guidebooks have been "fleeting" at best (4). In this essay, I respond to Laderman's call for further research into travel guides by subjecting representative examples of midwestern guidebooks and road atlases to critical analysis. My approach is necessarily interdisciplinary, since the study of travel guidebooks and road atlases draws on so many academic specializations, including American history, literary studies, and technical communication.

As Nicholas T. Parsons suggests in his exhaustive history of the genre, the best travel guidebooks are powerful heuristic devices that help readers to know the world (280). Travel guidebooks instruct readers in how to navigate unfamiliar terrain, and they do so in both the physical and the ideological sense. As Laderman explains, while a guidebook tells a reader what sites to visit in a foreign country, that same guidebook also tells the reader how to interpret these sites (125). In urging its readers to visit a historic battlefield such as Gettysburg, for example, a guidebook will also provide readers with an ideologically charged historical and cultural narrative for understanding that battlefield. Laderman notes that while contemporary guidebooks to Vietnam describe former battlegrounds such as the city of Hue, where bloody fighting raged between US forces and the National Liberation Front (the Viet Cong) during the 1968 Tet Offensive, these descriptions are invariably presented in terms that coincide with dominant American conceptions of the Tet Offensive specifically and the Vietnam War more generally. For this reason, Laderman finds that most Western travelers in Vietnam perceive these guidebooks as relatively objective and true (8). Vietnamese readers, however, might not agree. In fact, a guidebook written by a Vietnamese author for a Vietnamese readership would no doubt give a substantially different account of the battle, but its audience would also be likely to perceive this account as both objective and true. Objectivity is relative, and what appears as commonsense truth to one group of readers might strike another group as subjective bias.

Scholars in a wide variety of fields recognize that truth is socially constructed, which simply means that what counts as the truth is mutually decided upon by groups of like-minded people. Different groups of people reach very different verdicts on what qualifies as truth. The concept of socially constructed truth is helpful for understanding why travel guidebooks, like all texts, are necessarily subjective. Guidebooks, however, typically claim to be objective, which suggests that they are ideologically neutral. Historian Paul Fussell even goes so far as to claim in *The Norton Book of Travel* (1987) that "guidebooks belong to the world of journalism" (15). While journalists might not agree with this assessment, many guidebook readers clearly do. Readers expect a journalistic tone, in fact, because they equate this tone with objectivity and truth.

To position guidebooks as objective, publishers perform a rhetorical sleight of hand that removes the author from the reader's view. A guidebook from a well-known publisher such as Lonely Planet, for example, does not typically feature the author's name on the front cover and instead emphasizes the brand name and logo. Guidebooks are also notable for the absence of the first-person voice, a convention of journalism that also works to remove the presence of the author. There is a definite commercial motive for scrubbing the author from a guidebook—the brand name gets the attention, rather than an individual author. Just as important, it is common practice in the guidebook industry for teams of authors to collaborate on guidebooks and for different authors to update new editions of the same guidebook. This can lead to confusion in determining who actually wrote a guidebook, but if the authors are removed from the front cover and their presence downplayed or even erased from the text, the issue becomes irrelevant. Most important, scrubbing the author from the text enhances the guidebook's veneer of objectivity. This objective gloss sells guidebooks, because, as Laderman reminds us, readers equate a guidebook's objectivity with its trustworthiness (8).

Trusting the brand, however, can leave the reader reliant on simplistic, one-dimensional renderings of countries and cultures. During his field research in Vietnam, for example, Laderman interviewed numerous Western tourists and found that many relied on the Lonely Planet guidebook *Vietnam* not only for practical how-to information about traveling in Vietnam but also for an interpretation of the nation's history. These tourists typically believed that Lonely Planet offered objective, truthful interpretations of historical events such as the Vietnam War (Laderman 8). However, Laderman observes, readers of the Lonely Planet guide to Vietnam might be taken aback to learn that one of its two authors,Robert Storey, was unapologetically subjective in his interpretation of Vietnam's history. During an interview with Laderman, Storey described himself as "very anti-communist," a position that led him to reject historical accounts that did not correspond to his own beliefs (7, 119). Storey freely admitted that when writing the guidebook, which includes substantial passages on the conflict in Vietnam, he ignored credible sources of information that ran counter to his own understanding of the war.

Storey's ideological position rendered his narrative of the Vietnam War highly subjective. However, readers perceived his narrative to be reliable and objective both because they trusted the Lonely Planet brand name and because the narrative tended to confirm common but nonetheless socially constructed assumptions held by Americans about the war. Ultimately, the Lonely Planet guide simply ignored counternarratives of the Vietnam War that might challenge its readers' assumptions about the conflict and, in so doing, provide them with a more comprehensive understanding of this complex war.

When readers confer authorship on a brand name rather than an individual writer, they tend to lose sight of the fact that guidebooks are written by real people who interpret the world subjectively based on the cultural and historical narratives they believe to be true. I am not suggesting that a guidebook author such as Storey consciously embarks on an ideological mission when drafting a travel guide. Rather, I am arguing that the tendency of guidebook publishers to downplay their authors in the service of supposed objectivity makes it easy for these authors to avoid having to conduct a rigorous self-evaluation of their own ideological leanings. Storey did not have to ask himself hard questions about the Vietnam War, for example, or account for sources of information that ran counter to the cultural and historical narratives that underpinned his interpretation of the events and locales his guidebook describes. As this example illustrates, when guidebooks erase their authors and claim to be objective, the writers of these guidebooks are able to present one-sided and even slipshod interpretations of history and culture. As a result, readers may encounter distorted and incomplete descriptions of cities, cultures, and countries.

If Laderman's critique of travel guidebooks to Vietnam can help us understand how the assumption of guidebook objectivity works to cloak the socially constructed nature of these texts, technical communication scholar Bradley Dilger's work can help us understand how a focus on usability allows authors to leave the ideological dimensions of their work implicit and unacknowledged. Dilger argues that technical writers and their employers are typically focused not merely on usability but on what he terms "extreme usability." According to Dilger, extreme usability and a corresponding "ideology of ease" have become the dominant consideration in the design of any technological product bound for consumer consumption, be it an Apple iPhone or a Dodge Dakota pickup truck (48, 51).

Within this ideology of ease, the primary objective of any instructional text written by a technical writer is ease of use, "making it easy," to the exclusion of all other factors (Dilger 47). Travel guidebooks are instructional texts designed primarily for how-to practicality and easy usability, and in this sense, guidebook authors are technical writers. This focus on the pragmatic serves the goal of extreme usability, which requires that the ideologies embedded in a text remain implicit and aligned with dominant lines of power. After all, including ideological assumptions in a guidebook that are dramatically at odds with the assumptions of its readership will not promote extreme usability but rather provoke confusion, frustration, fear, and anger, making the guidebook hard to use. As the next section of this essay illustrates, however, bringing such assumptions to the foreground can also promote genuine learning and foster deeper understandings of the places travelers visit.

Cartography and Cultural Narratives: The DeLorme *Michigan Atlas and Gazetteer*

Maps are an integral component of travel guidebooks and the primary component of road atlases. Readers trust maps to direct their travels and assume that they present objective representations of reality. Scholars of technical communication argue, however, that although maps are commonly accepted as factual depictions of reality, they are actually subjective depictions of one possible reality among many (Barton and Barton). For example, Europe and North America occupy the top portion of most globes not because there is some scientifically justifiable reason for this positioning but because European and North American nations have been dominant world powers for centuries. A globe that placed Australia, Africa, and South America at the top of the world would be no more or less accurate from a scientific standpoint, since *up* and *down* are arbitrary concepts in space. But Western cartographers put their own continents at the top of the globe to represent symbolically the dominance of the northern over the southern hemisphere. As this example illustrates, maps work to normalize as objective fact certain favored ideological assumptions, such as the preeminence of Europe and North America. In normalizing such assumptions, maps serve dominant lines of power and privilege certain cultural narratives while simultaneously repressing counternarratives.

With their trademark red covers and large ten-by-fifteen-inch pages, DeLorme's series of road atlases—one for each of the fifty states—may well be the most commonly used brand in the United States. In fact, road atlases produced by DeLorme and rival publishers are even more widely used than travel guidebooks, since motorists often consult them for local travel, and even travelers who use guidebooks are likely to consult a road atlas on occasion. The popularity of road atlases, which can be found tucked beneath the passenger seats or stashed in the trunks of cars throughout the Midwest, gives the genre the power to shape road trips to an even greater degree than travel guidebooks.

The attractively designed maps contained in DeLorme road atlases feature obscure details of the landscape, such as windmills and abandoned railroad grades. They also depict the boundaries of towns, cities, counties, and states with great precision. However, road atlases such as the DeLorme *Michigan Atlas and Gazetteer* do not depict the boundaries of Native American tribal lands, and in this way the maps support dominant cultural narratives about land ownership. The boundaries of the 1836 Ceded Territory, for example, do not appear on any map in the *Michigan Atlas and Gazetteer*, despite their contemporary cultural, political, and historical significance. In the 1836 Treaty of Washington, the Native American bands collectively known as the Ottawas relinquished their ownership of the northwestern portion of Michigan's Lower Peninsula and the eastern half of the state's Upper Peninsula. These lands, which became known as the 1836 Ceded Territory, make up about a third of Michigan's total land area. The treaty granted the Ottawas a number of reservations as well as subsistence hunting, fishing, and gathering rights throughout the territory and on the waters of the Great Lakes. While the treaty stripped the Ottawas of their traditional homeland, the tribal leaders—the *ogemuk*—understood that they had no choice but to accept the terms of the treaty, as the US military stood ready to force them from Michigan should they resist signing (McClurken).

While the US government failed to honor many aspects of the Treaty of Washington, allowing the public sale of reservation lands just five years after signing it, the subsistence rights granted to the Ottawas remained in force and have been repeatedly upheld in court. Within the boundaries of the territory, for example, the Ottawas have subsistence hunting and fishing rights not granted to other citizens of Michigan. The various bands also practice wildlife and natural-resource management on state and federal lands, such as the Manistee National Forest. The bands conduct this management on an equal basis with the Michigan Department of Natural Resources, the US Forest Service, and similar agencies. More broadly, the boundaries of the 1836 Ceded Territory continue to assert Native American treaty rights.

From a usability standpoint, placing the borders of the 1836 Ceded Territory on maps in the *Michigan Atlas and Gazetteer* might have little practical value for most readers. However, by making extreme usability the primary criterion for determining what to include in their road atlas maps, DeLorme implicitly upholds dominant cultural narratives while suppressing counternarratives. To put it simply, failing to include the boundaries of the 1836 Ceded Territory on maps of Michigan implicitly supports the dominant cultural narrative of land-use rights and land ownership in Michigan. According to this narrative, the issue of land rights and ownership was resolved in the 1800s, when Euro-American immigrants began to settle uninhabited and unclaimed land in Michigan. The narrative also suggests that Native Americans have largely disappeared and that the few who remain no longer have any special claims to Michigan beyond the boundaries of their small reservations—which also fail to appear on DeLorme maps. By adhering to this narrative, the *Michigan Atlas and Gazetteer* implicitly erases not only Native American land-use rights but also Native American culture and history. Even more significant, adhering to this narrative erases some particularly shameful aspects of Euro-American history, such as the taking of Native American land by force or unequal treaty. Such an erasure accords with dominant ideological assumptions already held by Euro-American readers, who consequently judge the atlas to be objective in its rendering of Michigan's political and historic topography. Such an erasure also aligns with extreme usability. After all, DeLorme would be unlikely to remain a top seller of road atlases in Michigan if it chose to map the state in a way that depicted boundaries drawn according to Native American cultural narratives, particularly since this would require the use of Native American languages such as Ojibwa (Anishinaabemowin). For most readers, such an approach would be seen as an impediment to usability and an indictment of the atlas as biased and subjective. These same readers would be unlikely to view the decision to omit Native American cultural narratives from road atlas maps as a biased cartographic decision that privileges dominant Euro-American cultural assumptions.

Design Templates and Cultural Narratives: Lonely Planet's *Great Lakes* Guide

The technical writers, cartographers, and visual designers who produce DeLorme state road atlases must adhere to the company's master design template when creating or revising individual atlases in the series. This template governs all aspects of design, from the size of the map pages to the colors on the front cover. As a result, all of the road atlases in the DeLorme series look almost exactly alike. In addition to simplifying design and production, this uniform appearance benefits DeLorme by fostering brand recognition.

Like DeLorme, the travel-guidebook publisher Lonely Planet requires its authors to follow master design templates. These templates allow guidebooks to be produced with production-line efficiency, as evidenced by the fact that Lonely Planet has some five hundred titles in its catalogue and has sold over eighty million copies, according to the company's website. Lonely Planet templates differ depending on the specific series of guides, but all of these templates emphasize extreme usability as the primary design goal. The road-trip guidebook series remains the ultimate manifestation of this focus on extreme usability. *Lonely Planet Road Trip: Lake Michigan*, for example, is a sixty-four-page guide that jettisons historical and cultural information in favor of practical information about what to see and do as well as where to eat and sleep. Whether the author of the guide wished to include more cultural and historical background so that the reader could better understand the context of the guide's how-to information is irrelevant; the design template's demand for extreme usability overrode such concerns. As this example illustrates, in-house design templates are powerful tools that dictate the content and visual appearance of guidebooks. Parsons even suggests that these templates often have a greater influence on contemporary guidebook design than the authors of the guidebooks (xxi).

This certainly remains the case with the Lonely Planet series of regional and country guides, which all look the same and read as if they were all written by the same person. Lonely Planet promotes this conformity as a virtue and announces at the beginning of its *Great Lakes* regional guide that "all Lonely Planet guidebooks follow the same format." For example, chapters are always organized in the same way, as the *Great Lakes* guide rather proudly explains: "We always start with background, then proceed to sights, places to stay, places to eat, entertainment, getting there and away, and getting around information—in that order" (Ver Berkmoes, Huhti, and Lightbody 12). All Lonely Planet guides have a "Facts for the Visitor" chapter containing the same subsections on topics ranging from money to public holidays. The rigidity of Lonely Planet's design template prevents the kind of flexibility that might better serve readers, however. After all, a guide to the Great Lakes region of the United States might require a rather different set of "Facts for the Visitor" than a guide to Russia or North Africa.

Lonely Planet's design template shows similar rigidity in regard to guidebook audiences, which are presumed to be homogeneous. Catering to a more heterogeneous audience would compromise extreme usability by requiring more complex and multifaceted approaches to usability, so the template plays to dominant cultural narratives about what constitutes an average individual instead. This average reader is typically assumed to be able bodied, heterosexual, white, and male. Lonely Planet's design template ensures that guidebooks will be constructed in ways that implicitly privilege such readers while simultaneously marginalizing readers holding alternative identities.

As in all Lonely Planet regional guides, the "Facts for the Visitor" chapter of the *Great Lakes* guide contains three subsections titled "Women Travelers," "Gay and Lesbian Travelers," and "Disabled Travelers." These perfunctory 350-word subsections are required by the design template but do not actually contain much useful information. In some cases, these subsections have a rather patronizing tone. Female readers, for example, hardly need to be told that they should "avoid situations that leave [them] vulnerable, and conduct [themselves] in a commonsense manner." The subsections also give false impressions, such as when the guide warns that "gay travelers should be careful—holding hands in public might get [them] bashed" (Ver Berkmoes, Huhti, and Lightbody 52). The implication is that violent gay bashing is common throughout the Great Lakes region, which is factually inaccurate and caters to stereotypes of an overly conservative and culturally unsophisticated Midwest.

In fact, the subsections in the "Facts for the Visitor" chapter frequently cater to stereotypical views that align with dominant cultural narratives about who and what should be considered abnormal, dangerous, and deviant. For example, the "Gay and Lesbian Travelers" subsection includes a listing for the National HIV/AIDS Hotline, which implicitly positions HIV/AIDS as a health issue of concern only to gay men (Ver Berkmoes, Huhti, and Lightbody 52). However, as technical communication scholar J. Blake Scott points out in *Risky Rhetoric: AIDS and the Cultural Practices of HIV Testing* (2003), HIV/AIDS should be associated with certain actions and behaviors rather than certain identities. Information about HIV/AIDS would therefore be more appropriate for the "Health" subsection.

Finally, the subsections in the "Facts for the Visitor" chapter reinforce that the guides are written for straight, white, able-bodied male readers by listing resources that readers who do not hold these identities should consult to find travel information relevant to them, such as the gay city guides *Places for Women* and *Places for Men* or the website *Global Access: A Network for the Disabled* (Ver Berkmoes, Huhti, and Lightbody 52–53). The implication is that the *Great Lakes* guide cannot truly serve readers who are female, gay or lesbian, or disabled because the guide was written for a default audience of straight, able-bodied males.

Although the Lonely Planet design template allows for superficial acknowledgements of female, gay and lesbian, and disabled readers, it also works to streamline and homogenize reader identity in the service of extreme usability and, by extension, dominant cultural narratives about what constitutes a normal or average reader. As a result, certain reader identities are simply erased. The *Great Lakes* guide, for example, has no subsections devoted to Latino, African American, Native American, Asian, or multiracial readers. When such identities appear in the guide, they appear as part of the description of the Great Lakes region and its inhabitants—for example, in a description of the region's Native American history and culture. The guide is sensitive to ongoing debates involving Native Americans, such as the controversy surrounding University of Illinois sports mascot Chief Illiniwek (Ver Berkmoes, Huhti, and Lightbody 169), but it does not account for the possibility that its readers could be Native American. As a result, it plays to the same cultural narratives embedded in the DeLorme road atlases, which work to erase indigenous peoples from North American history, culture, and geography.

Lonely Planet authors often have identities that correlate with the design template's presumed average reader. This is certainly true in the case of the *Great Lakes* guide, which was written by three white male authors, two of whom mention having wives. The gender, race, sexual orientation, and degree of able-bodiedness of these three authors may make it easier for them to adhere to the demands of the design template. That said, these authors may well be aware of how the template promotes extreme usability and privileges dominant cultural narratives about what constitutes an average person. The authors may even wish to push back against these narratives and play to a more diverse sense of reader identity by replacing the subsections in the "Facts for the Visitor" chapter with more nuanced subsections—for example, one about race and racism in the United States. Such a subsection would be relevant and useful to readers of all backgrounds, and it would also provide an opportunity to explore a key element of US history and culture that the *Great Lakes* guide largely ignores.

What the authors of the *Great Lakes* guide may have wanted is largely irrelevant, however, since the demands of the Lonely Planet design template take precedence over any authorial intentions and desires. Indeed, as I have described earlier, the template works to erase the author from the text by requiring the removal of the authorial voice in the service of objectivity—regardless of whether the author wishes to be present. This effacement of the author does not necessarily serve the reader. Parsons suggests, for example, that the lack of an authorial voice discourages travelers from reading guidebooks with a critical eye. He argues that "authorial quirks, even prejudices, may well encourage the reader to think rather harder about what is being described than passionless consensual prose" (xxii). Getting the reader to think harder about what is being said, I would argue, is the single most important function of a good travel guidebook.

New Design Templates and the Challenging of Cultural Narratives

In his study of travel guides to Vietnam, Laderman concludes that for many international travelers, "guidebooks were instrumental in framing and shaping their touristic experiences and memories" (122). The same can certainly be said of Michigan guidebooks and road atlases, which shape how travelers come to understand the state's cultural, historic, political, and geographic landscape. In the process, these guides and atlases work to uphold dominant cultural narratives and position these narratives as uncontested, commonsense truths. Consequently, these guides and atlases can powerfully shape Michigan road quests in ways that reinforce and promote certain cultural narratives while suppressing and erasing others. However, I want to argue that rather than simply confirming dominant narratives, travel guidebooks and atlases should challenge them instead. This will require the replacement of current design templates, which focus on objectivity and extreme usability at the expense of all other considerations, privileging certain reader identities and the dominant cultural narratives that underpin them. By contesting these narratives, guides and atlases can render the ideologies embedded in them visible and open up space for counternarratives told by Native Americans and other groups who are rarely given voice in travel guidebooks. In doing so, guidebooks can provide travelers with more nuanced understandings of the cities, counties, and cultures they encounter on their midwestern road quests. For a midwestern road quest to reach its full potential, it must challenge and broaden the traveler's assumptions about this remarkably diverse region of the United States.

Works Cited

Barton, Ben F., and Marthalee S. Barton. "Ideology and the Map: Toward a Postmodern Visual Design Practice." *Central Works in Technical Communication.* Ed. Johndan Johnson-Eilola and Stuart A. Selber. New York: Oxford UP, 2004. 232–52. Print.

Bryson, Bill. *The Lost Continent: Travels in Small-Town America.* New York: Harper, 1989. Print.

Dilger, Bradley. "Extreme Usability and Technical Communication." *Critical Power Tools: Technical Communication and Cultural Studies.* Ed. J. Blake Scott, Bernadette Longo, and Katherine V. Wills. Albany: State U of New York P, 2006. 47–68. Print.

DuFresne, Jim. *Lonely Planet Road Trip: Lake Michigan.* Oakland: Lonely Planet, 2005. Print.

Fussell, Paul, ed. *The Norton Book of Travel.* New York: Norton, 1987. Print.

Gilbert, Elizabeth. *Eat, Pray, Love: One Woman's Search for Everything across Italy, India, and Indonesia.* New York: Penguin, 2006. Print.

Jenkins, Peter. *A Walk across America.* New York: Harper, 2001. Print.

Laderman, Scott. *Tours of Vietnam: War, Travel Guides, and Memory.* Durham: Duke UP, 2009. Print.

Lonely Planet. "About Lonely Planet: How to Make a Guidebook." *Lonely Planet.* BBC Worldwide, 2011. Web. 2 May 2012.

McClurken, James M. *Our People, Our Journey: The Little River Band of Ottawa Indians.* East Lansing: Michigan State UP, 2009. Print.

Michigan Atlas and Gazetteer. Yarmouth: DeLorme, 2006. Print.

Parsons, Nicholas T. *Worth the Detour: A History of the Guidebook*. Stroud: Sutton, 2007. Print.

Polo, Marco. *The Travels of Marco Polo*. Ed. Manuel Komroff. New York: Modern Library, 2001. Print.

Scott, J. Blake. *Risky Rhetoric: AIDS and the Cultural Practices of HIV Testing*. Carbondale: Southern Illinois UP, 2003. Print.

Storey, Robert, and Daniel Robinson. *Vietnam*. 4th ed. Hawthorn: Lonely Planet, 1997. Print.

Ver Berkmoes, Ryan, Thomas Huhti, and Mark Lightbody. *Great Lakes*. Melbourne: Lonely Planet, 2000. Print.

A Moving Story: The Recurrence of the Kiowa Tsoai Legend in the Work of N. Scott Momaday _____

Matthew Low

> Four days I lived on tea and sage
> And dreamed in symbols of an age,
> A beast incising on the tree:
> I am the bear Tsoai-talee
> —N. Scott Momaday, "Vision Quest"

As the first location to be designated a national monument by Theodore Roosevelt in 1906, Devils Tower in eastern Wyoming holds a unique place in the American landscape and in the writings of N. Scott Momaday. While national-monument status was initially granted to preserve Devils Tower and the land surrounding it from development, today that status upholds Devils Tower as an emblem of the tourist industry in America and especially in the West, which has been built around places of peculiar geology or geography, increasingly rare concentrations of natural phenomena, and the commemoration of battle (or massacre) sites. Because of its proximity to the Black Hills in western South Dakota, Devils Tower has most recently been absorbed into the same motorized tourist itinerary that includes such places as the Badlands, Wall Drug, and Mount Rushmore.

For the last half century or so, Devils Tower has also been a popular rock-climbing destination, and those who associate it with controversy or view it as contested space are generally thinking of the verbal and legal battles between rock-climbing enthusiasts and several American Indian communities, which the National Park Service tried in vain to mediate. This is the aspect of Devils Tower highlighted in the documentary *In the Light of Reverence* (2001), which features testimony from prominent natives and non-natives about the importance of the site to the cultural customs and practices of numerous native cultures.

The frustrations felt by those who want to see greater cultural sensitivity and courtesy administered at Devils Tower are perhaps best articulated by Lakota scholar Vine Deloria Jr., who notes in the film, "It's not that Indians should have exclusive rights at Devils Tower. It's that that location is sacred enough so that it should have time of its own. . . . Then the people who know how to do ceremonies should come and minister to it." It is easy to imagine that most of the tourists who visit Devils Tower would generally concur with Deloria's position and that few, apart from rock climbers themselves, would protest limitations on—if not outright abolition of—climbing on the monolith. But even such limitations would not wholly resolve the issue of giving the place "time of its own" because, paradoxically, many of those who want a personal experience with Devils Tower do so precisely because its cultural significations are just as resonant as its physical topography is awe inspiring.

All of which is to say that few places in North America can compare to Devils Tower with regard to layers of interpretation and cultural complexity, and this certainly plays a large role in its success as a tourist destination. Critiques of its "touristy" appeal are certainly valid, and infringement upon native cultural practices is both insensitive and hypocritical. Yet there is no denying that a place so highly contested is so in part because of the draw it has for so many different groups of people, a fact demonstrable in the cultural history of Devils Tower for the past several centuries. Adrian J. Ivakhiv has written extensively on similar places with divergent and competing interpretations, and one of his conclusions is that sacred space—a broad category that would include Devils Tower several times over—is "produced through the spatial, material, and discursive practices of social groups. As such, [sacred space] does not exist apart from the human meanings, sedimented over time in actual landscapes and places, which imbue them with their 'sanctity' and which are always subject to reinterpretation and contestation" (45). Likewise, Mike Crang argues that any place that is visited routinely, whether as an extension of ritual or as part of a tourist itinerary, takes part in a process of "writing the earth, labeling it and filling it with meanings," a process that often creates "its own momentum, whereby the very popularity of a site can make it 'sacred,' such that people feel compelled to include it in their itinerary; or it can go the other way . . . with the cachet of a site perhaps depending upon its exclusivity, and thus its popularity may diminish the aura of sacrality for some visitors" (38). In other words, sites like Devils Tower—which is considered "sacred" by numerous native cultures, wilderness lovers, environmental advocates, and even rock climbers—acquire scales of sanctification in accordance with the amount of physical interaction, religious observance, or written documentation to which they are subjected. And the upshot of these processes of sanctification is for better or for worse, depending on one's perspective, position, or degree of access in relation to the site in question.

The points raised by Ivakhiv, Crang, and other likeminded cultural geographers dealing with the topic of sacred (and contested) space bring up the importance of frequency as a measure of how much attention a given site receives by those who have or want close connections to it. For instance, repeated visits to a site by an individual, group, or culture are bound to create a lasting, deeply felt emotional, psychological, or religious association. On occasion, the recurrence of visits is so profound that a sense of sacredness is attached to that place. Deloria, for instance, writes of this uniquely human phenomenon in his introduction to *God Is Red* (1973), noting that "the remembrance of human activities at certain locations vested them with a kind of sacredness that could not have been obtained otherwise" (ix). However, in this sentiment, Deloria also recognizes that the process of creating sacred places does not solely depend on a repetition of physical proximity. Indeed, an individual, group, or culture may make but a single visit to a place, or even none at all, and it may eventually become elevated to the status of sacred space through the perpetuation of its memory via imaginative acts such as prayer, song, or especially storytelling—both oral and written. One need look no further than the Abrahamic religions to find examples of places (Jerusalem, Mecca, the Jordan River) that have not been subject to repeated visits, if any, by the vast majority of their adherents, yet have become among the most recognizably sacred in the world through the continual retelling and eventual written documentation of key stories. What Christian, for example, would fail to assert the need to maintain, protect, and revere the Church of the Nativity in Bethlehem, despite the fact that he or she may well never set foot on its grounds? Hearing the Gospel account of the Christmas narrative with great frequency is enough to establish this place as sacred, in some ways making the perpetuation of the narrative as important as the preservation of the place itself.

With respect to the Devils Tower site in particular, the matter of frequency is worth further attention for a number of reasons, including, of course, the history of claims to its importance (or sacredness) by so many different groups of people and the ensuing controversies. As it relates to travel literature, Devils Tower plays an important role in one of the most iconic and unconventional works of road literature of the twentieth century: N. Scott Momaday's *The Way to Rainy Mountain* (1969).

In the introduction to that work, Momaday tells the story of Tsoai, meaning "rock tree," the name the Kiowas use to refer to Devils Tower. The story of Tsoai is central to the larger narrative of the Kiowa migration from the Rocky Mountains to the Great Plains during the late seventeenth and early eighteenth centuries, which is one reason that it is featured so prominently in *The Way to Rainy Mountain*. In this text, Momaday gives two dozen prose English translations of traditional Kiowa stories and legends as a means of recounting the Kiowas' historic migration, as well as documenting his own physical and imaginative journey along the same route some two centuries later. The Tsoai story accounts for the creation of not only Devils Tower but also the Big Dipper, and for Momaday, it serves as an important connection to bear mythology. But perhaps the most notable feature of the Tsoai legend is that, in addition to its central role in what is arguably Momaday's most important text, the same version of the story that appears in *The Way to Rainy Mountain* is also incorporated into nearly every other text that Momaday has written.[1] The story itself is quite brief, the entire narrative fulfilled in just ten sentences, and in *The Way to Rainy Mountain*, the story is attributed to Momaday's grandmother Aho's voice:

> Eight children were there at play, seven sisters and their brother. Suddenly the boy was struck dumb; he trembled and began to run upon his hands and feet. His fingers became claws, and his body was covered with fur. Directly there was a bear where the boy had been. The sisters were terrified; they ran, and the bear after them. They came to the stump of a great tree, and the tree spoke to them. It bade them climb upon it, and as they did so it began to rise into the air. The bear came to kill them, but they were just beyond its reach. It reared against the tree and scored the bark all around with its claws. The seven sisters were borne into the sky, and they became the stars of the Big Dipper. (8)

As it appears in *The Way to Rainy Mountain*, the story is accompanied by illustrator Al Momaday's striking image of a bear at the base of Devils Tower, gazing up at the stars of the Big Dipper. But most essential to the analysis at hand is that this story—closely identified with the migration of a prominent American Indian culture from one region of the country to another, serving as the foundation for a contemporary travel narrative that is in part recounting that migration—itself moves as a whole from text to text, each time taking on a different, though no less important, position or role. By following the journey taken by the Tsoai legend over the course of Momaday's written work, we uncover some of the most compelling attempts to use language and narrative to uphold the sacredness of a specific place in the American landscape, a place that happens to be highly contested and under the constant pressures that accompany heavy use for tourism, recreational activities, and extreme sports.

The first text in which Momaday includes the Tsoai story is his earliest published work, *The Journey of Tai-me* (1967), a collection of Kiowa stories that is the precursor to *The Way to Rainy Mountain*. Between *The Journey of Tai-me* and *The Way to Rainy Mountain*, Momaday published his Pulitzer Prize–winning novel *House Made of Dawn* (1968), in which the story of Tsoai appears as part of a sermon delivered by the character Tosamah near the end of the book—a sermon that matches the introduction to *The Way to Rainy Mountain* nearly verbatim. The Tsoai story next appears in Momaday's memoir *The Names* (1976), an imaginative exploration of his heritage and lineage that features a lengthy account of how he came by the Kiowa name Tsoai-talee ("rock-tree boy"). Returning to fiction, the story next appears in the novel *The Ancient Child* (1989), serving as the prologue to a longer work that blurs realism with historical fantasy and the bear mythology central to the Tsoai story. In the essay collection *The Man Made of Words* (1997), Momaday offers one of his clearest reflections on the story in an essay titled "Revisiting Sacred Ground," which considers Devils Tower alongside other sacred sites, such as Bighorn Medicine Wheel along the Montana-Wyoming border. Yet perhaps the most creative reflection on the Tsoai story comes in the collection *In the Bear's House* (1999), a book-length examination—in the form of drama, poetry, and prose poetry—of Momaday's connection to this story and to the bear in particular.

Beyond these texts written by Momaday himself, the story is also included in several other secondary works, such as *Ancestral Voice* (1989), a collection of interviews with Momaday conducted by Charles L. Woodard, and the 1996 Ken Burns–produced PBS television documentary series *The West*, in which Momaday's significant presence includes an ad-lib recitation of the Tsoai story early in the first episode of the series; Momaday concludes his telling of the story with the assertion that it is "a wonderful story because it accounts for the rock, Devils Tower, this monolith that rises nearly a thousand feet into the air, and it also relates man to the stars."[2]

Before delving into the specific role of the Tsoai story in these individual texts, it is worth giving some attention to the concept of narrative frequency, returning to the earlier discussion of frequency as an important element in the creation of sacred space. It is the story's movement from text to text, its repetition in essentially the same form, though for vastly different purposes, that makes Momaday's recurrent use of this story both confounding and profound. Without a doubt, the most authoritative voice on narrative frequency is Gérard Genette, who devotes an entire chapter to the topic in his seminal work *Discours du récit* (1972; *Narrative Discourse*, 1980). Frequency, according to Genette, is one of five main components of narrative discourse, and he groups it together with order, duration, voice, and mood in his analysis of the common features found mostly in the works of modernist fiction that are his principal interest.

Despite a limited generic scope, Genette's writing on frequency is nonetheless instructive in considering the significance of the reappearance of the Tsoai story in so much of Momaday's work. At its most basic, the concept of frequency is fairly self-explanatory. As Genette points out: "Symmetrically, a narrative statement is not only produced, it can be produced again, can be repeated one or more times in the same text" (*Narrative Discourse* 114). Though not accounting for what happens when a "narrative statement" is reproduced not just in the same text but also across texts—that is, not just intratextually but intertextually as well—Genette nonetheless underscores the relatively infinite circumstances through which one may encounter a given narrative, including its repeated repetition. Again, despite the considerable distance separating Genette's primary literary examples and Momaday's postmodern or, to borrow a term from Gerald Vizenor, postindian , uuse of traditional storytelling, this basic understanding of narrative frequency is quite similar to Momaday's notion that he has spent his entire writing life "telling one story" (*Conversations* xv). What Momaday means by this is that there are common themes, images, and ideas that are consistent across his writing, and that each individual work is trying to give answers to a narrow set of essential questions, mostly pertaining to the sacred nature of the world at large and especially of language. The frequency with which Momaday engages the story of Tsoai is but one overt example of this phenomenon at work in his writing.

Within his analysis of narrative frequency, Genette further defines this concept by creating four categories into which different types of frequency may occur: narrating once what happened once, narrating n times what happened n times, narrating n times what happened once, and narrating one time what happened n times. The category that most closely expresses the function of the Tsoai story in Momaday's work is the third category, "Narrating n times what happened once, $(nN/1S)$" (Genette, *Narrative Discourse* 115). In other words, the singular event recounted in the Tsoai story can be said to have happened only one time during the Kiowa migration from the Rocky Mountains to the Great Plains—the action that constitutes the narrative has not been re-peated since its initial occurrence—yet Momaday himself has told this story over and over again, so that it has been narrated n times. The n has a true sense of variability because it is impossible to know how often Momaday has told and retold this story in interviews, conversa-tions, and lectures beyond the scope of the printed texts of which it is a part. Of this category of frequency, Genette offers an interesting quali-fication, noting that "children love to be told the same story several times—indeed, several times in a row—or to reread the same book, and that this predilection is not entirely the prerogative of childhood" (*Narrative Discourse* 115). Taking this a step further, the act of retell-ing the same story is also a key component in both the preservation of an oral tradition—the precise undertaking of both *The Journey of Tai-me* and *The Way to Rainy Mountain*—and the importance of the Tsoai story to Momaday's own childhood, a point that will be addressed in some detail below.

Clearly there is an important connection between the frequency with which a given narrative is told and the lasting impact it has on its audience, which may be one reason why, at the close of this section on frequency, Genette refers to the *nN/1S* category as "ritual narrative" (*Narrative Discourse* 116), a term for which he offers little elaboration but which seems to refer to the process of repeated narrative actions, events, or occurrences taking on the guise of ritual. For Momaday, of course, this notion of "ritual narrative" has even deeper implications, as his frequent retelling of the Tsoai story in text after text becomes its own sort of ritual, wherein repeating this signature event of the Kiowas' migration creates an indelible link between his disparate works. Moreover, establishing the Tsoai legend as a "ritual narrative" makes an imposing claim on the sacredness of Devils Tower for the Kiowas— a claim that will outlast the constant threats facing the Kiowa language, culture, and oral tradition, which serve as the impetus for much of Momaday's writing.

It is unlikely that Momaday plotted out a multidecade, multiwork endeavor to preserve the Tsoai story through its frequent repetition in his writing. Nevertheless, the fact that this story has become ritualized in his fiction, essay, and memoir, thus ensuring its preservation, is arguably Momaday's single greatest service to Kiowa history and culture. Writing about the Laguna Pueblo novelist Leslie Marmon Silko in *The Sacred Hoop* (1986), Paula Gunn Allen observes that if a writer demonstrates that "clear understanding of a given narrative depends on proper understanding of the stories attached to each significant word," it will also become apparent that "stories themselves are ritual events" (96). Looking at the three texts that Momaday published between 1967 and 1969—*The Journey of Tai-me*, *House Made of Dawn*, and *The Way to Rainy Mountain*—it does seem likely that Momaday himself had a similar realization about the Tsoai story's potential as a ritual narrative, just as he also realized his need to write almost exclusively about his Kiowa ancestry and cultural heritage.

With regard to these three works, the story's placement in *The Way to Rainy Mountain* in many ways informs its placement and use in the other two and signals the direction in which the story will travel in Momaday's later writing. Staying with this text for a moment, it is worth considering how travel functions in *The Way to Rainy Mountain* both as literal event—the historical journey of the Kiowas and Momaday's own undertaking two centuries later—and as literary device that sets up, and sets in motion, the retelling of the Kiowa oral legends that constitute the body of the work. Indeed, the first section of the work, titled "The Setting Out," includes several stories about the Kiowas beginning their journey or events that happened to them along the way. It would make organizational sense, therefore, to include the Tsoai story in this section of the book, because it fits with the thematic organization that Momaday establishes in the section title and the types of stories he includes in the early pages of the body of *The Way to Rainy Mountain*. This is precisely how the story appears in *The Journey of Tai-me*, placed sequentially in that short text where it makes most sense in the chronological and geographical contexts of the Kiowas' migration. However, by preceding all of the other stories in *The Way to Rainy Mountain* with the story of Tsoai, including the Kiowa origin story of coming into the world through a hollow log, Momaday begins his own—and the reader's—journey through the Kiowa oral tradition with the narrative he asserts "represents to me, in the best sense, the cultural memory of the migration of the Kiowas" (qtd. in Woodard 211). Opening the text with a story that chronologically comes after the Kiowa origin story may appear illogical from the perspective of traditional linear history and storytelling, but this organization is consistent with other works of postmodern travel literature, which tend to "subvert and revise the form of the travel narrative itself to reflect their alternative paths" (Russell 11).

The path Momaday establishes for the Tsoai legend in his later writing is thus initiated in the opening pages of *The Way to Rainy Mountain*. Just as, according to Kimberly Blaeser, "Momaday does not see the migration history as static or timebound in the traditional sense," he also does not see the Tsoai story itself as "static or timebound"—or even text bound, for that matter (40). In other words, the fluidity and flexibility at the heart of *The Way to Rainy Mountain* is later embodied in the narrative frequency of the Tsoai story as it moves from text to text. All of this is reinforced by Kai Mikkonen's observation of a "sense of profound openness in travel writing" and his insistence that "what comes after in the temporally ordered events in travel is not necessarily triggered by what went before" (293), a sentiment that applies to both *The Way to Rainy Mountain* itself and the manner in which the Tsoai story takes on a life and meaning of its own throughout the arc of Momaday's written work. Because Momaday chooses to, as Mikkonen describes it, "break down the temporal frame of representation" (297), the Tsoai story takes its place as the foundational narrative of the Kiowa migration and therefore becomes integral to, yet independent within, the works in which it appears beyond *The Way to Rainy Mountain*. Taking a closer look at the function of that story in these other texts will help illustrate just how influential it becomes in Momaday's conception of the power of language, the sacredness of places like Devils Tower, and his identity as Kiowa storyteller and universal mythmaker.

The placement of the Tsoai story in *House Made of Dawn* is perhaps the most challenging or perplexing appearance of the story in any of Momaday's works, as it is included in a sermon that is essentially a word-for-word reproduction of the introduction to *The Way to Rainy Mountain*—and thus yet another occurrence of repetition in Momaday's work, though on a much larger scale. The sermon in question is the second of two delivered by the character Tosamah, whose ambivalence in the novel, especially in relation to the novel's protagonist, Abel, seemingly contradicts the biographical similarities shared with Momaday himself.[3] For these reasons, the inclusion of the Tsoai story feels somewhat out of place, as the Kiowa migration narrative of which it is a part is culturally and geographically far removed from the main action of the novel. At the same time, an argument can be made that its inclusion marks an essential moment of healing for Abel, whose fractured memories and poor life choices undermine his clear desire for a deeper connection to the shared past of this family and his culture. As Christina M. Hebebrand points out, inclusion of the Tsoai story in

Tosamah's second sermon, therefore, "stresses tribal people's need to define and orient themselves in the world through their relationship with the homeland" (102). Just as one function of the introduction to *The Way to Rainy Mountain* is to highlight the process through which Momaday deepened his connection to his Kiowa forebears, Tosamah's sermon in *House Made of Dawn* pushes Abel to undertake a similar inner journey of discovery. This scene of the novel may be the most striking instance of Momaday's occasional efforts to universalize parts of Kiowa oral tradition, and the Tsoai story in particular, as its resonance with Abel, who is not of Kiowa descent, is no less moving or powerful. It is an instance of Momaday mining his own biography to exemplify the capacity of myth and storytelling to undo the traumatic disconnection from language, culture, and family—just as the boy experiences in the Tsoai story itself.

Momaday's own efforts to reconnect with language, culture, and family come together most explicitly in his memoir *The Names*. Early on in this work, Momaday reveals, "When I was six months old my parents took me to Devil's Tower, Wyoming, which is called in Kiowa Tsoai, 'rock tree'" (42). This is not a detail that is revealed anywhere in *The Way to Rainy Mountain*—or *House Made of Dawn*, for that matter—and yet it adds an essential layer to Momaday's personal relationship with Devils Tower and the Tsoai story, by creating a link from birth among writer, place, and story. The Tsoai legend is, at its most basic, a story about children, perhaps even what some today might call a children's story, and in *The Names*, Momaday reveals that he too was in the presence of this place at a very early age—too young, in fact, to be able to form a memory of the event himself. This is also the first work in which Momaday tells the story of how he acquired his Kiowa name, Tsoai-talee, a direct reference to the young boy in the story who is transformed into a bear. Again, because he was too young to actually remember this event, what Momaday tells in *The Names* is his reimagining of the moment in which the storyteller Pohd-lohk bestows the name upon him and, later, when his great-grandmother recites the same version of the Tsoai story that appears in *The Journey of Tai-me*, *The House Made of Dawn*, and *The Way to Rainy Mountain*. This is clearly a momentous occasion in the formation of Momaday's Kiowa identity, as Chadwick Allen notes:

> In Momaday's imagined account of the naming ceremony, the authenticating Kiowa elder, who represents the link to the past, positions the boy and his contemporary encounter with Tsoai within the larger tradition of Kiowa narratives stretching back to the period of creation. Both . . . are made integral parts of this ongoing Kiowa narrative of defining themselves as a people in the American landscape. (216)

That the version of the Tsoai story that Momaday envisions his great-grandmother reciting here is typographically the same as the version appearing in both his early and his later work is significant because it further establishes a unified telling across multiple works, regardless of storyteller, in an expression of Genette's *nN/1S* narrative frequency. Thus, the story itself is taking its own sort of journey, across texts and through genres, yet maintaining an internal coherence that is solidifying its place as the defining narrative of Momaday's—and possibly the Kiowas'—connection to Devils Tower as sacred space.

Returning to fiction, the appearance of the Tsoai story in Momaday's second novel, *The Ancient Child*, is unique—a rare instance in which the story is allowed to stand alone, as a prologue to the rest of the novel, without any commentary from Momaday on the relationship between the story and his Kiowa ancestry or a specific trip he himself made to Devils Tower. Numerous critics have written about the importance of the Tsoai story to *The Ancient Child*, in particular as it focuses so heavily on blurring the line between myth and reality, going so far as to establish itself as a postmodern exploration on the process of myth discovery and mythmaking in contemporary Western society. Of most interest to this study, however, is Momaday's decision not to imbed the Tsoai story somewhere within the text itself, as in all of the earlier texts that contain the story, but to place it outside the body of the novel, in what Genette refers to as the *paratext*. In using this term—often associated with such extratextual items as a book's title, cover image, and about-the-author paragraphs—Genette is actually envisioning something far more complex:

> More than a boundary or a sealed border, the paratext is, rather, a *threshold* . . . a "vestibule" that offers the world at large the possibility of either stepping inside or turning back. It is an "undefined zone" between the inside and the outside, a zone without any hard or fast boundary on either the inward side (turned toward the text) or the outward side (turned toward the world's discourse about the text) . . . a zone between text and off-text, a zone not only of transition but of *transaction*: A privileged place of a pragmatics and a strategy, of an influence on the public, an influence that—whether well or poorly understood and achieved—is at the service of a better reception for the text and a more pertinent reading of it. (*Paratexts* 1–2; ital. in orig.)

Of all of Momaday's works, *The Ancient Child* actually best lends itself to a consideration of paratextuality, as there is a great deal going on in the early pages before the actual text of the novel begins to unfold. In addition to the prologue containing the Tsoai story, there is a quote from Jorge Luis Borges—"For myth is at the beginning of literature, and also at its end"—and a list of characters in the novel, both of which precede the prologue; then "An Ethnographic Dictionary of the Navajo Language" that quotes a number of words relating to the bear and another epigraph containing lines from "Cotton Eye Joe" both follow the prologue (2–7). The need to include so much paratextual material is understandable, as the novel, easily Momaday's longest work, is demanding enough to warrant these "transactional" pages. That the Tsoai story is centered within the paratext demonstrates that Momaday at this point expects (or hopes) that his reader is already familiar with the story, and his use of it in particular; coupled with the Borges quote, it is also an indication that the treatment of myth in the novel will not be cursory or condescending but, in fact, integral. Finally, placing the story in what Genette terms an "undefined zone" is a reminder of the fluidity Momaday bestows upon this narrative as it moves from text to text and its unlimited potential for filling vital roles in each text.

In two more recent works in which the Tsoai story appears, Momaday moves in seemingly opposite directions—on the one hand universalizing the story in the broadest terms yet, and on the other hand interrogating the story as it relates most closely to his unique individual self and identity. The essay "Revisiting Sacred Ground" in *The Man Made of Words* is an explicit return to Momaday's earlier attention to the story and place, especially in *The Way to Rainy Mountain*, as parts of that work are quoted in the essay (including, of course, the Tsoai legend). Consciously elevating the stakes of the story, which is consistent with the focus of many of the essays in *The Man Made of Words*, Momaday writes, "This story, which I have known from the time I could first understand language, exemplifies the sacred for me. The storyteller, that anonymous, man who told the story for the first time, succeeded in raising the human condition to the level of universal significance" (123). This is arguably the moment in the whole of Momaday's writing in which he elevates the Tsoai story to the point of its greatest influence. Perhaps indicative of the comfort and familiarity Momaday himself feels toward the story, he clearly expects that the reader, seeing the Tsoai story quoted in full and given concise but weighty commentary from Momaday, will appreciate and be equally captivated by its profundity. Furthermore, the story is now nearly separated in full from the Kiowa oral tradition in which it was contextualized in the earlier works, with the expectation that it will hold up to the claims of universality that Momaday bestows upon it in this brief essay. One does not need to be Kiowa, or even familiar with Kiowa culture, to understand how powerfully the Tsoai story is linked to the place it tells about, nor to be moved by it.

The last of Momaday's texts that this study will consider is *In the Bear's House*, a short work more in the vein of *The Way to Rainy Mountain* with its genre-defying format than the more conventional novels, memoirs, and essays that fall in between. This is also the work in which Momaday takes the story of Tsoai in the most inward direction, writing, "Through the power of stories and names, I am the reincarnation of that boy. From the time the name Tsoai-talee was conferred on me as an infant, I have been possessed of Bear's spirit" (*In the Bear's House* xi). Rather than taking such a statement as metaphor, hyperbole, or even hubris on Momaday's part, Chadwick Allen suggests reading *In the Bear's House* as the result of "a more than thirty-year exploration of [Momaday's] personal, familial, and communal relationships to American Indian sacred geographies and oral traditions" (217–18). From this perspective, the statement can be clearly seen as the sentiment of a person who has dwelled upon and within this particular story for a long time. It is this decades-long narrative indwelling that has given Momaday the confidence in the final section of *In the Bear's House*, fittingly titled "The Transformation," to not only open with the Tsoai legend quoted boldly in full but also expand upon the story in his own imaginative explorations of what happened to the principal characters—the sisters, the boy/bear, and Tsoai itself—after the close of the brief Kiowa legend. Pulled from their scattered locations in *The Ancient Child* and set in juxtaposition to one another in this text, these ruminations give a profound sense of culmination (but not quite closure) to Momaday's long-standing relationship with this story. Of the sisters, we learn that they were never seen again and their names were soon forgotten. A hunter, Momaday imagines, once came across a bear who "cried in a human voice," and a Kiowa legend suggests that the boy may have reappeared in a Piegan camp. Finally, of the rock-tree itself, Momaday concludes, "No one said so, but each man in his heart acknowledged Tsoai, and the first thing he did upon waking was to cast his eyes upon it, thus to set his belief, to know that it was there and that the world remained whole, as it ought to remain. And always Tsoai was there" (95–96).[4]

There is a sense in these final lines of what Gerald Vizenor calls *survivance*, by which he means "an active sense of presence over absence, deracination, and oblivion"; most importantly for the argument being made here, "survivance is the *continuance of stories*" ("Aesthetics" 1; emphasis added). Tsoai—both the story and the place—is undoubtedly an active presence throughout Momaday's writing, from his earliest work to his most recent. And the open-ended nature of these lines from *In the Bear's House*, the certainty that Tsoai is "always . . . there," ensures the potential for this story to take up its journey once again in Momaday's writing, a journey that lends a sense of connection, continuity, and perpetuity to his body of work. The power of language and the sacredness of Devils Tower that are at the heart of Momaday's recurrent use of the Tsoai legend will journey onward as well, superseding the claims of tourists and rock climbers, empowered by the cumulative force of an unending ritual narrative.

Notes

1. In his contribution to *The Cambridge Companion to Native American Literature* (2005), Chadwick Allen notes that this story "can be traced across four of [Momaday's] major works, which span the thirty-year period of his career" (214), referring to *The Way to Rainy Mountain*, *The Names*, *The Ancient Child*, and *In the Bear's House*. As this essay argues, it is also worth considering the presence of this story in *The Journey of Tai-me*, *House Made of Dawn*, and *The Man Made of Words*, in addition to the secondary sources (interviews and documentaries) in which Momaday cites the story directly, as a means of fully accounting for the trajectory of this story in Momaday's work.

2. As a point of comparison with the version that appears in all of the printed texts addressed in this essay, an excerpt of the version Momaday tells in the documentary *The West* reads as follows:

   Kiowa story has it that eight children were playing in the woods; there were seven sisters and their brother. The boy is pretending to be a bear and he is chasing his sisters, who are pretending to be afraid, and they're running. And a terrible thing happens in the course of the game. The boy actually turns into a bear. And when the sisters see this, they are truly terrified and they run for their lives, the bear after them. They pass the stump of a tree, and the tree speaks to them and says, "If you will climb up on me I will save you."

3. When questioned on the similarities between Tosamah and himself, one compelling response that Momaday gives is, "Tosamah is my mouthpiece in a certain way. I use him to present some of my views concerning language" (qtd. in Woodard 124). This commentary further reinforces the significance of the Tsoai story to Momaday's career-long exploration of the limitless potential of human language, especially as used in the oral tradition.

4. The very last passage in this concluding section of the work is the penultimate scene of *The Ancient Child*, in which Set, the protagonist of that novel, undergoes a physical transformation into the bear. Unlike *The Ancient Child*, however, *In the Bear's House* ends not with an epilogue that ties back into the original story but with Set's transformation.

Works Cited

Allen, Chadwick. "N. Scott Momaday: Becoming the Bear." *The Cambridge Companion to Native American Literature*. Ed. Joy Porter and Kenneth M. Roemer. Cambridge: Cambridge UP, 2005. 207–20. Print.

Allen, Paula Gunn. *The Sacred Hoop: Recovering the Feminine in American Indian Traditions*. Boston: Beacon, 2004. Print.

Blaeser, Kimberly. "*The Way to Rainy Mountain*: Momaday's Work in Motion." Vizenor, *Narrative Chance* 39–54.

Crang, Mike. "Travel/Tourism." *Cultural Geography: A Critical Dictionary of Key Concepts*. Ed. David Atkinson et al. London: Tauris, 2005. 34–40. Print.

Deloria, Vine, Jr. *God Is Red: A Native View of Religion*. Golden: Fulcrum, 2003. Print.

Genette, Gérard. *Narrative Discourse: An Essay in Method*. Trans. Jane E. Lewin. Ithaca: Cornell UP, 1980. Print.

___. *Paratexts: Thresholds of Interpretation*. Trans. Jane E. Lewin. Cambridge: Cambridge UP, 1997. Print.

Hebebrand, Christina M. *Native American and Chicano/a Literature of the American Southwest: Intersections of Indigenous Literatures*. New York: Routledge, 2004. Print.

In the Light of Reverence. Dir. Christopher McLeod. Bullfrog Films, 2001. DVD.

Ivakhiv, Adrian J. *Claiming Sacred Ground: Pilgrims and Politics at Glastonbury and Sedona*. Bloomington: Indiana UP, 2001. Print.

Mikkonen, Kai. "The 'Narrative Is Travel' Metaphor: Between Spatial Sequence and Open Consequence." *Narrative* 15.3 (2007): 286–305. Print.

Momaday, N. Scott. *The Ancient Child*. New York: Harper, 1990. Print.

___. *Conversations with N. Scott Momaday*. Ed. Matthias Schubnell. Oxford: UP of Mississippi, 1997. Print.

___. *House Made of Dawn*. New York: Harper, 1999. Print.

___. *In the Bear's House*. Albuquerque: U of New Mexico P, 2010. Print.

___. *The Journey of Tai-me*. Albuquerque: U of New Mexico P, 2009. Print.

___. *The Man Made of Words: Essays, Stories, Passages*. New York: St. Martin's, 1997. Print.

___. *The Names: A Memoir*. Tucson: U of Arizona P, 1976. Print.

___. "Vision Quest." *Again the Far Morning: New and Selected Poems*. By Momaday. Albuquerque: U of New Mexico P, 2011. 108. Print.

___. *The Way to Rainy Mountain*. Albuquerque: U of New Mexico P, 1969. Print.

Russell, Alison. *Crossing Boundaries: Postmodern Travel Literature*. New York: Palgrave, 2000. Print.

Stevens, Jason W. "Bear, Outlaw, and Storyteller: American Frontier Mythology and the Ethnic Subjectivity of N. Scott Momaday." *American Literature* 73.3 (2001): 599–631. Print.

Vizenor, Gerald. "Aesthetics of Survivance: Literary Theory and Practice." *Survivance: Narratives of Native Presence*. Ed. Vizenor. Lincoln: U of Nebraska P, 2008. 1–23. Print.

___. *Manifest Manners: Narratives on Postindian Survivance*. Lincoln: U of Nebraska P, 1999. Print.

___, ed. *Narrative Chance: Postmodern Discourse on Native American Indian Literatures*. Norman: U of Oklahoma P, 1993. Print.

The West. Dir. Stephen Ives. 1996. PBS Home Video, 2003. DVD.

Woodard, Charles L. *Ancestral Voice: Conversations with N. Scott Momaday*. Lincoln: U of Nebraska P, 1989. Print.

RESOURCES

Additional Works on American Road Literature _____

Algeo, Matthew. *Harry Truman's Excellent Adventure: The True Story of a Great American Road Trip.* Chicago: Chicago Rev., 2009. Print.

Berg, Elizabeth. *The Pull of the Moon.* New York: Random, 1996. Print.

Betts, Doris. *Heading West.* New York: Knopf, 1990. Print.

Binding, Paul. *Separate Country: A Literary Journey through the American South.* Jackson: UP of Mississippi, 1988. Print.

Brinkley, Douglas. *The Majic Bus: An American Odyssey.* New York: Harcourt, 1993. Print.

Bryson, Bill. *The Lost Continent: Travels in Small-Town America.* New York: Harper, 1989. Print.

Cain, Chelsea. *Dharma Girl: A Road Trip across American Generations.* Seattle: Seal, 1996. Print.

Carter, Michelle. *On Other Days While Going Home.* New York: Morrow, 1987. Print.

Cassady, Carolyn. *Heart Beat: My Life with Jack and Neal.* Berkeley: Creative Arts, 1976. Print.

Cassady, Neal. *The First Third.* San Francisco: City Lights, 1971. Print.

Cole, Michelle, and Stuart Black. *Checking It Out: Some Lower East Side Kids Discover the Rest of America.* New York: Dial, 1971. Print.

Crews, Harry. *Car.* New York: Morrow, 1972. Print.

Dickinson, Charles. *The Widows' Adventures.* New York: Avon, 1989. Print.

Dodge, Jim. *Not Fade Away.* New York: Atlantic, 1987. Print.

Duncan, Dayton. *Out West: An American Journey.* New York: Viking, 1987. Print.

Faulkner, William. *The Reivers: A Reminiscence.* New York: Random, 1962. Print.

Fish, Cheryl. *Black and White Women's Travel Narratives: Antebellum Explorations.* Gainesville: U of Florida P, 2004. Print.

Fonda, Peter, et al. *Easy Rider.* New York: New Amer. Lib., 1969. Print.

Fox, Barbara, and Gwenda Gofton. *Bedpans and Bobby Socks: Five British Nurses on the American Road Trip of a Lifetime.* London: Sphere, 2011. Print.

Gaiman, Neil. *American Gods.* New York: Harper, 2001. Print.

Hawkes, John. *Travesty.* New York: New Directions, 1976. Print.

Herlihy, James Leo. *Midnight Cowboy.* New York: Simon, 1965. Print.

Kemp, Harry. *Tramping on Life: An Autobiographical Narrative.* New York: Boni, 1922. Print.

Kerouac, Jack. *The Dharma Bums.* New York: Viking, 1958. Print.

___. *Visions of Cody.* New York: McGraw, 1972. Print.

Kerouac, Jan. *Baby Driver.* New York: St. Martin's, 1981. Print.

___. *Trainsong.* New York: Holt, 1988. Print.

Kesey, Ken. *The Further Inquiry.* New York: Viking, 1990. Print.

Kuralt, Charles. *My Life on the Road.* New York: Ivy, 1990. Print.

Least Heat-Moon, William. *Blue Highways: A Journey into America.* New York: Little, 1983. Print.

Majerus, Janet. *Grandpa and Frank.* Philadelphia: Lippincott, 1976. Print.

McCarthy, Eugene. America Revisited: 150 Years after Tocqueville. Garden City: Doubleday, 1978. Print.

McMurtry, Larry. *Cadillac Jack.* New York: Simon, 1987. Print.

Miller, Henry. *The Air-Conditioned Nightmare.* New York: New Directions, 1945. Print.

Morris, Jan. *Destinations: Essays from* Rolling Stone. New York: Oxford UP, 1980. Print.

Moyers, Bill. *Listening to America: A Traveler Rediscovers His Country.* New York: Harper, 1971. Print.

Patermik, Michael. Driving Mr. Albert: A Trip across America with Einstein's Brain. New York: Dial, 2000. Print.

Phillips, Jayne Anne. *Fast Lanes.* New York: Dutton, 1987. Print.

___. *Machine Dreams.* New York: Dutton, 1984.

Pirsig, Robert M. *Zen and the Art of Motorcycle Maintenance.* New York: Morrow, 1974. Print.

Raban, Jonathan. *Old Glory: An American Voyage.* New York: Simon, 1981. Print.

Reeves, Richard. *American Journey: Traveling with Tocqueville in Search of Democracy in America.* New York: Simon, 1982. Print.

Robbins, Tom. *Even Cowgirls Get the Blues.* New York: Bantam, 1976. Print.

Robinson, Marilynne. *Housekeeping.* New York: Farrar, 1980. Print.

Robinson, Rose. *Eagle in the Air.* New York: Crown, 1969. Print.

Roiphe, Anne. *Long Division.* New York: Simon, 1972. Print.

Rosen, Gerald. *The Carmen Miranda Memorial Flagpole.* San Rafael: Presidio, 1977. Print.

Saroyan, William. *Short Drive, Sweet Chariot.* New York: Phaedra, 1966. Print.

Seals, David. *The Powwow Highway.* New York: Penguin, 1979. Print.

Sigal, Clancy. *Going Away: A Report, A Memoir.* Boston: Houghton, 1962. Print.

Simpson, Mona. *Anywhere but Here.* New York: Vintage, 1987. Print.

Steinbeck, John. *The Grapes of Wrath.* New York: Viking, 1939. Print.

___. *Travels with Charley: In Search of America.* New York: Penguin, 1962. Print.

Sukenick, Ronald. *Out.* Chicago: Swallow, 1973.

Williams, John A. *This Is My Country Too.* New York: New Amer. Lib., 1965. Print.

Wolfe, Tom. *The Electric Kool-Aid Acid Test.* New York: Farrar, 1968. Print.

Wolitzer, Hilma. *Hearts.* New York: Farrar, 1980. Print.

Yogi, Stan, ed. Highway 99: A Literary Journey through California's Great Central Valley. Berkeley: Heyday, 1996. Print.

Zelazny, Roger. *Roadmarks.* New York: Ballantine, 1979. Print.

Bibliography

Belasco, Warren James. *Americans on the Road: From Autocamp to Motel, 1910–1945*. Cambridge: MIT P, 1979. Print.

Bendixen, Alfred, and Judith Hamera, eds. *The Cambridge Companion to American Travel Writing*. Cambridge: Cambridge UP, 2009. Print.

Bluefarb, Sam. *The Escape Motif in the American Novel: Mark Twain to Richard Wright*. Columbus: Ohio State UP, 1972. Print.

Braidotti, Rosi. *Nomadic Subjects: Embodiment and Sexual Difference in Contemporary Feminist Theory*. New York: Columbia UP, 1994. Print.

Brinkley, Douglas, ed. *Windblown World: The Journals of Jack Kerouac, 1947–1954*. New York: Viking, 2004. Print.

Casey, Roger N. *Textual Vehicles: The Automobile in American Literature*. New York: Garland, 1997. Print.

Conde, Rosina. *Women on the Road*. San Diego: San Diego State UP, 1994. Print.

Cook, Bruce. *The Beat Generation*. New York: Scribner, 1971. Print.

Cox, John David. *Traveling South: Travel Narratives and the Construction of American Identity*. Athens: U of Georgia P, 2005. Print.

Dettelbach, Cynthia Golomb. *In the Driver's Seat: The Auto in American Literature and Popular Culture*. Westport: Greenwood, 1976. Print.

Flink, James J. *The Car Culture*. Cambridge: MIT P, 1975. Print.

Emery, Brook. "The Road Novels of Jack Kerouac." MA thesis. U of Sydney, 1983. Print.

Ganser, Alexandra. *Roads of Her Own: Gendered Space and Mobility in American Women's Road Narratives, 1970–2000*. Amsterdam: Rodopi, 2009. Print.

Groom, Eileen. *Methods for Teaching Travel Literature and Writing: Exploration of the World and Self*. New York: Lang, 2005. Print.

Hill, Lee. *Easy Rider*. London: BFI, 1996. Print.

Holmstrom, Darwin, and Melinda Keefe. *Life Is a Highway: A Century of Great Automotive Writing*. Minneapolis: Motorbooks, 2010. Print.

Holland, Patrick, and Graham Huggan. *Tourists with Typewriters: Critical Reflections on Contemporary Travel Writing*. Ann Arbor: U of Michigan P, 1998. Print.

Hotz, Jeffrey. *Divergent Visions, Contested Spaces: The Early United States through the Lens of Travel*. New York: Routledge, 2006. Print.

Imbarrato, Susan Clair. *Traveling Women: Narrative Visions of Early America*. Athens: Ohio UP, 2006. Print.

Jakle, John A. *The Tourist: Travel in Twentieth-Century America*. Lincoln: U of Nebraska P, 1985. Print.

Kennedy, Todd. *Hitting the American Highway: The Ontology of the Hobo Hero in Twentieth-Century American Culture*. New York: ProQuest, 2007. Print.

Kowalewski, Michael. *Temperamental Journeys: Essays on the Modern Literature of Travel*. Athens: U of Georgia P, 1992.

Krim, Arthur. *Route 66: Iconography of the American Highway*. Santa Fe: Center for Amer. Places, 2005. Print.

Lackey, Kris. *Road Frames: The American Highway Narrative.* Lincoln: U of Nebraska P, 1997. Print.

Laderman, David. *Driving Visions: Exploring the Road Movie.* Austin: U of Texas P, 2002. Print.

Lipton, Lawrence. *The Holy Barbarians.* New York: Messner, 1959. Print.

Leland, John. *Why Kerouac Matters: The Lessons of* On the Road (*They're Not What You Think*). New York: Viking, 2007. Print.

Marling, Karol Ann. *The Colossus of Roads: Myth and Symbol along the American Highway.* Minneapolis: U of Minnesota P, 1984. Print.

McCarthy, Eugene. *America Revisited: 150 Years after Tocqueville.* Garden City: Doubleday, 1978. Print.

McNally, Dennis. *Desolate Angel: Jack Kerouac, the Beat Generation, and America.* New York: Da Capo, 2003. Print.

Mills, Katie. *The Road Story and the Rebel: Moving through Film, Fiction, and Television.* Carbondale: Southern Illinois UP, 2006. Print.

Newlin, Keith, ed. *Critical Insights: The Grapes of Wrath.* Ipswich: Salem, 2010. Print.

Paes de Barros, Deborah. *Fast Cars and Bad Girls: Nomadic Subjects and Women's Road Stories.* New York: Lang, 2004. Print.

Patton, Phil. *The Open Road: A Celebration of the American Highway.* New York: Simon, 1986. Print.

Primeau, Ronald. *Romance of the Road: The Literature of the American Highway.* Bowling Green: Bowling Green State U Popular P, 1996. Print.

Roberson, Susan. *Antebellum American Women on the Road: American Mobilities.* New York: Routledge, 2011. Print.

Russell, Alison. *Crossing Boundaries: Postmodern Travel Literature.* New York: Pelgrave-St. Martin's, 2000. Print.

Scharff, Virginia. *Twenty Thousand Roads: Women, Movement, and the West.* Berkeley: U of California P, 2002. Print.

Sherrill, Rowland. *Road-Book America: Contemporary Culture and the New Picaresque.* Urbana: U of Illinois P, 2000. Print.

Siegel, Kristi. *Gender, Genre, and Identity in Women's Travel Writing.* New York: Lang, 2004. Print.

___. *Issues in Travel Writing: Empire, Spectacle, and Displacement.* New York: Lang, 2002. Print.

Turner, Victor. *The Ritual Process.* Ithaca: Cornell UP, 1969. Print.

Steadman, Jennifer Bernhardt. *Traveling Economies: American Women's Travel Writing.* Columbus: Ohio State UP, 2007. Print.

Stout, Janis P. *The Journey Narrative in American Literature: Patterns and Departures.* Westport: Greenwood, 1983. Print.

Teale, Tamara M. *The Liberty-Genocide Paradox: American Indians in European and American Travel Literature, 1795–1991.* Ann Arbor: U of Michigan P, 1999. Print.

Thompson, Carl. *Travel Writing.* New York: Routledge, 2011. Print.

Vogel, Andrew Richard. *Narrating the Geography of Automobility: American Road Story, 1893–1921.* Columbus: Ohio State UP, 2007. Print.

Wallis, Michael. *Route 66: The Mother Road.* 75th anniv. ed. New York: Griffin-St. Martin's, 2001. Print.

Williams, Mark. *Road Movies: The Complete Guide to Cinema on Wheels.* New York: Proteus, 1982. Print.

Wesley, Marilyn C. *Secret Journeys: The Trope of Women's Travel in American Literature.* Albany: State U of New York P, 1999. Print.

Wrobel, David M. *Global West, American Frontier: Travelers' Accounts from the Nineteenth and Twentieth Centuries.* Albuquerque: U of New Mexico P, 2013. Print.

Ziff, Larzar. *Return Passages: Great American Travel Writing, 1780–1910.* New Haven: Yale UP, 2000. Print.

CRITICAL
INSIGHTS

About the Editor _____

Ronald Primeau is professor of English and former director of the master of arts program in humanities at Central Michigan University. He is the author of books on Herbert Woodward Martin, Paul Laurence Dunbar, Edgar Lee Masters, critical theory, the writing process, and the rhetoric of television, as well as *Romance of the Road: The Literature of the American Highway* (1996). His career-long interest in the highways through the heartland has resulted in many articles on Jack Kerouac, Robert M. Pirsig, William Least Heat-Moon, Elizabeth Berg, and various authors of the American Midwest. He has received numerous honors and grants, including the MidAmerica Award from the Society for the Study of Midwestern Literature in recognition of distinguished research; grants from the National Endowment for the Humanities, the Michigan Humanities Council, and the US Department of Education; and an Excellence in Teaching Award and recognition as Honors Faculty Member of the Year from Central Michigan University. With filmmaker David B. Schock, he has produced the films *Distinct and Midwestern* (2008), a documentary on David D. Anderson, who founded the Society for the Study of Midwestern Literature; *Jump Back, Honey: The Poetry and Performance of Herbert Woodward Martin* (2009); and the prize-winning *Star by Star: Naomi Long Madgett, Poet and Publisher* (2011), about Detroit's poet laureate. Works in progress include a book on Chicago literature and a film about Toi Derricotte.

Contributors _____

Ronald Primeau is professor of English and former director of the master of arts program in humanities at Central Michigan University. He is the author of numerous books, including *Romance of the Road: The Literature of the American Highway* (1996). With filmmaker David B. Schock, he has produced the films *Distinct and Midwestern* (2008), a documentary on David D. Anderson, who founded the Society for the Study of Midwestern Literature; *Jump Back, Honey: The Poetry and Performance of Herbert Woodward Martin* (2009); and the prize-winning *Star by Star: Naomi Long Madgett, Poet and Publisher* (2011), about Detroit's poet laureate.

Ann Brigham teaches English and women's and gender studies at Roosevelt University in Chicago. She has published numerous articles on the constructions of space, place, and spatial relations in twentieth- and twenty-first-century American literature, film, and popular culture. She is coeditor of the interdisciplinary volume *Making Worlds: Gender, Metaphor, Materiality* (1998). Her recent manuscript *Constructing Mobility: Shifting Pursuits in the American Road Narrative* focuses on how road narratives re-create the meanings of mobility as an ideological and spatial practice.

Marilyn Judith Atlas teaches American literature at Ohio University, specializing in the American Renaissance, realism, naturalism, modernism, the Chicago Renaissance, Jewish American literature, African American and ethnic literature, and women's studies. She has published widely on authors ranging from Leo Tolstoy and Toni Morrison to Margaret Fuller and Etgar Keret.

Barry Alford teaches English at Mid Michigan Community College. He has published on community-college issues, language theory, assessment, and postmodernism. He taught a class on American road literature at Central Michigan University for twenty years.

John Rohrkemper teaches American literature and creative writing at Elizabethtown College. He is also an actor and a playwright.

Dominic Ording teaches English at Millersville University in Lancaster, Pennsylvania. His teaching and research focus on American literature and culture, gender and sexuality studies, and comparative spiritualities.

Joseph J. Wydeven is professor emeritus of English and humanities at Bellevue University and the author of *Wright Morris Revisited* (1998). He is the recipient of the 2010 Midamerica Award for Distinguished Research on Midwestern Literature from the Society for the Study of Midwestern Literature.

Richmond Adams received his doctorate from Southern Illinois University Carbondale in 2011, having written his dissertation on Harold Frederic's *The Damnation of Theron Ware* (1896). He earned his bachelor of arts from the University of Memphis and his master of divinity degree from Vanderbilt University. His interests include postbellum American fiction.

Deborah Paes de Barros is professor of English at Palomar College. She is the author of *Fast Cars and Bad Girls: Nomadic Subjects and Women's Road Stories* (2004), the poetry collection *On Kevin's Boat* (2012), and many articles on American literature.

David Bain teaches writing at an Indiana community college and is the author of *Gray Lake: A Novel of Crime and Supernatural Horror* (2012) and several short-story collections. He has well over one hundred publications in venues such as *Weird Tales Magazine* and *Poems and Plays*. His fiction recently appeared in *Dark Highways: Five Road Trips into Terror* (2012).

Christian Knoeller specializes in the teaching of writing and literature at the secondary level at Purdue University and is the author of *Voicing Ourselves: Whose Words We Use When We Talk about Books* (1998). He is researching cultural and ecological memory in Native American and Midwestern literature. His first collection of poems, *Completing the Circle* (2000), received the Millennium Prize from Buttonwood Press. The Society for the Study of Midwestern Literature has awarded him both the Midwestern Heritage Prize for literary criticism and the Gwendolyn Brooks Prize for poetry.

Caroline Maun teaches creative writing and American literature at Wayne State University in Detroit. She is the editor of *The Collected Poems of Evelyn Scott* (2005) and the author of *Mosaic of Fire: The Work of Lola Ridge, Evelyn Scott, Charlotte Wilder, and Kay Boyle* (2012). Her poetry publications include *The Sleeping* (2006) and *Cures and Poisons* (2009).

Maureen N. Eke teaches African diaspora literatures, postcolonial literature and theory, world literature, and women writers at Central Michigan University. She is a past president of the African Literature Association (ALA) and is the editor of the ALA Annuals series. Her publications include four coedited volumes as well as numerous articles on African literature and cinema. She serves on the editorial boards of several international publications and is at work on a book of collected essays on Nigerian playwright Tess Onwueme.

Mary Beth Pringle is professor of English at Wright State University, where she teaches modern and contemporary literature and women's studies. Travel literature, both fiction and nonfiction, has been a decades-long fascination.

Arvid F. Sponberg teaches Midwestern literature and twentieth-century drama at Valparaiso University and writes most often about the unnatural history of American playwrights. With Stuart Hecht of Boston College, he is editing a book of essays from the first Chicago Theatre Symposium, held in 2011 at Columbia College.

Phil Patton is the author of many books, including *Open Road: A Celebration of the American Highway* (1986), *Made in USA: The Secret Histories of the Things That Made America* (1992), and *Bill Traylor: High Singing Blue* (1997). He has served as curator for many museum exhibitions, including *Different Roads: Automobiles for the Next Century* at the Museum of Modern Art in New York. He appears frequently on TV interview shows, writes regularly for the *New York Times,* and teaches in the design-criticism program at the School of Visual Arts.

Steven K. Bailey teaches composition and rhetoric at Central Michigan University. He is the author of several guides to the history and culture of Asian cities, including *Exploring Hong Kong: A Visitor's Guide to Hong Kong Island, Kowloon, and the New Territories* (2009) and a more recent book on Hanoi.

Matthew Low's research interests include writing on the environment, Native American literature, studies of place, and hands-on prairie conservation and restoration fieldwork. He has been published in *ISLE: Interdisciplinary Studies in Literature and Environment*, *Mosaic*, *Mid America*, *Prairie Fire*, and other journals. He lives and teaches in Omaha, Nebraska.

Index _____

King, Stephen, 170
King Philip's War, 152
Kiowa migration narrative, 310
language, use of
    Huckleberry Finn, in (Twain), 69, 73
    The Road, in (McCarthy), 146
Led-Horse Claim, The (Foote), 160
Life, A (Morris), 134–136
Life on the Mississippi (Twain), 65–68
light as symbol, 221
"Lines Composed a Few Miles above
    "Tintern Abbey" (Wordsworth).
    See "Tintern Abbey" (Wordsworth)
Lonely Planet guidebook series,
    294–295, 300–304
"Longing, The" (Roethke), 191–198
"Long Waters, The" (Roethke), 203–204
*Lost Continent: Travels in Small-Town
    America, The* (Bryson), 291
male privilege, 51
Malvin, John, 242
Man Made of Words, The (Momaday),
    321
maps, subjectivity of, 297
Maria (*Play It As It Lays*), 164–165
masculinity
    crying and, 98
    desire for, 84
    kidnapping as an act of, 109
    selfishness as, 94
"Meditation at Oyster River" (Roethke),
    198–199
Mencken, H. L., 35
Metacom's War. *See* King Philip's War
Mexico, 128–129
Michigan, 234, 268, 298–300
Michigan Central Station, 225
Midnight Cowboy (film), 86
"Mission Accomplished" speech
    (George W. Bush), 218
Mississippi Delta, 282

mobility
    American identity and, 102
    physical leading to social, 106
    self-education through, 119
    self-reliance, through, 113
    social tension and, 103–104
    threat, as, 114
    un-American ideals, hindered by,
    112
Model T. *See* Ford Model T
moral allegory, 172–173
Moriarty, Dean (*On the Road*), 86–99
Morris, Mary, 248–264
Morris, Wright, 122–129
mortality, awareness of, 135, 202
mother-child relationship, 154–155,
    165–166
Move under Ground (Mamatas),
    187–188
"Mrs. Todd's Shortcut" (King), 173
mythology, 177–178
My Uncle Dudley (Morris), 129–132
narrative frequency, 313–315
*Narrative of the Life of Frederick
    Douglass* (Douglass), 158
Native Americans
    American identity and, 197
    cultures, 52
    land ownership and, 298
    Puritan attitudes toward, 156–157
No Country for Old Men (McCarthy),
    140–144
"North American Sequence" (Roethke),
    190–210
Northeast blackout (2003), 221
Nothing to Declare (Morris), 250–254
Oglala, 197
Ohio, 234
Once upon a River (Campbell), 268–271
One Door away from Heaven (Koontz),
    182